GRE

Reading Comprehension:
Detailed Solutions to 200 Questions

○ 200 solved RC questions for exhaustive practice

○ Comprehensive test-taking strategies to give you a competitive edge

○ Passage summaries and detailed answer keys to develop your RC skills

○ Examples on all RC question formats for all-round preparation

VP **Vibrant Publishers**

www.vibrantpublishers.com

GRE® Reading Comprehension: Detailed Solutions to 200 Questions

ISBN-10: 1479216925
ISBN-13: 978-14-79216-92-5
Library of Congress Control Number: 2012916201

This publication is designed to provide accurate and authoritative information in regard to the subject matter covered. The Author has made every effort in the preparation of this book to ensure the accuracy of the information. However, information in this book is sold without warranty either expressed or implied. The Author or the Publisher will not be liable for any damages caused or alleged to be caused either directly or indirectly by this book.

Vibrant Publishers books are available at special quantity discount for sales promotions, or for use in corporate training programs. For more information please write to
bulkorders@vibrantpublishers.com

Please email feedback / corrections (technical, grammatical or spelling) to
spellerrors@vibrantpublishers.com

To access the complete catalogue of Vibrant Publishers, visit **www.vibrantpublishers.com**

Table of Contents

1

Overview of the GRE revised General Test

The Graduate Record Examinations (GRE) General Test is required for admission to most graduate programs. The most competitive programs tend to require comparatively higher scores. As of August 1, 2011, the current GRE General Test will be replaced by the GRE revised General Test. This book is designed to prepare students for the GRE revised General Test. Note that some graduate programs require applicants to take specialized GRE Subject Tests which will not be covered in this book. Before preparing to take the GRE, please review the admissions criteria for the programs that you are interested in applying to so that you know whether you need to take subject tests in addition to the GRE General Test. To learn more about subject tests visit the Subject Tests section at ets.org.

The GRE revised General Test is not designed to measure your knowledge of specific fields. It does not measure your ability to be successful in your career or even in school. It does, however, give a reasonably accurate indication of your capabilities in certain key areas for graduate level work, such as your ability to understand complex written material, your understanding of basic mathematics, your ability to interpret data, and your capacity for reasoning and critical thinking. By using this book to prepare for the GRE revised General Test, you will not only improve your chances of scoring well on the test, you will also help to prepare yourself for graduate level study.

General Information of the Format of the GRE revised General Test

Whether you are taking the paper or computer version of the GRE revised General Test, the format of the test will be essentially the same. The test consists of three main components: Analytical Writing, Verbal Reasoning and Quantitative Reasoning. The total time for the test will be between 3 ½ and 3 ¾ hours, depending on the version you are taking.

The first section of the test is always the Analytical Writing component which is broken into two sections. In the first, you will be asked to write an argumentative essay that takes a position on an issue of general interest. In the second, you will be asked to analyze an argument for logical validity and soundness. You will be given 30 minutes for each section.

The remainder of the test will be split between sections devoted to Verbal Reasoning and sections devoted to Quantitative Reasoning. There will be two sections devoted to Verbal Reasoning, and another two devoted to Quantitative Reasoning. You will be given between 30-40 minutes to complete each section, and each section will contain approximately 20 questions. At any point during the test, you may be given an unscored section on either Verbal or Quantitative Reasoning; since this section will not be identified, it is important that you try your best at all times. Also, it is possible that you will be asked to complete a research section that will allow ETS to test the efficacy of new questions. If you are given a research section, it will appear at the end of your General Test. Unscored and research sections may vary in number of questions and time allotted.

As of August 1, 2011, all students taking the GRE General Test will take a revised version of the test that will add several new features while removing some others.

Whether you have taken the GRE before or are taking it for the first time, it is important that you gear your preparation for the revised version of the test. This book is designed to help to prepare you for the GRE revised General Test.

What's New about the GRE revised General Test

This book is designed for those who plan on taking the GRE revised General Test, which will be implemented as of August 1, 2011. The GRE revised General Test will have new features that are designed to make the test more user-friendly and more directly related to the sort of skills that students need as they pursue a graduate or professional degree. The tasks in the Analytical Writing portion of the test are now more focused, and feature more detailed instructions. The Verbal Reasoning section now places a greater emphasis on your reading comprehension and your ability to reason with written material. The Quantitative Reasoning component still tests you competence with basic math, but now places a greater emphasis on applying quantitative skills to real-world scenarios and data. The following is an overview of some of the features that are new to the revised General Test:

General Changes to the GRE

- Greater emphasis on skills that are directly applicable to graduate study

- A more user-friendly interface for the computer based version of the test

Changes to the Analytical Writing Section

- You will no longer have more than one option to write on for either of the Analytical Writing tasks, making the assignments more focused

- The prompts for the Analytical Writing tasks are now more specific, and you will be scored based on your ability to write logically and coherently about the subject while addressing the specific points in the prompt

Changes to the Verbal Reasoning Section

- The Verbal Reasoning portion of the test no longer includes any vocabulary out of context; antonym and analogy questions have been removed

- New Text Completion questions on the Verbal Reasoning portion that test your ability to interpret and evaluate passages, and apply vocabulary in context

- New Sentence Equivalence questions on the Verbal Reasoning portion that evaluate your ability to complete sentences based on context

- New types of Reading Comprehension questions on the Verbal Reasoning portion that allow you to choose more than one correct answer or highlight a section of text to answer the question

Changes to the Quantitative Reasoning Section

- New multiple choice format on the Quantitative Reasoning section that will ask you to select one or more correct answers for some questions

- New numeric entry questions on the Quantitative Reasoning Section that will ask you to enter a numeric value rather than choose from several options

- Onscreen calculator for those taking the computer-based version of the test allowing more emphasis on reasoning over calculation

Outline of the GRE revised General Test

The following will briefly introduce the three main components of the GRE revised General Test.

Analytical Writing Assessment

The first section of the GRE revised General Test is the Analytical Writing assessment. This component of the GRE is designed to test your ability to use basic logic and critical reasoning to make and assess arguments. The Analytical Writing assessment is broken into two assignments, each of which must be completed within 30 minutes. In the first assignment, you will be asked to develop a position on an issue of general interest. You will be given an issue and a prompt with some specific instructions on how to approach the assigned issue. You will be expected to take a position on the issue and then write a clear, persuasive and logically sound essay defending your position in correct English. You will be assessed based on your ability to effectively defend your positions with supporting evidence and valid reasoning, your skill in organizing your thoughts, and your command of English. In the second assignment, you will be presented with a passage in which the author sketches an argument for their position on an issue. Here, you will be expected to write and essay that critically evaluates their argument in terms of the evidence they use and the logical validity of their reasoning. You will be assessed based on your ability to parse the author's argument and effectively point out the strengths and weaknesses of their reasoning using good organization and correct English.

Task	Time Allowed	Answer Format
Analyze an Issue	30 minutes	Short essay on an issue of general interest that clearly and carefully addresses the prompt
Analyze an Argument	30 minutes	Short essay that analyzes another person's argument for validity, soundness and supporting evidence

The Analytical Writing assessment tests your ability to:

- Coherently develop complex ideas

- Write in a focused, organized manner

- Identify relevant evidence and use it to support your claims

- Critically evaluate another person's argument for clarity and effectiveness

- Command the elements of standard written English

Verbal Reasoning

The Verbal Reasoning portion of the GRE assesses your reading comprehension, your ability to draw inferences to fill in missing information, and your vocabulary. You will be given two sections on Verbal Reasoning, each consisting of approximately 20-25 questions and lasting 30-35 minutes. Verbal Reasoning questions on the GRE revised General Test are mostly multiple choice, and will be drawn from the following three types: Reading Comprehension, Text Completion, and Sentence Equivalence. Reading Comprehension questions will ask you to read a short passage several paragraphs long, and then answer questions about the passage. Text Completion questions will have a short passage with 1-3 blanks which you will need to fill in by choosing the best of several multiple choice options. The Sentence Equivalence section will ask you to fill in the blank in a passage using the two words that will complete the sentence in such a way that the meaning will be as similar as possible.

Question Type	Time	Answer Format
Reading Comprehension	You will have 30-35 minutes to complete the entire section, which will include a mixture of different question types	Multiple choice: select one answer choice Multiple choice: select one or more answer choices Highlight a section of text
Text Completion		Multiple choice: fill in one or more blanks to complete the text
Sentence Equivalence		Multiple choice: select the two options that produce two sentences with the most similar meanings

The Verbal Reasoning section tests your ability to:

- Comprehend, interpret and analyze complex passages in standard written English

- Apply sophisticated vocabulary in context

- Draw inferences about meaning and authorial intent based on written material

Quantitative Reasoning

The Quantitative Reasoning section of the GRE evaluates your ability to use basic mathematics, read and interpret graphs and figures and engage in basic reasoning involving math and numbers. You will be given two sections on Quantitative Reasoning, each with about 20-25 questions. You will have 35-40 minutes to complete each section. There are two basic question types, multiple choice and numerical entry. For multiple choice questions, you will be asked to choose the best answer or answers from several possibilities; for numerical entry questions, you will be asked to enter a numerical answer from your own calculations. Some questions will be designed to test your knowledge of basic algebra and geometry; others will be designed to test your ability to read and interpret different presentations of data.

Question Type	Time	Answer Format
Multiple Choice		Select one answer choice Select one or more answer choices
Numeric Entry	You will have 30-35 minutes to complete the entire section, which will include a mixture of different question types	Solve the problem through calculation and enter a numeric value
Quantitative Comparison		Evaluate two quantities to decide whether one is greater than the other, whether they are equal, or whether a relationship cannot be determined
Data Interpretation		Multiple choice: choose the best answer or answers Numeric entry: enter a value

The Quantitative Reasoning section tests your ability to:

- Use mathematical tools such as basic arithmetic, geometry, algebra and statistics

- Understand, interpret and analyze quantitative information

- Apply basic mathematical and data interpretation skills to real-world information and problems

Paper Based and Computer Based GRE revised General Test

The Paper Based GRE revised General Test

If you are taking the paper-based version of the test, the format will be slightly different than the computer-based version. The typical format for the paper version of the test will be as follows:

Component	Number of Questions	Time Allowed
Analytical Writing	1 Analyze an Issue	30 minutes
	1 Analyze an Argument	30 minutes
Verbal Reasoning (2 sections)	25 questions per section	35 minutes per section
Quantitative Reasoning (2 sections)	25 questions per section	40 minutes per section

Note that if you are taking the paper based test, you will not be given an unscored section or a research section. Also, there are several changes to the GRE revised

General Test that will apply specifically to those taking the paper based test:

- You will now enter all answers in your test booklet, and not on a separate sheet

- You will be provided with an ETS calculator for doing computations. You will not be allowed to use your own calculator

The Computer Based GRE revised General Test

If you are taking the computer-based version of the test, the format will be slightly different than the paper-based version. Also, unlike the paper-based test, the Verbal Reasoning and Quantitative Reasoning sections of the computer based version is partially adaptive. This means that the computer will adapt the test to your performance. Since there are two sections each of Verbal Reasoning and Quantitative Reasoning, the difficulty of the second section will depend on how well you did on the first section. The format for the computer-based version of the test will be as follows:

Component	Number of Questions	Time Allowed
Analytical Writing	1 Analyze an Issue	30 minutes
	1 Analyze an Argument	30 minutes
Verbal Reasoning (2 sections)	Approximately 20 questions per section	30 minutes per section
Quantitative Reasoning (2 sections)	Approximately 20 questions per section	35 minutes per section
Unscored	Variable	Variable
Research	Variable	Variable

There are several changes to the GRE revised General Test that will apply specifically to those taking the computer based test:

- The Verbal Reasoning and Quantitative Reasoning sections are partially adaptive; this means that the difficulty of the second section will depend upon your performance on the first section

- You can now review and preview questions within a section, allowing you to budget your time to deal with the questions that you find most difficult

- You will now be able to mark questions within a section and return to them later. This means that if you find a question especially difficult, you will be able to move on to other questions and return to the one that you had trouble with, provided that you stay within the time limit for the section

- You will now be able to change or edit your answers within a section. This means that if you realize that you made a mistake, you can go back and correct yourself provided you stay within the time limit for the section

- You will now have an onscreen calculator during the Quantitative Reasoning portions of the test, allowing you to quickly complete any necessary computations

Registering for the GRE

Before you register to take the GRE, be sure to consider your schedule and any special accommodations that you may need. Be aware that the availability of testing dates may vary according to your location, and that paper based testing only takes place on certain set dates. Be sure to give yourself plenty of time to prepare for the GRE, and be sure that you know the deadlines for score reporting and application deadlines for all the schools you are applying to. For general information about deadlines and the GRE, visit GRE section at ets.org. For more information on how to register for the GRE, visit the Register for GRE section at ets.org. For information on special accommodations for disabled students, visit Disabilities section at ets.org.

How the GRE revised General Test is Scored

The GRE revised General Test features a revised scoring system. If you have taken the GRE before, or seen a sample score report, you will know that the Verbal and Quantitative Reasoning portions of the current test are scored on a scale of 200-800 while the Analytical Writing section is scored on a 6-point scale. The Analytical Writing measure will continue to use the same scoring system, however, the Verbal Reasoning and Quantitative Reasoning sections will now be scored on a new scale of 130-170.

Scoring for the Analytical Writing Section

The scoring for the Analytical Writing section will remain the same from the previous version of the GRE General Test. You will be scored on a scale of 0-6 in increments of .5. The Analytical Writing measure emphasizes your ability to engage in reasoning and critical thinking over your facility with the finer points of grammar. The highest scores of 5.5-6.0 are given to work that is generally superior in every respect - sustained analysis of complex issues, coherent argumentation and excellent command of English language. The lowest scores of 0.0-0.5 are given to work that is completely off topic or so poorly composed as to be incoherent.

Scoring for the Verbal and Quantitative Reasoning Sections

Previously, the Verbal and Quantitative Reasoning sections of the GRE were scored on a scale of 200-800 in 10 point increments. These sections are now scored on a scale of 130-170 in 1 point increments. This means that minor discrepancies in performance that were amplified by the previous scoring system have been greatly reduced. If two test-takers performed similarly on the GRE with only a one or two point difference in their score, the old system would have translated that minor discrepancy into a difference of 10-20 points, making the variation in performance look larger than actual. The new scoring system eliminates the amplification of minor differences in scores, making it easier to compare scores.

General Strategies for Taking the GRE

There are strategies you can apply that will greatly increase your odds of performing well on the GRE. The following is a list of strategies that will help to improve your chances of performing well on the GRE:

- Review basic concepts in math, logic and writing

- Work through the test-taking strategies offered in this book

- Work through mock GRE tests until you feel thoroughly comfortable with the types of questions you will see

- As you are studying for the GRE, focus your energy on the types of questions that give you the most difficulty

- Learn to guess wisely. For many of the questions on the Verbal and Quantitative Reasoning Sections, the correct answer is in front of you - you only need to correctly identify it. Especially for questions that you find difficult, you should hone your ability to dismiss the options that are clearly wrong and make an educated guess about which one is right

- Answer every question. You won't lose any points for choosing the wrong answer, so even a wild guess that might or might not be right is better than no answer at all

Preparing for Test Day and Taking the GRE

How you prepare for the test is completely up to you, and will depend on your own test-taking preferences and the amount of time you can devote to studying for the test. At the very least, before you take the test, you should know the basics of what is covered on the test along with the general guidelines for taking the GRE. This book is designed to provide you with the basic information you need, and give you the opportunity to prepare thoroughly for the GRE revised General Test.

Although there is no set way to prepare for the GRE, as a general rule you will want to

- Learn the basics about the test - what is being tested, the format, and how the test is administered

- Familiarize yourself with the specific types of questions that you will see on the GRE revised General Test

- Review skills such as basic math, reading comprehension, and writing

- Learn about test-taking strategies

- Take a mock GRE test to practice applying your test-taking skills to an actual test.

Remember, you don't need to spend an equal amount of time on each of these areas to do well on the GRE - allot your study time to your own needs and preferences. The following are some suggestions to help you make the final preparations for your test, and help you through the test itself:

Preparing for Test Day

- In the time leading up to your test, practice, then practice some more. Practice until you are confident with the material

- Know when your test is, and when you need to be at the testing center

- Make a "practice run" to your testing center, so that you can anticipate how much time you will need to allow to get there

- Understand the timing and guidelines for the test and plan accordingly. Remember that you are not allowed to eat or drink while taking the GRE, although you will be allowed to snack or drink during some of the short breaks during testing. Plan accordingly

- Know exactly what documentation you will need to bring with you to the testing center

- Relax, especially in the day or night before your test. If you have studied and practiced wisely, you will be well prepared for the test. You may want to briefly glance over some test preparation materials, but cramming the night before will not be productive

- Eat well and get a good night's sleep. You will want to be well rested for the test

The Test Day

- Wake up early to give yourself plenty of time to eat a healthy breakfast, gather the necessary documentation, pack a snack and a water bottle, and make it to the testing center well before your test is scheduled to start

- Have confidence: You've prepared well for the test, and there won't be any big surprises. You may not know the answers to some questions, but the format will be exactly like what you've been practicing

- While you are taking the test, don't panic. The test is timed, and students often worry that they will run out of time and miss too many questions. The sections of the test are designed so that many students will not finish them, so don't worry if you don't think you can finish a section on time. Just try to answer as many questions as you can, as accurately as possible

- Remember the strategies and techniques that you learn from this book, and apply them wherever possible

Frequently Asked Questions

General Questions

What is new about the GRE revised General Test?

The test has several new features:

- The Verbal Reasoning and Quantitative Reasoning sections now feature new types of questions that focus more on skills you will require in graduate school, such as understanding texts and interpreting data. Antonyms and questions that test vocabulary out of context have been removed

- The Analytical Writing measure is now more focused - you will be asked to write to a prompt rather than choose from among possible topics

- Scoring has been revised to better indicate whether two test-takers performed similarly

- The computer based test now features a more user-friendly format, allowing you to review and return to previous questions, use an on-screen calculator, etc.

Why was the GRE revised?

The test was revised in order to more accurately determine your proficiency with the skills you need for graduate or professional school. The test has also been revised to make the test-taking experience smoother and more user-friendly.

How do I get ready to take GRE revised General Test?

To take the GRE revised General Test, there are several steps you'll need to take:

- Find out what prospective graduate/professional programs require: Does the program you're interested in require additional testing beyond the GRE revised General Test? What is the deadline for receipt of scores?

- Sign up for a test date. You need to sign up for any GRE testing. For computer based testing, there will generally be numerous dates to choose from, although acting in a timely manner is essential so that you have plenty of time to prepare and are guaranteed that your scores will be sent and received on time. For paper based testing, testing dates are much more restricted, so if you know that you will need to take the paper based GRE revised General Test, make arrangements well in advance of the application deadline for your program

- Use this book and the resources provided by ETS to familiarize yourself with both the format of the GRE and the types of questions you will face. Even if you are confident about taking the test, it is essential to prepare for the test

Does the GRE revised General Test Measure my proficiency in specific subject areas?

No. The GRE revised General Test is designed to measure general proficiency in reading, critical reasoning, and working with data, all abilities that are critical to graduate work. However, you won't be tested on your knowledge of any specific field.

Where can I get additional information on the GRE revised General Test?

Educational Testing Service (ETS), the organization that administers the GRE, has an informative website entirely devoted to information about the test at the GRE section at ets.org. There, you can find links that further explain the differences between the old GRE General Test and the GRE revised General Test, as well as information on how to sign up for testing, fees, score reporting and much more.

Preparing for the Test

How should I start to prepare for the test?

The first thing you should do is thoroughly familiarize yourself with the format of the GRE revised General Test. Once you've decided whether you're taking the paper based test, or the computerized version, learn exactly what you can expect from the version of the test you're taking - how many sections there are, how many questions per section, etc. You can find general information about the structure of the test earlier in this chapter.

How do I prepare for the questions I will be asked on the GRE revised General Test?

There are plenty of resources by Vibrant Publishers, including this book to help you prepare for the questions you will face on the GRE revised General Test. A list of books is provided at the end of this book. You may have a detailed look at them at www.vibrantpublishers.com.

How much should I study/practice for the GRE?

Study and practice until you feel comfortable with the test. Practice, practice and practice some more until you feel confident about test day!

Are there additional materials I can use to get even more practice?

Yes. ETS offers a free full-length practice test that can be downloaded from the GRE section at ets.org. Also, after you have signed up for testing through ETS, you are eligible for some further test preparation materials free of additional charge.

Test Content

How long the GRE revised General Test is?

- The computer based version of the test is around 3 hours and 45 minutes including short breaks

- The paper based version of the test will take around 3 ½ hours

What changes have been made to the content of the GRE?

The content of the GRE revised General Test will be noticeably different than the content of the current version of the test. The specific changes are:

- **The Analytical Writing portion:** You will be given only one topic to write an essay on rather than a choice of topics. This makes the Analytical Writing measure more focused and will allow you to focus your attention on writing a well-crafted essay rather than on choosing a topic

- **The Verbal Reasoning section:** There will no longer be questions that test your vocabulary out of context - the old antonym and analogy questions have been removed and replaced with Text Completion and Sentence Equivalence questions. These new types of question will test your ability to reason from what you read, as well as your ability to use sophisticated vocabulary in context

- **The Quantitative Reasoning section:** This section will now place less emphasis on computation and more emphasis on your ability to interpret data

What skills does the GRE test?

In general, the GRE is designed to test your proficiency in certain key skills that you will need for graduate level study. More specifically:

- **The Analytical Writing section** tests your ability to write about complex ideas in a coherent, focused fashion as well as your ability to command the conventions of standard written English, provide and evaluate relevant evidence, and critique other points of view

- **The Verbal Reasoning section** tests your ability to understand, interpret and analyze complex passages, use reasoning to draw inferences about written material, and use sophisticated vocabulary in context

- **The Quantitative Reasoning section** tests your knowledge of basic, high school-level mathematics, as well as your ability to analyze and interpret data

What level of math is required for the Quantitative Reasoning section?

You will be expected to know high school level math - arithmetic, and basic concepts in algebra and geometry. You will also be expected to be able to analyze and interpret data presented in tables and graphs.

Scoring and Score Reporting

What's new about the score scale for the GRE revised General Test?

The scoring for the Verbal and Quantitative Reasoning sections of the GRE revised General Test is different than the scoring system for the current version of the test. The scoring for the Analytical Writing measure will remain the same:

- **The Verbal Reasoning section** will now be scored in 1-point increments on a scale of 130-170. This will replace the old system, which used 10-point increments on a scale of 200-800

- **The Quantitative Reasoning section** will now be scored in 1-point increments on a scale of 130-170. This will replace the old system, which used 10-point increments on a scale of 200-800

- **The Analytical Writing section** will continue to be scored on a scale of 0-6 in increments of .5

Why was the scoring system changed?

The scoring system was revised to better reflect relative differences in scores. The previous scoring system inflated differences in scores, making the scores of two test takers who performed similarly look larger than they actually were.

When will my score be reported?

It depends on which version of the test you are taking, and also when you decide to take the GRE revised General Test. In general, scores for the computer based version of the test are reported within two weeks; for the paper based test, they are reported within six weeks. Due to the fact that the revised test is new, the time for scores to be reported may vary during the first several months after the new test has been implemented. Check the GRE section at ets.org for updates on score reporting and deadlines.

How long will my scores be valid?

As with the old version of the GRE, your score for the GRE revised General Test will remain valid for five years.

Other Questions

Do business schools accept the GRE instead of the GMAT?

An increasing number of business schools accept the GRE as a substitute for the more standard test for admission to an MBA program, the GMAT. Before you decide to take the GRE instead of the GMAT, make sure that the programs you are interested in applying to will accept the GRE. You can find a list of business schools that currently accept the GRE in the GRE section at ets.org.

How is the GRE administered?

The GRE is administered at designated testing centers, where you can take the test free from distraction in a secure environment that discourages cheating. The computer based version of the test is administered continuously year round at designated testing centers. In areas where computer based testing is unavailable, the paper based version of the test is administered at most three times a year on designated dates. For information on testing centers in your area and important dates, visit the GRE section at ets.org.

I have a disability that requires me to ask for special accommodation while taking the test - what sort of accommodations are offered?

ETS does accommodate test-takers with disabilities. For information on procedures, visit the GRE section at ets.org.

Will there be breaks during testing?

Yes. You will have a 10 minute break during the test. On the computer based version of the test, the 10 minute break will fall after you have completed the first three sections of the test. On the paper based version, you will be given a 10 minute break following the Analytical Writing sections.

Will I be given scratch paper?

If you are taking the computer based version of the test, you will be given as much scratch paper as you need. If you are taking the paper based version of the test, you won't be allowed to use scratch paper, however, you will be allowed to write in your test booklet.

Should I bring a calculator to the test?

No. If you are taking the computer based version of the test, there will be an onscreen calculator for you to use. If you are taking the paper based version of the test, an ETS-approved calculator will be issued to you at the testing center.

2

Reading Comprehension

R eading Comprehension questions are designed to test your ability to understand, interpret and analyze what you read. You will be asked to read a short passage between one or more paragraphs long and then answer several questions about the passage. To answer them you will need to recognize what the passage explicitly states, and be able to draw inferences about the implications of the passage.

The passages used for Reading Comprehension questions will be drawn from a variety of topics, including the physical, biological and social sciences, the arts and the humanities, business and everyday life. To answer the questions on these passages, you do not need to be an expert on the topic covered; you need only read the passage attentively enough to answer basic questions about it. You will not be asked to evaluate the passage for truth or falsity; you will only need to understand what the author said, and what implications can be drawn from what the author said.

The Verbal Reasoning portion of the revised GRE will generally have about 10 passages that you will need to read. Some will be several paragraphs in length, others just one paragraph. You will be asked to answer 1-6 questions per passage, with longer passages generally corresponding to more questions. The questions will appear in three formats: two types of multiple choice, and highlighting a section of the passage. The first type of multiple choice will ask you to choose the single best answer from several options. The second type of multiple choice will ask you to choose one or more answers from several options. For select-in passage, you will be asked to highlight the section of text that best addresses the question.

What does a Reading Comprehension question look like?

Reading Comprehension questions will always be based off a short passage of one or more paragraphs. You will be asked to read the passage and then answer 1-6 questions about it. Below is an example of what a Reading Comprehension question will look like on the GRE revised General Test:

Questions 1 to 3 are based on the following reading passage.

Sometimes hype can create impossible expectations. Nowhere is this phenomenon more pronounced than in the world of popular music. Two bands that came to prominence in the first years of the 2000s exemplify this. New York's The Strokes and England's Arctic Monkeys were both hailed by critics as the leaders of a garage rock revival, and more grandiosely, as saviors of rock music. Despite successes and considerable popularity, neither band has entirely lived up to these overblown expectations. Although both bands helped to bring greater awareness to the burgeoning indie music scene, rock music still struggles to compete with other genres of popular music. And although both bands have gained considerable popularity, they still don't have the ability to fill stadiums and arenas the way that some of their older and less heralded peers do.

Select only one answer choice.

1. Which of the following statements best characterizes the main idea of the passage?

    A Popular music is more diverse than many people realize

    B The Strokes and Arctic Monkeys are both highly successful bands

    C A single band can revolutionize popular music

    D Critics of popular music sometimes create exaggerated expectations for bands

    E Older bands draw bigger crowds than newer bands

Consider each of the three choices separately and select all that apply.

2. The author most likely uses the phrase "saviors of rock music" to:

    A characterize the strokes

    B make a plea for the future of the genre

    C indicate the hyperbolic expectations created by music critics

3. Select the sentence that suggests rock music's struggles competing with other types of popular music.

Answer Key

The correct answers to the questions are:

1. D. Critics of popular music sometimes create exaggerated expectations for bands

2. C. indicate the hyperbolic expectations created by music critics

3. Although both bands helped to bring greater awareness to the burgeoning indie music scene, rock music still struggles to compete with other genres of popular music.

What skills do Reading Comprehension questions test?

Reading Comprehension questions test your ability to understand, interpret and analyze complex passages of the kind you will encounter in graduate school. Some key skills that are tested include your ability to

- understand a text holistically and be able to determine the meaning of individual components

- distinguish major and minor points

- succinctly summarize the meaning of an entire passage

- use inference to draw conclusions about implied meaning and intent

- understand how individual parts of a text support the key points

- identify an authors assumptions, biases and perspective

- determine the potential strengths and weaknesses of the author's position

Key Facts about Reading Comprehension questions

- Questions will be based off short passages of one or more paragraphs

- There will be approximately 10 passages on the Verbal Reasoning portion of the test; you will be required to answer 1-6 questions per passage

- Passages will be on a variety of topics including the physical, biological and social sciences, the arts and the humanities, business and everyday life

- Questions will be answerable based on the passage alone - you will not need any prior knowledge of the subject matter being discussed

- Questions will ask you to select one or more correct answers from several, or highlight a relevant portion of the passage

Strategies for Reading Comprehension questions

Depending on what version of the GRE you are taking, you will have 30 or 35 minutes to complete each Verbal Reasoning section. To complete a section successfully, you will need to budget your time well, and this is especially important with Reading Comprehension questions. It is essential that you not lose too much time reading passages too carefully. Remember, to do well on Reading Comprehension questions you do not need to have a mastery of the material covered in a given passage - you just need to be able to answer a few highly directed questions about the passage. If you are able to read the passage both thoroughly and quickly, so much the better; however, if you find yourself taking too much time over a passage, it is better to gather key information quickly than to grasp absolutely everything and lose too much time. As you read passages for Reading Comprehension questions, your reading should be goal-oriented: read quickly and "loosely" and focus only on information that is important. Remember, you won't need to remember anything about the passage after the test, and you only need to grasp key points while taking the test.

Another key consideration is how to approach passages that cover unfamiliar material. Remember, passages can be drawn from many different fields, and chances are you will come across a passage that deals with something you are unfamiliar with. However, the questions about the passage will not demand any prior knowledge of the subject matter. Don't panic if you are asked to read about something that you know nothing about, since the questions will not ask you to evaluate the truth of the claims made in the passage. By the same token, don't let any expertise that you may possess lead you to make unnecessary judgments about the passage. Focus your attention on answering the questions and always keep in mind that your knowledge or lack of knowledge about the subject matter will have no bearing on how well you are able to answer those questions.

Finally, keep in mind that the key skills for Reading Comprehension are skimming and paraphrasing. To skim effectively, you will need to read quickly and gather key information. To paraphrase, you will need to be able to summarily restate the key points of the passage in other words. Skimming will help you quickly understand what the passage is about while paraphrasing will allow you to recognize which possible answers are the best.

- Don't lose too much time reading a passage carefully; read quickly, and read with the goal of answering the questions

- Don't worry too much about understanding everything - remember, you don't need to learn the material covered in the passage thoroughly, you simply need to answer a few highly directed questions

- Don't let your knowledge, or lack of knowledge, of the subject matter distract you - every question you are asked will be answerable solely on the basis of the information in the passage

- Use your abilities to skim and paraphrase to your advantage; gather relevant information rapidly, and be able to reformulate it to determine what answer choice best answers the question

- What follows are some more specific strategies for answering Reading Comprehension questions. Later in this section, you'll have a chance to put your skills to the test and learn how to hone them in several in-depth worked examples.

Determine What the Passage is About

Your first task as you read a passage should be to find out what is being discussed. You should immediately look for clues as to what the main idea of the passage is - doing so will help you address any broad questions about the big picture that the passage is trying to convey. The following three questions will help you find the main idea of the passage:

- What is the passage about? This question should be the easiest of the three to answer, and could be fairly broad (e.g. "European history")

- What is the scope of the passage? This question asks how narrowly/broadly the passage addresses its subject matter

- What is the purpose of the passage? Here you are asking why the author wrote the passage to begin with - is it to educate? To persuade? Who is the intended audience, and what reaction is the author trying to get?

Some of the questions you will be asked will be directly answered by answering one or more of the above questions.

Skim the Passage

You need to gather key information quickly to do well, and one of the best ways to do that is to skim. As you skim the passage, keep several key points in mind. First of all, skim to determine what the passage is about. You shouldn't need to read every word carefully to be able to address the questions listed in the section above. Also, as you skim the passage, try to keep in mind how the passage is organized - try to have a general idea of what information can be found where. Some questions will ask you to refer to very specific sections of the text - by skimming effectively, you can form an idea of where you'll need to look to address specific questions. Finally, don't be afraid to skip over sentences or phrases that you don't understand. In many cases, you will be able to learn all you need to from a passage without understanding every word. In those rare cases when a question directly addresses something that you didn't understand on the first read-through, you can always read the section again more carefully when you are trying to answer the question.

As you are reading the passage, try to get a quick feel for the structure of the text. If there is more than one paragraph, how are the paragraphs organized? What is the topic and purpose of each paragraph? How is evidence and supporting material presented?

Understanding the Questions

After skimming the passage as described above, you will need to be prepared to answer questions about it. You can use the following strategies to help you answer the questions well:

- Read the question carefully. While you usually don't need to read more than a small part of the passage carefully, it's important that you read the question and the possible solutions with care - you need to have a clear sense of what you are being asked in order to find the right answer

- If the question is in multiple choice format, read every possible answer choice. Even if you think you can identify the right answer immediately, make sure you read all of the options

- If the question is general and asks you to describe what the passage is about, or what the purpose is, you should already have a pretty good idea of what the answer is from skimming and determining what the main idea of the passage is

- If the question is specific, you may need to find a particular section of the passage and read over it more carefully. Make "mental bookmarks" as you skim the passage to give you some idea of where to find which idea, so that when you're asked to answer a question on something very specific, you'll know where to find it

- Be prepared to use the information in the passage to draw an inference to a conclusion that was not explicitly stated. Sometimes you'll be asked to determine the next step in a passage - given what's said in the passage, what sort of conclusions can be drawn?

- Paraphrase. Sometimes you will find that you just can't understand the way that a particular question applies to the passage. By trying to reformulate the question, or the relevant section of the passage, or both, in your own words, you can often grasp the key idea that you need to address

Answering the Questions

Once you have read and understood the questions, you'll need to select the best answer (or in some cases, answers).

- Be sure you know what kind of answer you need to find. Some questions will be straight multiple choice, where you pick only one answer; others will allow you to choose more than one answer, and still others will ask you to highlight a portion of the text. Be aware of what you're expected to provide in your answer

- Be sure you are answering the question that was asked. Just because an answer choice is true, doesn't necessarily mean that it is right. Sometimes you will have more than one option that correctly addresses a point made by the passage - be sure that you choose the option that answers the question asked

- Don't allow any personal opinion or prior knowledge of a topic distract you - again, you should only answer the question as it bears on the passage. You are not being asked to express your opinions about a passage, or critique the content

- Use logic. To correctly answer some questions, you will need to use basic logic. Learn to recognize implicit assumptions made by the author, and draw inferences to see what unstated conclusions might follow from a passage

- Apply the process of elimination. For multiple choice questions, you will often be given several potential answers that are more obviously wrong than others. Be sure to dismiss these answers first of all, since even if you don't know which of the remaining options is the right answer, you'll increase your odds of choosing it by dismissing those that are clearly wrong

Types of Questions

There are several types of Reading Comprehension questions that you can expect to find. Reviewing the kinds of questions you can expect to be asked, and looking at strategies for answering them, will help you prepare for the test. The following is a list of typical questions:

- What is the main idea?

- What is the purpose?

- Identify specific details

- Identify the purpose of specific details

- Infer a conclusion based on evidence presented in the passage

- Identify assumptions made by the author

- Identify additional evidence that might undermine/bolster the author's argument

- Highlight a specific section of text that addresses a question

- Other

Main Idea

Some questions will be quite straightforward - you will be asked to answer a "big picture" question about the passage, such as questions about the main topic, intended audience, and scope.

Assuming that you have skimmed the passage well and answered the questions listed above in the section on determining what the passage is about, answering this type of question should be quite easy. Practice reading passages to quickly grasp the key points, and then have confidence in your ability to apply this skill on test day.

Purpose

Some questions will ask you to say something about the purpose of the passage. Here you are being asked to make an educated guess as to why the author bothered to write the passage - did they intend to educate? To entertain? To undermine a commonly held belief? To develop an argument as to why their perspective is better than another?

When answering questions about the purpose of a passage, look for clues in structure and wording. Does the author develop and then dismiss a certain view? What is the tone - is it adversarial or merely stating facts? Does the passage present a course of action, or does it simply present information? Answering questions such as these will help you determine some basic points about the passage, such as whether the author is advocating something or just trying to educate. You can then look of over some of the details of the passage to gain a sense of exactly what position the author is advocating, or who the intended audience might be for the information given.

Details

Some questions will ask you to identify specific points within the passage. Here you are being asked to find the place in the passage where the author discusses some particular aspect of the main topic or a detail that supports something that they have said.

To answer these questions, you will need to have developed good skimming skills. As you skim, learn to mentally bookmark the passage so that you know where to find certain information whether or not you have read it carefully or understood it perfectly. Doing this will allow you to quickly refer back to the right section of the passage to find the specific point you are being asked about.

Purpose of Detail

Some questions will ask you to identify why the author chose to use certain details in their discussion. If the author is making an argument, you will need to think why they chose to include a certain point to support it; if they are attempting to educate, you will need to decide why they thought a given detail would help make the discussion more informative.

To do well with these types of questions, you will need to have a good grasp on the topic and purpose of the passage, and you will need to know where to find the relevant detail to see where and how it fits into the whole discussion. As you read through the passage, try to read actively rather than passively - ask yourself why the author has chosen to include particular information, and how it fits into the piece as a whole. If you can get a good sense of how and why things hang together in the passage as you skim through it, you will be able to answer this type of question much more rapidly.

Additional Conclusions

Sometimes you will be asked to put together the evidence provided in a passage to draw a conclusion. In some cases, the author will have stated a clear conclusion and you will be asked to use the evidence presented to find other implied conclusions. In others, the author will have left their conclusions implied, and you will be asked to say something about them given the evidence.

To answer questions about implied conclusions, you need to have grasped the main idea of the passage. There is no way to answer questions about what conclusion you might draw from the passage without knowing the basic big picture information about the passage. Once you have that, you can use clues from the author's tone and the details they provide to determine what conclusions can be inferred.

Assumptions

Some questions may ask you what assumptions are implied in the passage. Here, you will need to consider what the author is assuming to develop their position - what do they consider so completely uncontroversial that they rely on it without even mentioning it?

To answer questions about assumptions, you will need to have a solid grasp of what the author is trying to say and why, and how they have structured the passage. You need to focus on ideas or points that are essential to what the author is trying to say but have been left unstated.

Bolster/Undermine

Sometimes you will be asked to identify another point that would either strengthen or weaken the author's case in the passage. Here you are looking for any additional evidence that can be brought to bear on the passage.

To answer this type of question, you need to have a clear grasp of the main idea, purpose and structure of the passage. Focus on only those potential answers that have a direct bearing on the topic, and weigh how the additional information would affect the development of the passage.

Highlight

Sometimes you will be asked to find a specific point in the passage and highlight it. For these questions, rather than being given possible answers, you will need to find the answer in the text and highlight it.

If you have skimmed the passage well and know where to find different points, these questions will be quite similar to multiple choice questions that ask for specific details. Focus your attention only on those parts of the passage that deal specifically with the question asked, and answer the question based on that.

Other

You may be asked other types of question about passages, although any additional type of question will test the same skills that the types listed test. To answer other question types, apply the techniques discussed above in the appropriate combination.

General Tips for answering Reading Comprehension questions

- Be sure that you read the instructions for the question carefully. Remember that Reading Comprehension questions can appear in three distinct formats, and to correctly answer a given question, you'll need to understand the format first of all

  - **For all types of multiple choice questions,** always review every potential answer before you choose the correct answer or answers

- **For multiple choice questions that ask for the single best answer** select only the option that best addresses the question

- **For multiple choice questions that ask you to select one or more answers** don't be alarmed if more than one of the options looks correct. For this type of question, you can select all of the options that accurately answer the question

- **Don't be deceived by answers that are only partially true**, or do not completely address the question - make sure that you select only those answers that fully and appropriately answer the question you were asked, especially for those questions that ask you to select a single option out of several or a passage

---

KEY STRATEGY # 1

Always use process of elimination. Many multiple choice questions of any type will have some options that are more obviously wrong than some others - perhaps they fall beyond the scope of the question, perhaps they produce an absurd result. If you are not immediately certain of the correct answer, dismiss those answers that are obviously wrong first of all and work with what remains. Even if you end up having to guess the right answer, you'll increase your odds of guessing right by eliminating answers that are obviously incorrect.

KEY STRATEGY # 2

Some questions on the test are designed to make you waste time if you haven't read effectively. If you did not do a good job of skimming the passage, you could easily waste minutes searching through the passage trying to determine which answers are right and which aren't. Don't let this happen. Hone your skimming skills so that you already have an idea of which information is right and which isn't before you look back over the passage for any final confirmation.

KEY STRATEGY # 3

You should be careful not to let "fancy" options that sound like they relate to the passage fool you. Some answer choices will be designed to take advantage of the way your mind tends to associate information with the topic. Be wary of this and be sure to ask yourself whether you actually saw anything in the passage that substantiates a possible answer.

KEY STRATEGY # 4

As you work on Reading Comprehension questions, remember to use elementary logic to your advantage. One very basic rule of logic is the following: for two propositions p and q, if p then q and not q entails not p. In other words, if you know that it is true that proposition p implies proposition q, and you know that proposition q is not true, then you know that proposition p is also not true. Use this and other strategies from basic logic to answer Reading Comprehension questions that require reasoning.

This page is intentionally left blank

3

Practice Set 1 - Arts and Humanities

This chapter is devoted to helping you develop your skill with Reading Comprehension questions using concrete examples. You will find passages related to *Arts and Humanities* that are similar to the sorts of passages you will encounter on an actual GRE test. Each passage has a set of questions and a detailed explanation of the solution to each question. The questions and their solutions will be presented as follows:

In this chapter:

- A passage related to *Arts and Humanities* similar to what you can expect on an actual GRE test

- Several questions about the passage similar to those you will encounter on an actual GRE test

In *Explanatory Answers for Practice Set 1: Arts and Humanities*:

- A quick summary that paraphrases the main issues of the passage and points out important words or phrases that indicate the meaning or intent of the passage. Being able to answer a few basic questions about Reading Comprehension passages before you even see any of the questions is a key skill that will help you answer questions more quickly and more accurately. The summaries provided here will give you some sense of how to approach summarizing when looking at actual questions.

- Detailed solutions that explain what the correct answer is, and what strategy of strategies you could use to determine the correct answer. Explanatory answers will usually refer back to the summary.

Passage 1

Question 1 is based on the following passage.

It was supposed that Tezcatlipoca had guided the Nahua, and especially the people of Tezcuco, from a more northerly clime to the valley of Mexico. But he was not a mere local deity of Tezcuco, his worship being widely celebrated throughout the country. His exalted position in the Mexican pantheon seems to have won for him especial reverence as a god of fate and fortune. The place he took as the head of the Nahua pantheon brought him many attributes which were quite foreign to his original character. Fear and a desire to exalt their tutelar deity will impel the devotees of a powerful god to credit him with any or every quality, so that there is nothing remarkable in the spectacle of the heaping of every possible attribute, human or divine, upon Tezcatlipoca when we recall the supreme position he occupied in Mexican mythology. His priestly caste far surpassed in power and in the breadth and activity of its propaganda the priesthoods of the other Mexican deities.

1. Select the sentence in the passage that predicts the likelihood that a leader will need to deviate from his initial intentions.

Passage 2

Question 2 is based on the following passage.

A pleasant and elevated spot being fixed upon, Sheddad despatched a hundred chiefs to collect skilled artists and workmen from all countries. He also commanded the monarchs of Syria and Ormus to send him all their jewels and precious stones. Forty camel-loads of gold, silver, and jewels were daily used in the building, which contained a thousand spacious quadrangles of many thousand rooms. When finished, Sheddad marched to view it. Suddenly was heard in the air a voice like thunder, and Sheddad, looking up, beheld a personage of majestic figure and stern aspect, who said, "I am the angel of death, commissioned to seize thy impure soul." Sheddad exclaimed, "Give me leisure to enter the garden," and was descending from his horse, when the seizer of life snatched away his impure spirit, and he fell dead upon the ground. At the same time, lightnings flashed and destroyed the whole army of the infidel, and the rose garden of Irim became concealed from the sight of man.

Select only one answer choice.

2. Which of the following is an explanation for concealing the rose garden of Irim from the sight of man?

    - A   To prevent theft of the precious metals and gems used in its construction

    - B   To reserve its spectacular beauty for God and His angels

    - C   To prevent Sheddad's heirs from claiming it as their own

    - D   As a preventive against using the riches of other countries to promote oneself

    - E   As a moral lesson about the sin of excessive pride

Passage 3

Questions 3 to 5 are based on the following passage.

By the 1890s Social Darwinist ideas were popular and were making themselves felt, influencing social policies in the United States and elsewhere. Social Darwinism saw human society as based on a struggle for survival, in which the superior, the fittest, would triumph and the inferior would be swept to the wayside. It was more or less the ancient "predator ethic" -- the idea that might makes right, that the strong are entitled to oppress the weak - dressed up in pseudoscientific clothes. If the struggle for survival was the way of the world, then it was only natural that human society should operate in the same way. Social Darwinism also dovetailed with racist thinking: American segregationists used the idea to promote the second-class status of black folk as a positive good. In Germany, Ernst Haeckel took the idea even farther, using it as a framework to propose Aryan race-supremacy notions and German militarism.

3. Select the sentence that explains how humans justified the tenets of social Darwinism.

Consider each of the three choices separately and select all that apply.

4. Based on your understanding of predator ethic, select the events or actions that are examples of such behavior.

    A   Cyber- bullying

    B   Involuntary commitment to a mental institution

    C   The Holocaust

Select only one answer choice.

5. The use of the word "dovetailed" in the context of this passage most closely matches which of the following definitions?

    A   Coincided with

    B   Deviated from

    C   Fit together

    D   Having a series of indentations suggesting dovetails

    E   Split apart

Passage 4

Question 6 is based on the following passage.

The aim of this little work is, therefore, limited to the gathering of such facts and phenomena as may serve to throw light upon the nature of the magic powers with which man is undoubtedly endowed. Its end will be attained if it succeeds in showing that he actually does possess powers which are not subject to the general laws of nature, but more or less independent of space and time, and which yet make themselves known partly by appeals to the ordinary senses and partly by peculiar phenomena, the result of their activity. These higher powers, operating exclusively through the spirit of man, are part of his nature, which has much in common with that of the Deity, since he was created by God "in His own image," and the Lord "breathed into his nostrils the breath of life and man became a living soul.

Select only one answer choice.

6. Based on the information in this passage, what makes it likely that the author will find it difficult to conduct an objective investigation?

  A   His belief in God

  B   His preconceived idea that man has magical powers

  C   The lack of previous research on the subject

  D   The refusal of the church to cooperate in his endeavor

  E   The likelihood that the public will scoff at his ideas

Passage 5

Question 7 is based on the following passage.

I must confess, though, that I am a bibliophile with War books. Any book about the Great War is good enough for me. I am to that class of literature what little boys are to stamps. Yes; I know well the dread implication. I am aware of the worm in the mind; that I probe a wound; that I surrender to an impulse to peer into the darkness of the pit; that I encourage a thought which steals in with the quiet of midnight, and that it keeps me awake while the household sleeps. I know I consort with ghosts in a region of evil. I get the horrors, and I do not repel them. For some reason I like those ghosts. Most of them have no names for me, but I count them as old friends of mine; and where should I meet them again, at night, but amid the scenes we knew.

7. Select the sentence that suggests that the writer may be performing a cathartic act in this passage.

Passage 6

Questions 8 and 9 are based on the following passage.

Out we drove at last. It was December, but by luck we found a halcyon morning which had got lost in the year's procession. It was a Sunday morning, and it had not been ashore. It was still virgin, bearing a vestal light. It had not been soiled yet by any suspicion of this trampled planet, this muddy star, which its innocent and tenuous rays had discovered in the region of night. I thought it still was regarding us as a lucky find there. Its light was tremulous, as if with joy and eagerness. I met this discovering morning as your ambassador while you still slept, and betrayed not, I hope, any greyness and bleared satiety of ours to its pure, frail, and lucid regard. That was the last good service I did before leaving you quite. I was glad to see how well our old earth did meet such a light, as though it had no difficulty in looking day in the face. The world was miraculously renewed.

Select only one answer choice.

8. In the context of this passage, which of the following is the best definition for "lucid"?

    A   Easily understood

    B   Shining or bright

    C   Rational or sane

    D   Clear, transparent

    E   Evident

Consider each of the three choices separately and select all that apply.

9. Select the statement that can replace the second sentence of the passage without altering the overall meaning of the author's words.

    A   Although it was December, we were fortunate to discover tranquil weather that seemed a better fit for a warmer month

    B   It was December, and we discovered a holiday celebration that we had neglected to observe earlier in the year

    C   Because it was December, we felt as carefree on that morning as we had in the summer months

Passage 7

Questions 10 and 11 are based on the following passage.

Friends - This lecture has been delivered under these circumstances: I visit a town or city, and try to arrive there early enough to see the postmaster, the barber, the keeper of the hotel, the principal of the schools, and the ministers of some of the churches, and then go into some of the factories and stores, and talk with the people, and get into sympathy with the local conditions of that town or city and see what has been their history, what opportunities they had, and what they had failed to do - and every town fails to do something - and then go to the lecture and talk to those people about the subjects which applied to their locality. "Acres of Diamonds" - the idea - has continuously been precisely the same. The idea is that in this country of ours every man has the opportunity to make more of himself than he does in his own environment, with his own skill, with his own energy, and with his own friends.

Select only one answer choice.

10. Based on the information in this passage, select the word that best describes his purpose in delivering his presentation, "Acres of Diamonds".

- Ⓐ   Information
- Ⓑ   Confirmation
- Ⓒ   Innovation
- Ⓓ   Motivation
- Ⓔ   Intimidation

Select only one answer choice.

11. What is the relationship of the last two sentences to the preceding portion of the passage?

- (A) They invalidate the process of the writer's visiting local officials and work places.
- (B) They contrast the universality of the idea with the specificity of the points for each town or city.
- (C) They cast aspersions on the officials and townsfolk that he has visited.
- (D) They summarize the information that he has discovered from his visits to officials and work places.
- (E) They support the assumption of failure on the parts of the town's inhabitants.

Passage 8

Questions 12 and 13 are based on the following passage.

Nowhere is there anything just like them. In his best work - and his tales of the great metropolis are his best - he is unique. The soul of his art is unexpectedness. Humor at every turn there is, and sentiment and philosophy and surprise. One never may be sure of himself. The end is always a sensation. No foresight may predict it, and the sensation always is genuine. Whatever else O. Henry was, he was an artist, a master of plot and diction, a genuine humorist, and a philosopher. His weakness lay in the very nature of his art. He was an entertainer bent only on amusing and surprising his reader. Everywhere brilliancy, but too often it is joined to cheapness; art, yet art merging swiftly into caricature. Like Harte, he cannot be trusted. Both writers on the whole may be said to have lowered the standards of American literature, since both worked in the surface of life with theatric intent and always without moral background, O. Henry moves, but he never lifts.

Select only one answer choice.

12. Consider the words of this critic and select word or phrase that best identifies what is missing from O. Henry's writing.

    (A)   Tension

    (B)   Style

    (C)   Subtlety

    (D)   Plot

    (E)   Conflict resolution

Consider each of the three choices separately and select all that apply.

13. Which of the following statements, if true, would have altered this critic's opinion of both O. Henry's and Harte's literary endeavors?

    [A]   The readers of the stories crafted by Harte and O. Henry are left with a sense of satisfaction

    [B]   Harte's and O. Henry's stories continue to appear in secondary school anthologies

    [C]   The themes in the works of both writers provide significant insight into the motivations of human behavior

Passage 9

Questions 14 to 19 are based on the following passage.

Men's ideas root pretty far back. Their religious creeds are very old. By means of interest and hope and largely fear, they manage to hang on to the old, even when they know it is not true. The idea of man's importance came in the early history of the human race. He looked out on the earth, and of course he thought it was flat! It looks flat, and he thought it was. He saw the sun, and he formed the conception that somebody moved it out every morning and pulled it back in at night. He saw the moon, and he had the opinion that somebody pulled that out at sundown and took it in the morning. He saw the stars, and all there was about the stars was, "He made the stars also." They were just "also." They were close by, and they were purely for man to look at, about like diamonds in the shirt bosoms of people who like them.

This was not an unreasonable idea, considering what they had to go on. The people who still believe it have no more to go on. Blind men can't be taught to see or deaf people to hear. The primitive people thought that the stars were right nearby and just the size they seemed to be. Of course now we know that some of them are so far away that light traveling at nearly 286,000 miles a second is several million light years getting to the earth, and some of them are so large that our sun, even, would be a fly-speck to them. The larger the telescopes the more of them we see, and the imagination can't compass the end of them. It is just humanly possible that somewhere amongst the infinite number of infinitely larger and more important specks of mud in the universe there might be some organisms of matter that are just as intelligent as our people on the earth. So to have the idea that all of this was made for man gives man a great deal of what Weber and Field used to call "Proud flesh."

Man can't get conceited from what he knows today, and he can't get it from what intellectual people ever knew. You remember, in those days the firmament was put in to divide the water below from the water above. They didn't know exactly what it was made of, but they knew what it was. Heaven was up above the firmament. They knew what it was, because Jacob had seen the angels going up and down on a ladder. Of course, a ladder was the only transportation for such purposes known to Jacob. If he had been dreaming now, they would have been going up in a flying machine and coming down in the same way.

Our conceptions of things root back; and that, of course, is the reason for our crude religions, our crude laws, our crude ideas, and our exalted opinion of the human race.

Select only one answer choice.

14. In the context of this passage, which of the following definitions most closely fits the use of the word "crude" in the last sentence of the passage?

    A   Lacking in intellectual subtlety, perceptivity

    B   Unrefined or natural

    C   Lacking finish, polish, or completeness

    D   Lacking culture, refinement, tact

    E   Undisguised; blunt

Select only one answer choice.

15. What purpose is served by the author's using the speed of light in the second paragraph?

    A   To reveal the author's level of education

    B   To demonstrate how man's understanding of the universe has increased

    C   To help the reader understand the context of the passage

    D   To explain how distant the stars actually are

    E   To show the value of telescopes

Select only one answer choice.

16. What does the author's use of the words "blind" and "deaf" in the second paragraph reveal about his attitude toward his topic?

    A   They make evident his optimism for the human race

    B   They demonstrate his fear for the human race

    C   They show his scorn for members of the human race

    D   They reveal his feelings of superiority over other men

    E   They reinforce his sense of hopelessness about science in general

Consider each of the three choices separately and select all that apply.

17. Which of the following is akin to the story of Jacob's ladder?

  A President Kennedy's declaration that the United States would send a man to the moon by the end of the 1960's

  B The belief that the Earth is the center of the universe

  C Columbus' calling the natives of the New World Indians

Consider each of the three choices separately and select all that apply.

18. What does the author imply when he says at the beginning of the third paragraph that man can't get conceited from what he knows today?

  A Man has failed to make significant progress in knowledge

  B Man's current knowledge will be made insignificant by the knowledge of future generations

  C The knowledge that man possesses is not used for the advancement of the human race

19. Select the sentence that supports the author's opinion that man is conceited.

Passage 10

Question 20 is based on the following passage.

Is human nature intrinsically good or inherently evil? One of the most prominent and influential arguments for the latter was put forward by the British political philosopher Thomas Hobbes. In his seminal work, Leviathan, Hobbes established his theory of the social contract, in which he claimed that humans without government exist in a state of nature where each individual has a right to everything, engendering a "war against all". This environment creates a constant fear of death and prevents humans from both obtaining and hoping for the necessities needed to survive. It is only through the establishment of a civil society by way of a social contract that individuals are able to unite and thrive collectively. For Hobbes, society is what tames and controls the ultimately selfish and corrupt natural state of the human being.

20. Select the sentence that best illustrates Hobbes' view on human nature.

Passage 11

Questions 21 and 22 are based on the following passage.

The Pop Art movement is generally seen as the aesthetic expression of capitalism, its motifs and imagery centering on mass production and consumer culture. The hallmark of Pop Art is its ability to make the viewer feel that it is pretend and not worthy of serious critique. A good example of such a work is pop artist Andy Warhol's images of Campbell's Soup cans. While Pop Art seems superfluous at the surface level, it is actually produced with marked intentionality and has a message that splinters in two directions. In Britain, Pop Artists use the capitalist aesthetic to mock and critique the vapidity of American consumer society while American Pop Artists tend to use their work as a celebration of reality and a slight re-imagining of familiar surroundings.

Select only one answer choice.

21. How does British Pop Art differ from American Pop Art?

- (A)   There is no difference
- (B)   British Pop Art lampoons American consumer culture while American Pop Art focuses on re-creating reality
- (C)   British Pop Art is not worthy of serious critique while American Pop Art is highly valued as a legitimate form of aesthetic expression
- (D)   British Pop artists are more famous than American Pop artists
- (E)   British Pop artists avoid exploring capitalism in their work while American Pop artists use their work to address issues related to capitalism

Consider each of the three choices separately and select all that apply.

22. What traits of capitalistic culture does Pop Art seek to explore?

    A   Consumerism

    B   Mass production

    C   Free markets

Passage 12

Question 23 is based on the following passage.

One of the defining features of the Art Nouveau movement was its desire to distance itself aesthetically from previous methods of artistic expression. Art Nouveau arose at the turn of the 20th century as a reaction to the Neoclassicist movement's propensity to simply mimic the style of the Greeks and Romans. Art Nouveau artists sought to create a truly new and distinct way of representing the world and this is best exemplified in their architectural approach. They used asymmetry and curvy lines and forms in conjunction with leafs, vines, and other unusual patterns to construct and decorate their buildings in a way that had never before been seen.

23. Select the sentence that best describes why Art Nouveau artists were looking to radically alter artistic expression.

Passage 13

Questions 24 and 25 are based on the following passage.

Jacques Derrida famously proclaimed, "There is nothing outside the text." By this he meant that analyzing a work of literature could only be done by way of investigating its labyrinthine relationships to other contexts. As a literary critic and founder of deconstructionist theory, Derrida advocated the position that there is no true or objective reference that can serve as a hermeneutical springboard; narratives can only be understood by deconstructing the various frameworks that inform the interpretive process.

Select only one answer choice.

24. It can be inferred that Derrida prefers a subjective approach to literary analysis because

    A   Textual analysis is dependent on deconstructing complex narratives

    B   All texts are context sensitive and thus subjectivity is a more illuminating approach to finding meaning than objectivity

    C   Subjectivity accounts for the different ways readers experience and interpret a text

    D   Deconstructionist theory is predicated on the inner experience of each reader

    E   Subjectivity allows for a wider array of interesting interpretations of a given text

Consider each of the three choices separately and select all that apply.

25. Derrida's claim "There is nothing outside the text" can be taken to mean that

    A   Texts are connected to the myriad of contexts that contribute to their overall meaning

    B   Texts cannot be studied as independent entities

    C   There is no reality outside of the text

Passage 14

Question 26 is based on the following passage.

Modernist literature bloomed at the beginning of the 20th century and was characterized by concise language and precise imagery. Modernist writers such as Ezra Pound and T.S. Eliot used their poetry and prose to express sentiments of radical individualism and methodical order. However, this conviction quickly deteriorated from praise of autonomy to a more introspective, darker look at humanity and the role of the individual as the exactitude of form that modernists so cherished in their writing came to represent the meticulousness with which the industrialized world could extinguish human life during World War I and World War II.

Select only one answer choice.

26. Given the information in the passage, all of the following are true relative to modernist writing except

- (A) Modernist writing evolved to mirror cultural changes
- (B) Modernist writing lauds the primacy of coherent form
- (C) Modernist writing is at its crux deeply reflective.
- (D) Modernist writing eschews florid prose
- (E) Modernist writing is mechanical in nature

Passage 15

Questions 27 and 28 are based on the following passage.

Sun Tzu's The Art of War is one of the earliest and most celebrated books on military strategy in the world. The Art of War covers a variety of topics related to success on the battlefield and, astoundingly, people at nearly all levels of Chinese society in both the past and present are familiar with the text. One of the most influential themes in the book is its emphasis on the ability to evolve and change plans in the present moment instead of focusing solely on developing rigidly thought-out, long-term strategies. This efficacious strategy defined success as the ability to evolve and utilize a quick wit when the situation calls for such action.

Select only one answer choice.

27. The author's personal opinion on The Art of War can be best described as

- (A) Light-hearted
- (B) Aloof
- (C) Unaligned
- (D) Inert
- (E) Phlegmatic

Select only one answer choice.

28. The author intends the term efficacious in the passage to be analogous to

     A   Ambitious

     B   Useful

     C   Potent

     D   Adequate

     E   Unorganized

Passage 16

Questions 29 to 31 are based on the following passage.

A true visionary, Albert Camus changed the way we think about the world we live in. Although he rejected the label himself, Nobel Laureate Camus is most commonly associated with the 20th century existential movement in art, philosophy, and literature. Born in Algeria to French colonists, Camus used his writing to explore the philosophical idea of the absurd. In novels such as The Stranger and The Plague, Camus underscored his belief that human beings desire meaning and understanding in a world that cannot fulfill this need. This ultimately leads to the erection of civil societies that, if examined more closely, are mired in and permeated by the absurd "at every street corner."

Select only one answer choice.

29. Based on the information given in the passage, which of the following can be inferred about existentialism?

     A   Existentialism concerns itself mainly with the humanities

     B   Existentialism is a method of exploring the absurdity of modern life

     C   Existentialism is a school of philosophical thought

     D   Existentialism teaches people that life has no inherent meaning

     E   Existentialism helps delineate the various structures found in civil society

Consider each of the three choices separately and select all that apply.

30. Why are humans unable to extract meaning and understanding from the world?

 A   Because there is no meaning in the world

 B   Because humans do not yet possess the knowledge needed to understand the world

 C   Because they do not pay close enough attention to the way in which civil societies are structured

31. Select the sentence that best describes the hamartia of the search for meaning in the world according to Camus.

Passage 17

Question 32 is based on the following passage.

The latter half of the 20th century witnessed the rise of a new epistemological approach in the humanities: postcolonial theory. Postcolonial theory was a reaction to the Western meta-narratives of European Imperialism that had been deeply entrenched in global society. It sought to give the colonized and their experience a voice in literature, cultural studies, politics, and philosophy in order to illuminate the fact that global reality had been constructed by European cultural power and that cultural space is really a fluid interaction of a "multiplicity of positionalities."

Select only one answer choice.

32. According to the passage, what was the primary consequence of European Imperialism?

  (A) European imperialism created norms that dictated the structure of global society

  (B) European Imperialism made it difficult for diversity to thrive

  (C) The colonized were unable to participate in the political systems erected by colonial societies

  (D) European Imperialism had little effect on global society

  (E) European Imperialism promoted a cultural space comprised by a variety of cultural perspectives

Passage 18

Questions 33 to 38 below are based on the passage below.

Authorial intent is a vehemently debated topic within the realm of literary criticism. Some critics, such as the Marxists, believe that the author's intentions and ideological leanings shape the content of his or her work while others insist that the text is a completely independent artistic entity, impervious to external influences. Many scholars engaged with the New Criticism school of thought are proponents of the latter approach to textual analysis.

Narrowing the scope of the authorial intent debate, Franz Kafka is a writer whose narratives lend themselves well to this literary tiff. Kafka is widely regarded as one of the most prolific and inventive writers of the 20th century and is credited with changing the way many readers and writers viewed the form, content, and limits of fiction. His works are penetrated by alienation, persecution, and a metaphysical sense of magical realism that leave the doors wide open to the debate on whether or not Kafka's prose was an ideological tool or autonomous artistic expression. However, the consensus among scholars tends to hover around the conclusion that Kafka's texts were intentional metaphors for his ideological beliefs and experiences. Kafka's use of the law in his stories provides a compelling example of why this might be the case.

As a trained lawyer, Kafka was well aware of the ins and outs of the legal system in his native Prague - at that time a part of the Austro-Hungarian Empire. In his fiction, particularly in the aptly named The Trial or The Penal Colony, Kafka often portrayed the legal system as rigid, absurd, and tyrannical, as evidenced by arrests for unspecified crimes or the construction of elaborate tools for punishment. The images and metaphors that Kafka infuses his prose with regarding the law and the legal process are what constitute not only the meaning of his fiction but also his personal view on the law. His fiction is written with intention - the intention to show that the legal system is comprised of arbitrary signs and symbols that neither the lawmen nor laymen seem to understand. Thus, the images and themes in Kafka's works are intentionally placed to promote a deliberate message to the readership.

Kafka's use of the law is just one example of why many literary critics hold fast to the idea that every author produces a narrative that has intentional meaning - it is difficult to imagine that a writer can produce a text without having some kind of interpretive goal or objective in mind. However, since no hermeneutical approach to a fictional work's meaning is ever set in stone, the authorial intent debate, like all points of contention in literary criticism, is now and always will be open to a multiplicity of interpretations.

Select only one answer choice.

33. Which of the following can most reasonably be inferred from the passage?

- (A)   Kafka was anti-authoritarian
- (B)   The Marxist's have the best method of textual inquiry
- (C)   Kafka's fiction impacted the practice and implementation of law in the West
- (D)   Authorial intent can always be determined by properly analyzing the form and content of a piece of narrative fiction
- (E)   Literary criticism concerns itself primarily with the search for objective truth

Select only one answer choice.

34. Given the information in the passage, how would the author define the concept of authorial intent?

   A   Authorial intent is the aggregate of the author's personal opinions and experiences that can influence the meaning of a given text

   B   Authorial intent is best defined as the author's main impetus for writing a text

   C   Authorial intent is the sum of an author's subjective thoughts that always create the meaning of a given text

   D   Authorial intent is the term coined by the New Critics for a specific kind of writing style

   E   The passage does not give enough information to define authorial intent

Select only one answer choice.

35. The author intends the term hermeneutical in the last sentence to be analogous to

   A   Methodological

   B   Intentional

   C   Epistemological

   D   Explicative

   E   Remedial

Consider each of the three choices separately and select all that apply.

36. What postulation does the passage put forth to argue that Kafka's works convey his personal opinions on law and legality?

   A   Kafka used metaphor to describe how difficult it was for laymen to understand the law and legal process

   B   Kafka used images and themes of absurdity and tyranny in his fiction to reinforce his belief that the legal process was based on arbitrary authoritarian signs and symbols

   C   Kafka used his prose to show that he did not like the legal system because he was a reluctant lawyer

Consider each of the three choices separately and select all that apply.

37. According to the information given in the passage, Kafka believed the legal system to be

    | A | Intransigent |
    | B | Incongruous |
    | C | Inane |

38. Select the sentence that delineates Kafka's tropes.

This page is intentionally left blank

4

Practice Set 2 - Biological Sciences

This chapter is devoted to helping you develop your skill with Reading Comprehension questions using concrete examples. You will find passages related to *Biological Sciences* that are similar to the sorts of passages you will encounter on an actual GRE test. Each passage has a set of questions and a detailed explanation of the solution to each question. The questions and their solutions will be presented as follows:

In this chapter:

- A passage related to *Biological Sciences* similar to what you can expect on an actual GRE test

- Several questions about the passage similar to those you will encounter on an actual GRE test

In *Explanatory Answers for Practice Set 2: Biological Sciences*:

- A quick summary that paraphrases the main issues of the passage and points out important words or phrases that indicate the meaning or intent of the passage. Being able to answer a few basic questions about Reading Comprehension passages before you even see any of the questions is a key skill that will help you answer questions more quickly and more accurately. The summaries provided here will give you some sense of how to approach summarizing when looking at actual questions

- Detailed solutions that explain what the correct answer is, and what strategy of strategies you could use to determine the correct answer. Explanatory answers will usually refer back to the summary

Passage 19

Question 39 is based on the following passage.

We may note here the meaning of certain terms we shall be constantly employing. The head end of the rabbit is anterior, the tail end posterior, the backbone side of the body-- the upper side in life-- is dorsal, the breast and belly side, the lower side of the animal, is ventral. If we imagine the rabbit sawn asunder, as it were, by a plane passing through the head and tail, that would be the median plane, and parts on either side of it are lateral, and left or right according as they lie to the animal's left or right. In a limb, or in the internal organs, the part nearest the central organ, or axis, is proximal, the more remote or terminal parts are distal. For instance, the mouth is anteriorly placed, the tongue on its ventral wall; the tongue is median, the eyes are lateral, and the fingers are distal to the elbow. The student must accustom himself to these words, and avoid, in his descriptions, the use of such terms as "above," "below," "outside," which vary with the position in which we conceive the animal placed.

Consider the answer choices separately and select all that apply.

39. Select the scenario below that best reflects the writer's purpose in this passage.

   - [A] Sailing a yacht in the America's Cup race
   - [B] Performing brain surgery
   - [C] Repairing a truck engine

Passage 20

Question 40 is based on the following passage.

In the jungles of India, which preserve a state of things which has existed for immemorial years, we find the tiger, his stripes simulating jungle reeds, his noiseless approach learnt from nature in countless millions of lessons of success and failure, his perfectly powerful claws and execution methods; and, living in the same jungle, and with him as one of the conditions of life, are small deer, alert, swift, light of build, inconspicuous of colour, sharp of hearing, keen-eyed, keen-scented-- because any downward variation from these attributes means swift and certain death. To capture the deer is a condition, of the tiger's life, to escape the tiger a condition of the deer's; and they play a great contest under these conditions, with life as the stake. The most alert deer almost always escape; the least so, perish.

Consider the answer choices separately and select all that apply.

40. Which of the following events would cause a decline in the number of tigers in the jungles of India?

    A   Commercial harvesting of the jungle reeds

    B   Destruction of the food source for the deer

    C   A mutation causing a change in the deer's ability to see clearly

Passage 21

Question 41 is based on the following passage.

From this you can see that it is especially important to know all you can about the life of injurious insects, since it is often easier to kill these pests at one stage of their life than at another. Often it is better to aim at destroying the seemingly harmless beetle or butterfly than to try to destroy the larvae that hatch from its eggs, although, as you must remember, it is generally the larvae that do the most harm. Larvae grow very rapidly; therefore the food supply must be great to meet the needs of the insect.

Select only one answer choice.

41. Consider the information in this passage and select what relationship it likely has to the text that precedes it.

    A   It functions as the conclusion

    B   It functions as an explanation of an idea from the preceding paragraph

    C   It functions as a warning about a situation mentioned in the previous paragraph

    D   It serves as a transition between the previous paragraph and the conclusion

    E   It reinforces the idea presented in the previous portion of the text

Passage 22

Questions 42 to 44 are based on the following passage.

We have already given a description of the mammalian skull, and we have stated where the origin of the several bones was in membrane, and where in cartilage; but a more complete comprehension of the mammalian skull becomes possible with the handling of a lower type. We propose now, first to give some short account of the development and structure of the skull of the frog, and then to show briefly how its development and adult arrangement demonstrate the mammalian skull to be a fundamentally similar structure, complicated and disguised by further development and re-adjustment.

Select only one answer choice.

42. Which of the following is the most appropriate audience for the information in this passage?

   - Ⓐ   Herpetologists
   - Ⓑ   Zoologists
   - Ⓒ   Endocrinologists
   - Ⓓ   Thoracic surgeons
   - Ⓔ   Craniologists

Select only one answer choice.

43. Select from the following list the definition of "fundamentally" that most closely matches the use of the word in this context.

   - Ⓐ   Primarily
   - Ⓑ   Basically; underlying
   - Ⓒ   Of or affecting the foundation or basis
   - Ⓓ   Originally
   - Ⓔ   Indispensably

Consider each answer choice separately and select all that apply.

44. Based on the information in this passage, which of the following is likely to be true about the study of human anatomy.

    | A | Every aspect of human anatomy has a corresponding structure in a lower life form |
    | B | Examining amphibian anatomy leads to a better understanding of human anatomy |
    | C | Examining anatomical structures of other life forms may lead to a better understanding of human anatomy |

Passage 23

Questions 45 to 47 are based on the following passage.

Many attempts have been made and are still being made to increase the length of the staple of the upland types. The methods used are as follows: selection of seed having a long fiber; special cultivation and fertilization; crossing the short-stapled cotton on the long-stapled cotton. This last process, as already explained, is called hybridizing. Many of these attempts have succeeded, and there are now a large number of varieties which excel the older varieties in profitable yield. The new varieties are each year being more widely grown. Every farmer should study the new types and select the one that will best suit his land. The new types have been developed under the best tillage. Therefore if a farmer would keep the new type as good as it was when he began to grow it, he must give it the same good tillage, and practice seed-selection.

45. Select the sentence in the passage that justifies the writer's purpose in this piece.

Select only one answer choice.

46. Which of the following is a reasonable conclusion based on the content of the passage?

    A   Hybridization is a long and costly endeavor

    B   The benefit or a hybrid is that it can adapt to any conditions

    C   Fertilization produces the best results with hybrid plants

    D   Overlooking one of the cultivation criteria will reduce the success of a hybrid seed

    E   Farmers should select the hybrid that demands the highest price after harvesting

Select only one answer choice.

47. The use of the word "tillage" in this context implies that which of the following is most important to insure crop success?

    A   Good soil preparation

    B   Correct nutrient application

    C   Sufficient use of pesticides

    D   Adequate irrigation

    E   Widespread application of mulch

Passage 24

Question 48 is based on the following passage.

The reason for mixing clover and grass is at once seen. The true grasses, so far as science now shows, get all their nitrogen from the soil; hence they more or less exhaust the soil. But, as several times explained in this book, the clovers are legumes, and all legumes are able by means of the bacteria that live on their roots to use the free nitrogen of the air. Hence without cost to the farmer these clovers help the soil to feed their neighbors, the true grasses. For this reason some light perennial legume should always be added to grass seed.

48. Select the sentence in this passage that demonstrates that growing clover is preferable to adding nitrogen-rich fertilizer to the soil.

Passage 25

Questions 49 to 51 are based on the following passage.

It may seem somewhat superfluous to say that fish cannot live in any water unless that water contains the food supply necessary for them to thrive upon, and yet this is the point most often overlooked in stocking waters with fish. Small attempts at stocking with creatures suitable for food, particularly after the fish have been already introduced, are not at all likely to succeed. Such an important matter when treated as a small afterthought is almost sure to end in failure of the whole business of stocking.

49. Select the sentence that most closely exemplifies the adage, "An ounce of prevention is worth a pound of cure".

Select only one answer choice.

50. What assumption about fish is the reader apt to make after reading this passage?

    A   Fish have specific diets

    B   Fish in a pond with no food source will be easier to catch

    C   Fish are slow to adapt to a new food source

    D   Fish become cannibalistic when deprived of a natural food source

    E   Fish will migrate to a source of food

Select only one answer choice.

51. In a presentation on stocking a pond with fish, where, in the sequence, is the best place for the information in this passage?

    (A)   The introduction

    (B)   The conclusion

    (C)   Immediately following a discussion of the types of food necessary for fish to thrive in a pond

    (D)   Immediately prior to a discussion of the types of food necessary for fish to thrive in a pond

    (E)   Immediately prior to a discussion of the vegetation needed in the pond

Passage 26

Questions 52 to 54 are based on the following passage.

Whether, therefore, a tree might possibly continue living and growing forever is a question of less entertainment than the question of its possible duration in the common state of nature and under the irreversible conditions of climate, soil, and the elements. What age may we ascribe to some of our largest specimens, either still existing or recorded in trustworthy history? Is the period of one thousand years, the favorite figure of tradition, a common or probable period of arboreal longevity, or have our proudest forest giants attained their present size in half the time that is commonly claimed for them?

In the discussion of this question we have but few known data to guide us, since statistics of the rate of growth, as afforded by careful measurement, date only from about the beginning of the eighteenth century. Of such statistics we may dismiss at once measurement of height or of the spread of a tree's boughs, the measurement of girth being far easier and more conclusive.

52. Select the sentence that implies that the ages of apparently old trees were arbitrarily determined.

Select only one answer choice.

53. Select the most accurate definition of entertainment as it appears in the first sentence of this passage.

     (A)   Amusement

     (B)   Something affording pleasure

     (C)   A performance

     (D)   An agreeable occupation of the mind

     (E)   Consideration

Select only one answer choice.

54. Use the progression of ideas in this passage to select which of the following is the most probable topic of the writer's next paragraph.

     (A)   Other means of determining the age of trees

     (B)   How soil and climate conditions contribute to arboreal longevity

     (C)   The progress made in aging trees between the end of the eighteenth century and the end of the nineteenth century

     (D)   An argument for replacing the one-thousand-year measurement for very old trees with a more moderate five-hundred-year measurement

     (E)   The part of the world that is home to the oldest trees

Passage 27

Questions 55 to 58 are based on the following passage.

Of course you know my friend the squirting cucumber. If you don't, that can be only because you've never looked in the right place to find him. On all waste ground outside most southern cities-Nice, Cannes, Florence; Rome, Algiers, Granada; Athens, Palermo, Tunis, where you will-the soil is thickly covered by dark, trailing vines which bear on their branches a queer, hairy, green fruit, much like a common cucumber at that early stage of its existence when we know it best in the commercial form of pickled gherkins. As long as you don't interfere with them, these hairy, green fruits do nothing out of the common in the way of personal aggressiveness. Like the model young lady of the books on etiquette, they don't speak unless they're spoken to. But if peradventure you chance to brush up against the plant accidentally, or you irritate it of set purpose with your foot or your cane, then, as Mr. Rider Haggard would say, "a strange thing happens ": off jumps the little green fruit with a startling bounce, and scatters its juice and pulp and seeds explosively through a hole in the end where the stem joined on to it. The entire central part of the cucumber, in short (answering to the seeds and pulp of a ripe melon), squirt out elastically through the breach in the outer wall, leaving the hollow shell behind as a mere empty windbag.

Naturally, the squirting cucumber knows its own business best, and is not without sufficient reasons of its own for this strange and, to some extent, unmannerly behavior. By its queer trick of squirting, it manages to kill at least two birds with one stone. For, in the first place, the sudden elastic jump of the fruit frightens away browsing animals, such as goats and cattle. Those meditative ruminants are little accustomed to finding shrubs or plants take the aggressive against them; and when they see a fruit that quite literally flies in their faces of its own accord, they hesitate to attack the uncanny vine which bristles with such magical and almost miraculous defenses. Moreover, the juice of the squirting cucumber is bitter and nauseous, and if it gets into the eyes or nostrils of man or beast, it impresses itself on the memory by stinging like red pepper. So the trick of squirting serves in a double way as a protection to the plant against the attacks of herbivorous animals and other enemies.

But that's not all. Even when no enemy is near, the ripe fruits at last drop off of themselves, and scatter their seeds elastically in every direction. This they do simply in order to disseminate their kind in new and unoccupied spots, where the seedlings will root and find an opening in life for themselves. Observe, indeed, that the very word "disseminate" implies a general vague recognition of this principle of plant-life on the part of humanity. It means, etymologically, to scatter seed; and it points to the fact that everywhere in nature seeds are scattered broadcast, infinite pains being taken by the mother-plant for their general diffusion over wide areas of woodland, plain, or prairie.

Consider each answer choice separately and select all that apply

55. Which of the following examples of adaptation is similar to that of the squirting cucumber?

    A   The camel's ability to go for long periods of time without water

    B   The remora's ability to establish a host relationship with a shark

    C   The chameleon's ability to camouflage itself

Select only one answer choice.

56. Consider the style elements in this passage to determine the writer's tone.

    A   Satiric

    B   Sarcastic

    C   Admiring

    D   Awestruck

    E   Antagonistic

Select only one answer choice.

57. Which of the following designate the main points of this passage?

    A   Repulsion and reproduction

    B   Accident and intention

    C   Offense and defense

    D   Adaptation and mutation

    E   Allusion and illusion

58. Select the sentence that expresses the same warning as the familiar adage, "Let sleeping dogs lie."

Passage 28

Question 59 is based on the following passage.

Research on barn swallows gives us insight into the ways in which hormones affect the behavior of various species, including our own. Male barn swallows with the most vibrantly colored feathers are most attractive to females and thus mate much more frequently than their dull-feathered male counterparts. Scientists, however, have discovered that simply darkening the feathers of the lusterless males with a marker can change their hormone levels, turning beta males into alpha males since their mating rates increase dramatically. This is due not only to an increase in attractiveness to females but also an increase in the confidence of the males, consequently engendering higher levels of testosterone.

Select only one answer choice.

59. Given the information in the passage, what is the relationship between confidence and hormones in male barn swallows?

- (A) Confidence plays a minor role in the increase of certain hormones in male barn swallows
- (B) Physically attractive male barn swallows are more confident and thus experience higher levels of testosterone
- (C) Only inherently attractive alpha male barn swallows have confidence due to high testosterone levels
- (D) Confidence is the sole factor in raising the testosterone levels of male barn swallows
- (E) Confidence plays no role in the hormonal patterns of male barn swallows; mating is the key factor in fluctuating hormone levels

Passage 29

Questions 60 to 62 are based on the following passage.

According to anthropologists, observing primates in Senegal is like opening a window to the world of understanding the behavior of early humans, particularly related to sharing. They have found that the chimpanzees display an intentional willingness to share food and rudimentary hunting tools with each other, an important detection since it was previously thought that chimpanzees usually only shared meat. However, this sharing is not altruistically motivated. Since it is an exchange that primarily takes place from males to females, anthropologists have postulated a "food for sex" theory. This claim is further backed up by the fact that sexually receptive females in their reproductive years were most likely to receive food and supplies from males.

Select only one answer choice.

60. What is inferred by the "food for sex" theory in primates?

- Ⓐ   Attractive females have the best chances for survival
- Ⓑ   Sexual gratification is the primary motivation of male primates
- Ⓒ   Male primates are ultimately exploitative
- Ⓓ   Primates display a high level of magnanimity
- Ⓔ   Male primates are lazy

Select only one answer choice.

61. According to the passage, understanding group behavior in primates is important because

- Ⓐ   Primates are closely related to humans and thus can help us better understand our own species
- Ⓑ   Group behavior in primates can help us understand specifically the way males and females share
- Ⓒ   Primates can help humans see why it is important to learn to be altruistic
- Ⓓ   Group behavior in primates is the key to understanding behavior patterns in all species
- Ⓔ   The sexual habits of primates can enlighten humans as to their own motivations for sex

62. Select the sentence that makes use of the rhetorical device of the trope.

Passage 30

Question 63 is based on the following passage.

Starvation-induced antibiotic resistance is one of the primary reasons many bacteria are elusive when it comes to treatment and as a result some infections are actually impossible to cure. This situation proves paradoxical to scientists, as many of the bacteria that are antibiotic-sensitive still exhibit remarkable survival skills. As soon as bacteria, which typically gather in clusters, sense that their supply of nutrients is waning, they issue a chemical warning that causes them to modify their metabolic rates as a means of defending against starvation, which in turn halts their growth. Many forms of antibiotic treatment, which target active bacteria, are then rendered ineffective since starving bacteria stall cellular growth and lie dormant.

Consider each of the three choices separately and select all that apply.

63. According to the passage, starvation protects bacteria from medications by

  A Modifying its growth patterns

  B Making it impervious to antibiotic attack

  C Changing its chemical composition

Passage 31

Questions 64 to 66 are based on the following passage.

Ocean acidification due to the absorption of atmospheric carbon dioxide is a major threat to coral reef ecosystems worldwide and scientists are looking for ways to both understand and combat this phenomenon. This is an especially vital area of exploration since coral reefs are home to 25% of all marine species. Studies pertaining to ocean acidity and the coral reef have been conducted at the submarine springs near the Yucatan Peninsula in Mexico, a perfect environment due to the naturally occurring high acidity (low pH). They have found that the type of coral that serves as the foundation of the reef is unable to calcify and grow in high acidity, which means that the continued absorption of carbon from the atmosphere could halt or dramatically change the growth of the ocean's coral reefs - a terrible catastrophe for the delicate balance of life undersea.

Select only one answer choice.

64. From the information given in the passage, what are the implications of the continued occurrence of low pH levels in the world's oceans?

- A   The atmosphere will continue to absorb carbon from the high acidity ocean
- B   At least 25% of all marine species will die
- C   The low acidity will negatively impact the growth of the foundation of the coral reefs
- D   Since many types of coral can grow in high acidity, coral reefs are not in any dramatic danger
- E   Continued acidification will make it difficult for coral reefs to grow and support marine life

Select only one answer choice.

65. The rhetorical goal of this passage is

- A   To delineate the danger atmospheric carbon dioxide poses to the world's oceans
- B   To invoke an emotional response in the reader relative to ocean acidification
- C   To persuade the reader that ocean acidification is harmful
- D   To delve deeper into the specifics of how pH levels affect coral reefs
- E   To persuade the reader that the coral reefs are in grave danger

66. Select the sentence that best describes the importance of coral reefs in the ocean ecosystem.

Passage 32

Question 67 is based on the following passage.

Malaria is a mosquito-borne disease that attacks its victims by way of parasites within the red blood cells that cause serious illness that can result in coma and death.

Researchers have recently gained a crucial understanding of the disease after discovering why people who have sickle-cell anemia, a prominent hereditary mutation of the red blood pigment hemoglobin, are immune to malaria. The successful transmission of malaria requires that the red blood cells infected by the parasite establish a trafficking system that allows the parasite to access the exterior of the blood cells via its adhesive proteins known as adhesins. However, the mutated hemoglobin present in sickle cell anemics causes these adhesions to occur rarely and often not at all. Thus, mutated hemoglobin (which does not only occur in sickle cell anemia) protects the human body from the malaria parasite.

Consider each of the three choices separately and select all that apply.

67. Which of the following, if true, would weaken the author's contention?

   - [ ] A   Hemoglobin mutations facilitate the bonding of adhesins
   - [ ] B   Adhesins have the ability to attach to blood cells
   - [ ] C   Malaria is able to infect the blood cells of sickle cell anemics

Passage 33

Questions 68 to 70 are based on the following passage.

Oxytocin, also known as the love hormone, bonds mothers to their children and promotes intimacy and relationships in various species including humans. Researchers have recently discovered that administering oxytocin nasally enhances prosocial choices among macaque monkeys. Exposure to the oxytocin caused the monkeys to more frequently share their juice without the expectation of receiving something in return. Scientists believe that it is important to understand how the hormone can impact the behavior in a positive way and monkeys provide valuable information in this regard since they are so closely related to humans.

Select only one answer choice.

68. Based on the information given in the passage, what can be inferred about the scientific motivation to study oxytocin relative to humans?

    A   Humans are closely related to macaques and thus will behave in the same way as them under the influence of oxytocin

    B   Understanding the behavior of macaque monkeys under the influence of oxytocin can help scientists discern how oxytocin can potentially affect behavior in humans

    C   Scientists can find ways of treating antisocial behavior in humans with oxytocin

    D   Scientists can learn how to reproduce oxytocin synthetically as a treatment for depression

    E   Humans are not the focal point of scientific motivation for studying oxytocin

Select only one answer choice.

69. What is meant by "prosocial choices" in the second sentence?

    A   Choices that promote the well-being of others

    B   Choices that are made as a result of higher levels of altruism

    C   Choices that create a hierarchy in the community

    D   Choices that influence hormonal patterns

    E   Choices that cannot be made without the influence of oxytocin

70. Select the sentence that best describes why oxytocin is a crucial component of social attachment.

Passage 34

Question 71 is based on the following passage.

Scientists have taken another step in the direction of better understanding the biological underpinnings of various psychiatric disorders. They have homed in on the gene named RNF123 because of affect on the hippocampus, the area of the brain that is altered in people with major depression. They hope to be able to then ascertain more information about the relationship between the gene, the hippocampus, and the subjective experiences of the patient in order to establish a more holistic approach to understanding the delicate amalgamation of nature vs. nurture in psychiatry and mental health treatment.

71. Select the sentence that best indicates scientists' initial interest in the role of genetics in depression.

Passage 35

Questions 72 to 74 are based on the following passage.

Stem cells are found in all multicellular organisms and their value in research is their ability to differentiate into specialized types of diverse cells as a result of mitosis (cell division). Medical researchers are convinced that human embryonic stem cell therapy has the potential to treat or cure various diseases and physical ailments from cancer to muscle damage; many even go as far as to claim it is a miracle treatment. However, many people stand in opposition to embryonic stem cell therapy, as they believe it is interfering with and exploiting natural life. Furthermore, some scientists believe that stem cell therapy could potentially aggrandize medical conditions rather than cure them. Thus, human embryonic stem cell research remains a highly controversial method of medical treatment.

Select only one answer choice.

72. Mitosis is a specifically important factor in stem cell research because

   A   Mitosis allows scientists to use large quantities of stem cells since they reproduce so quickly

   B   Stem cells after mitosis are stronger and easier for scientists to study

   C   Mitosis generates cells that can be manipulated for a variety of medical purposes

   D   Mitosis is not really an important factor in stem cell research

   E   Stem cells undergo mitosis and become diversified as a result

Select only one answer choice.

73. The author would agree with all of the following except

     A   Stem cell therapy is a sensitive issue

     B   Medical benefits sometimes come at a cost

     C   The outcomes of scientific research do not always align themselves with social mores

     D   The exploitation of natural life is the white elephant in the room of stem cell therapy debate

     E   Stem cells are a testament to the regenerative nature of the human body

Consider each of the three choices separately and select all that apply.

74. According to the passage, stem cell therapy is an ethical conundrum because

     A   Some believe that, despite its efficacy, it is the immoral treatment of natural life

     B   Many maintain that it promotes a culture of death, despite the fact that it is an extremely useful form of medical treatment

     C   Despite its flexibility as a treatment, stem cell therapy can also have adverse effects

Passage 36

Questions 75 to 78 are based on the following passage.

It has been a long-held belief within the field of biology that our DNA is fixed and unchangeable. While environmental factors may cause us to gain weight, lose a limb, or contract a virus, our underlying genetic sequence will remain constant. However, this popular view among scientists is beginning to shift towards a more fluid definition of the human genome; a new subfield within genetics, epigenetics, is exploring how environmental factors can actually change the expression of our genetic code throughout the course of our lives.

Epigenetics is the study of heritable changes to the cellular phenotypes of the DNA sequence, changes that have occurred as a result of external environmental factors after conception. Environmental factors are able to stimulate a particular gene, switching it on or off or altering it in some way. Through cellular division, the changes to the gene then have the potential to be passed on as heritable traits in subsequent generations.

One way that scientists are delving into epigenetic inquiry is by studying heritability in animals. Scientists have been able to show that when a rat is subjected to a stressful environment during pregnancy, epigenetic changes to the fetus can engender behavioral problems in the rat's progeny as they mature and reach adulthood.

Scientists are also using human twins to better understand epigenetics and a related process called DNA methylation. DNA methylation causes genes to be expressed either stronger or weaker. By testing DNA samples taken from identical twins, scientists are able to identify areas where DNA methylation has impacted the expression of a particular gene in the sequence. Since identical twins have identical DNA, creating a methylation profile for each twin allows scientists to account for any subtle to extreme differences in behavior, opening the window to understanding how epigenetic processes affect both our personalities and our genetic code.

Epigenetics is still in the nascent stages of its development as a field of biological study, but it is nonetheless an incredibly exciting and groundbreaking area. It throws a wrench into Darwin's theory of evolution since it demonstrates how evolutionary changes can occur within one generation instead of spanning thousands of years. The possibility of such rapid evolutionary changes has major implications for how we think of not only life on earth but also the power we have to impact it, for better or worse.

Select only one answer choice.

75. What is meant by "nascent" in the last paragraph of the passage?

    A   Nascent means that epigenetics is an old and established field of study within the biological community

    B   Nascent means that epigenetics should not be seen as a valid method of biological inquiry

    C   Nascent means that epigenetics should be seen as a valid method of biological inquiry

    D   Nascent means that epigenetics is in the early stages of its development as a biological field of study

    E   Nascent means that epigenetics is at a confusing stage in its development as a method of biological inquiry

Select only one answer choice.

76. According to the passage, why are DNA methylation profiles of identical twins important to epigenetics?

    A   The DNA methylation profiles of identical twins are not important to epigenetics

    B   The DNA methylation profiles of identical twins can be compared to see how epigenetic changes affect the genetic code of identical DNA

    C   Investigating the DNA methylation profiles helps scientists better understand the process of cell division and how it affects the genetic code

    D   The DNA methylation profiles of identical twins help scientists understand how twins inherit their genetic code

    E   DNA methylation profiles show where DNA methylation has affected the gene sequence

Consider each of the three choices separately and select all that apply.

77. According to the information given by the author, why do scientists use twins in epigenetic studies?

    A   Twins have identical DNA

    B   Twins are ideal for testing the DNA methylation process and its effects on the genome

    C   Twins look alike and thus it is easier for scientists to identify the expression of a particular phenotype

78. The claims of epigenetics have major implications for the future of the field of biology. Select the sentence form the passage that best describes why.

This page is intentionally left blank

5

Practice Set 3 - Business

This chapter is devoted to helping you develop your skill with Reading Comprehension questions using concrete examples. You will find passages related to *Business* that are similar to the sorts of passages you will encounter on an actual GRE test. Each passage has a set of questions and a detailed explanation of the solution to each question. The questions and their solutions will be presented as follows:

In this chapter:

- A passage related to *Business* similar to what you can expect on an actual GRE test

- Several questions about the passage similar to those you will encounter on an actual GRE test

In *Explanatory Answers for Practice Set 3: Business:*

- A quick summary that paraphrases the main issues of the passage and points out important words or phrases that indicate the meaning or intent of the passage. Being able to answer a few basic questions about Reading Comprehension passages before you even see any of the questions is a key skill that will help you answer questions more quickly and more accurately. The summaries provided here will give you some sense of how to approach summarizing when looking at actual questions

- Detailed solutions that explain what the correct answer is, and what strategy of strategies you could use to determine the correct answer. Explanatory answers will usually refer back to the summary

Passage 37

Question 79 is based on the following passage.

Older workers have prospered in the recent economic downturn. Currently, workers aged 55-64 account for 12% of the nation's workers, an increase of nearly 2% since 2000, and by 2010, nearly one in three workers will be at least age 55. A number of factors and trends are contributing to the increase in older adults in the work force including demographics, financial concerns, changing concepts of retirement, longer and healthier life spans, and demand for the knowledge and skills possessed by the current generation of older workers.

Older adults in the work force are not the only ones who remain engaged in productive activities. Many adults who have retired look for expanded opportunities and options - either paid or unpaid - that may represent "a new chapter in life embodying a new definition of success". For these older adults, retirement represents another stage of life - which may extend for as much as 25 years - in which to accomplish many things. Because they have differing abilities, desires, and needs in terms of both paid and unpaid work, adults in late midlife are not homogeneous. As a group, however, they typify some of the changing conceptions of career.

Select only one answer choice.

79. What additional information does the reader need to calculate the impact of older citizens' remaining in the workforce on younger people's ability to obtain employment?

- (A) The number of people in each demographic group that is currently in college
- (B) The average annual salary of workers aged 55-64
- (C) The average amount of debt carried by workers aged 55-64
- (D) The percentage of the total population represented by workers aged 55-64
- (E) The geographic areas in which most of the workers aged 55-64 live

Passage 38

Questions 80 to 85 are based on the following passage.

By the early 20th century, paper currency was in widespread use all over the world. The failures in paper currency were not really due to the fact that the paper money wasn't adequately backed by gold or silver. Although many nations clung to the gold standard well into the 20th century, all money amounts to is a medium of exchange, allowing the citizens of a country to engage in transactions. The US finally completely abandoned the gold standard in 1971. All nations now use "fiat currencies", money which has no intrinsic value and is not backed by precious metals.

The problem with paper currencies was not that they were often inadequately backed by precious metals. The money circulating in a society, in a sense, mirrors the material wealth of a country. It is relatively easy to print more banknotes, but not so easy to increase the overall material wealth of a nation, and so if twice the number of banknotes is printed given the same amount of wealth, the value of each banknote is more or less cut in half. This happened automatically, as if by magic, every time a government cheated on the system. The most famous example was the Wiemar Republic that ran post-World War I Germany, where inflation took place by a factor of trillions. It was actually done more or less deliberately, to reduce the burden of foreign war reparations payments, at the expense of wiping out the savings of the citizens. More recently, the African nation of Zimbabwe printed their currency into worthlessness, to finally establish the US dollar as the national currency.

The idea that there is an "inherent" value even to gold and silver is something of an illusion. A money supply based on precious metals is not absolutely more stable than one based on paper. When the Spaniards and Portuguese conquered much of what would become Latin America in the 16th century, they seized large quantities of gold and also obtained rich gold and silver mines, with the result that the value of their gold and silver currencies plunged to about a third of their original value.

Some astrogeologists have calculated the value of the metals in a single typical metallic asteroid; if some future generation were able to nudge one into orbit around the Earth and then render it down, the haul would be so huge that it would dramatically devalue every precious metal in circulation. Even without such a monstrous kick in the teeth, the price of gold tends to fluctuate drastically, dropping or rising relative to relatively stable fiat currencies. Money, as the saying goes, "is worth what everyone thinks it's worth", and that rule applies just as much to gold as to paper bills. The real concern is discipline in the printing of money. If too much money is printed, it becomes devaluated. If too little is printed, it stifles commerce.

Mainstream economists will admit that it may be harder to cheat with a gold standard, but point to its restrictiveness as a crippling flaw; some accuse those who push the gold standard of simply trying to restore a system that would give them personal control over the money supply by hoarding gold. There is still a school of thought that believes money should at least have some hard currency backing, but it's well off the mainstream. In 1998, the highly respected US Federal Reserve chairman Alan Greenspan commented: "I am one of the rare people who still has some nostalgic view about the old gold standard but I must tell you I am in a very small minority among my colleagues on that issue." As for advocates of a strict gold standard, mainstream economists regarded them as pushing "the economic equivalent of leeching.

Select only one answer choice.

80. In this context, the word "fiat" most closely matches which of the following definitions?

  A   Decreed

  B   Sanctioned

  C   Acceptable

  D   Solvent

  E   National

Select only one answer choice.

81. What is implied by the information in the first sentence of the third paragraph?

     Ⓐ   Gold is the most appropriate foundation for a monetary system

     Ⓑ   Gold is an arbitrary choice of foundation for a monetary system

     Ⓒ   Latin America has greater quantities of gold than other areas of the world

     Ⓓ   Gold is an unreliable foundation for a monetary system

     Ⓔ   Spanish and Portuguese conquerors are responsible for gold's acceptance as the foundation of modern monetary systems

Select only one answer choice.

82. Based on your understanding of the information in the passage, what would be the likely result of the discovery of twenty previously unknown paintings by the nineteenth-century artist, Van Gogh?

     Ⓐ   They would be found to be counterfeit

     Ⓑ   They would be appraised based on the completeness, originality, and the quality of the work

     Ⓒ   The value of already known works of Van Gogh would be reduced

     Ⓓ   The value of already known work of Van Gogh would be inflated

     Ⓔ   They would be donated to a museum for tax purposes

Consider each of the three answer choices separately and select all that apply.

83. Which of the following scenarios has an effect similar to that of the Weimar Republic's devaluing its currency after World War I?

     ☐ A   A clothing store putting its seasonal merchandise on sale at the end of the season

     ☐ B   High-school students taking Advanced Placement courses to raise their GPAs

     ☐ C   A college admissions' policy that adds 100 points to the SAT scores of applicants from culturally deprived areas

Consider each of the three answer choices separately and select all that apply.

84. Use the information in this passage to determine which of the following is an example of a medium of exchange.

    A Replacing a traditional baby-shower gift with a coupon for 5 hours of free babysitting

    B Revising a writing assignment for a higher grade

    C A mechanic providing a free oil change for the electrician who did not charge him for replacing a faulty switch in his office

85. Select the sentence that explains the weakness inherent in the use of the gold standard.

Passage 39

Question 86 is based on the following passage.

In 1980, the federal government began encouraging academic-industry relationships by creating a uniform federal patent policy, allowing federal grantees to collaborate with commercial interests to promote inventions, and permitting universities to retain the title on inventions developed through government funding.

As a result, as many as 90 percent of life-science companies now have a financial relationship with academia. Corporate licensing of academic inventions account for more than $20 billion of the universities' annual revenue. In most cases, the researchers making the discoveries get some portion of the money.

Another recent byproduct of the increased privatization of research has been the right of companies under patent law to refuse to allow foreign competitors to create generic -- and often significantly cheaper -- treatments for life-threatening diseases. Poorer countries in Africa, particularly, say they need the less-expensive generic drugs to fight AIDS, leaving the federal government in the awkward position of equivocating between protection of U.S. corporate interests and global humanitarian interests.

Select only one answer choice.

86. Select a word from the following list that would be a better choice than equivocate in the final sentence of the passage.

  - A   Hesitate
  - B   Prevaricate
  - C   Pontificate
  - D   Vacillate
  - E   Abrogate

Passage 40

Question 87 is based on the following passage.

The United States has been the largest producer of greenhouse gases, so what we do makes a big difference. And the U.S. has been reluctant to act aggressively on curbing emissions, worried about the economic consequences. But this is generally agreed to be a global problem requiring worldwide action. Many European nations like Britain and France, and Japan as well, have acted much more aggressively on cutting emissions. They rely more on nuclear power and relatively clean natural gas than we do. They have also mandated significantly higher fuel efficiency standards for cars and invested more in mass transit and rail. The story is mixed in developing countries, especially the economic powerhouses like China and India. Because their economies are growing so rapidly, they are using much more energy and producing more greenhouse gases than they have in the past. At the same time, they have the chance to start fresh with cleaner and more efficient technologies if they can be persuaded to do so.

Select only one answer choice.

87. Use your understanding of this passage to determine which of the following can be inferred about the challenges faced by rapidly growing economies.

    A   They cannot train enough workers to meet the demands of industry

    B   They are reluctant to use examples set by other nations

    C   Their isolation makes them unaware of more efficient technologies

    D   They cannot institute more efficient technologies fast enough to keep pace with their growth

    E   They do not recognize their impact on global warming

Passage 41

Questions 88 and 89 are based on the following passage.

Not every government program is created equal. In fact, the federal government spends most of its money on just a few programs. Some programs, such as Social Security and Medicare, are "mandatory" programs (sometimes called "entitlements") that the government is obligated by law to provide. Other services, ranging from national defense to national parks, may be vitally important but, for budget purposes, are still considered "discretionary" (and are therefore easier to cut). In the early 1960s, two-thirds of the budget was considered discretionary spending. But entitlements have grown dramatically since then, and now only about a third of the federal budget is discretionary spending. That trend is likely to continue, since entitlement costs are rising faster than most other areas of the federal budget

Select only one answer choice.

88. The highlighted sentence in the passage is an example of which of the following?

    A   Point- counterpoint

    B   Question - and- answer

    C   Circular logic

    D   Cause-and-effect

    E   Loaded language

Select only one answer choice.

89. What effect on the passage is created by the use of parentheses?

    A   The parenthetical phrases make the tone of the passage more formal

    B   The parenthetical phrases provide further explanation of terminology used by the writer

    C   The use of parenthetical phrases adds sophistication to the writing

    D   The parenthetical phrases identify this passage as part of a government publication

    E   The parenthetical phrases create an informal tone in this passage

Passage 42

Questions 90 to 92 are based on the following passage.

Some proposals to reign in health costs include embracing a free-market approach to make the insurance marketplace more competitive and less expensive by using tax credits to encourage more people to buy health insurance on their own instead of receiving it from their employers. Supporters say one reason expenses are rising is that it's hard for most people to tell how much their health care really costs. Most people who have insurance only pay part of the cost through co-pays, deductibles or employee contributions – the insurance company pays the rest, and the patient may or may not ever see a bill. And since different insurance plans negotiate different deals with providers, the bills for two people with the same illness could be quite different. Many experts say that since the patient isn't bearing the real cost, there's no incentive to control costs.

Select only one answer choice.

90. Based on the information in this passage, which of the following adages might the writer use when speaking about health-care consumers?

    Ⓐ   Ignorance is bliss

    Ⓑ   No news is good news

    Ⓒ   A penny saved is a penny earned

    Ⓓ   Nothing ventured, nothing gained

    Ⓔ   A stitch in time saves nine

Select only one answer choice.

91. What can the reader infer about the possible role of doctors in the cost of health-care from the information in the passage?

    Ⓐ   There is a serious shortage of doctors

    Ⓑ   Doctors structure their charge for services around the cost of maintaining a practice

    Ⓒ   More doctors have left private practice and work for hospitals and medical centers

    Ⓓ   Doctors may accept insurance only from companies that pay more for services and procedures

    Ⓔ   Doctors order unnecessary tests

Select only one answer choice.

92. How might competition between health insurance providers lead to higher prices in the insurance marketplace?

   A   There will be a reduction in the number of group plans, forcing citizens to buy more expensive individual policies

   B   Larger companies can reduce their rates to levels that would force smaller companies to fail, once again reducing competition and raising rates

   C   Government regulations will add cumbersome costs to health insurance

   D   The public will remain ignorant about the real cost of health care

   E   Small hospitals will be forced to charge more for services

Passage 43

Question 93 is based on the following passage.

A nation's GDP (Gross Domestic Product) at purchasing power parity (PPP) exchange rates is the sum value of all goods and services produced in the country valued at prices prevailing in the United States. This is the measure most economists prefer when looking at per- capita welfare and when comparing living conditions or use of resources across countries. The measure is difficult to compute, as a US dollar value has to be assigned to all goods and services in the country regardless of whether these goods and services have a direct equivalent in the United States (for example, the value of an ox-cart or non-US military equipment); as a result, PPP estimates for some countries are based on a small and sometimes different set of goods and services. In addition, many countries do not formally participate in the World Bank's PPP project that calculates these measures, so the resulting GDP estimates for these countries may lack precision. For many developing countries, PPP-based GDP measures are multiples of the official exchange rate (OER) measure.

Select only one answer choice.

93. Based on your understanding of the information in this passage, which of the following statements is likely to be true?

    (A)   The difference between the OER- and PPP- denominated GDP values for developing countries is generally much smaller

    (B)   The difference between the OER- and PPP- denominated GDP values for most of the wealthy industrialized countries in generally much greater

    (C)   The difference between the OER- and PPP-denominated GDP values for countries who do not participate in the World Bank's PPP project is generally much greater

    (D)   The difference between the OER- and PPP-denominated GDP values for countries who do not participate in the World Bank's PPP project is generally much smaller

    (E)   The difference between the OER- and PPP- denominated GDP values for most of the wealthy industrialized countries is generally much smaller.

Passage 44

Questions 94 and 95 are based on the following passage.

The normal situation is that the business enterprise is aiming at net profits, having an interest in large sales, heavy transactions and gross profits only so far as these are expected to lead finally to net profits, the real goal. Now these net profits are, of course, the remainder of earnings left on hand after providing for all costs and expenses, for depreciation and every other factor causing loss, destruction, and deterioration during the business period under consideration. In short, the business capital as it was at the beginning of the period is first fully restored and made intact at the end of the period before a net profit emerges. This net profit therefore becomes in a true sense a creation of new capital and may indeed be retained in the business as an addition to capital funds. Even when it is paid out in dividends, partly or wholly, it becomes new capital in the hands of the individual stockholders who then in their private capacity may of course spend it, but by proper investment may keep it permanently stored as capital. It is the creation of capital then that is in reality the ultimate money-making making aim of the business enterprise.

Consider each of the three answer choices separately and select all that apply.

94. Which of the following statements is true based on the information in this passage?

   A   Large sales, heavy transactions and gross profits lead inevitably to net profits

   B   Gross profits must be greater than the initial capital in any fiscal period in order to create net profits

   C   Investors benefit most by spending their dividends from a company

Select only one answer choice.

95. Which of the following actions has the potential to increase net profits even though gross profits remain the same?

   A   Freezing wages and salaries

   B   Concealing losses

   C   Reducing inventory

   D   Installing energy efficient lights

   E   Staying open more hours

Passage 45

Questions 96 and 97 are based on the following passage.

Time is an asset that is critically important to the health of a business, particularly in the upper management domain; wasted time can be especially noxious to an organization's overall success. Despite the prevalence of the platitudes "time is money" and "time is of the essence", many people working in the higher echelons of a company are unaware of how they distribute their time relative to the tasks that they need to accomplish. Such oversight of fundamental management principles can cause a business to stagnate because it shows a lack of self-reflexivity that leads to disorganization, wasted resources, and a lack of solid leadership.

Select only one answer choice.

96. Based on the information in the passage, the reader can infer all of the following except

    A   Upper management in an organization is often characterized by disorganization

    B   The principles of business theory are not often practiced

    C   Time management skills correspond to money management skills

    D   A lack of organizational leadership is a harbinger of poor time management

    E   Successful organizations have the ability to critically evaluate themselves

Consider each of the three choices separately and select all that apply.

97. Poor time management is paradoxical in businesses because

    A   Upper management is the guilty party

    B   Businesses know that time is a valuable asset

    C   It leads to poor business decisions

Passage 46

Question 98 is based on the following passage.

In recent years, the business world has placed increasing emphasis on the inner-work lives of their employees. A recent study published in McKinsey Quarterly has shown that productivity, commitment, and creativity increase in the work place when employees' experience in the office includes a positive flow of emotions, motivations, and perceptions. This environment can best be fostered by leadership that promotes the connection between meaning and work tasks through active engagement and positive, consistent feedback.

Select only one answer choice.

98. Which of the following rhetorical strategies is employed by the author to discuss the work environment and the inner work life of employees?

    A   Logos rhetoric

    B   Pathos rhetoric

    C   Ethos rhetoric

    D   Comparative rhetoric

    E   Narrative rhetoric

Passage 47

Question 99 is based on the following passage.

According to a recent study conducted at the University of Minnesota, men spend more money when there is a dearth of women in their locale. Researchers were able to determine that U.S. cities with a higher male to female ratio had correspondingly higher levels of male debt. Consequently, men are much more willing to take financial risks and engage their consumer habits in the aforementioned areas than men in regions with gender equilibrium.

Select only one answer choice.

99. The author intends "a dearth of women" to be analogous to

    A   An abundance of women

    B   The rarity of women

    C   A surplus of men

    D   A total lack of women

    E   A paucity of women

Passage 48

Question 100 is based on the following passage.

Although professional women make up over 40% of the employees at organizations in the United States, they are still woefully underrepresented in the corporate upper echelons; only 21% of women serve among the ranks of business executives. However, in the post-feminism world this is not due to outright discrimination but rather covert bias. There is a strong pipeline of female talent that is fed into the corporate sphere but women rarely make the executive suite due to high levels of attrition that typically occur after they have reached the management level. Many researchers claim that this is due to the fact that U.S. businesses make it extremely difficult for women to advance up the chain of command when they decide to have a family - U.S. businesses do not focus on maternity leave options for women that allow them to easily re-access the upper levels of the company.

Select only one answer choice.

100. According to the passage, in what clandestine way are U.S. businesses anti-female?

- (A)   U.S. businesses do not provide women with the professional development needed for career advancement
- (B)   U.S. businesses do not afford women the opportunity to the management level
- (C)   U.S. businesses do not provide women with maternity leave
- (D)   U.S. businesses do not equip themselves to deal with issues important to women in the work place
- (E)   U.S. businesses do not place emphasis on family friendly policies

Passage 49

Questions 101 to 103 are based on the following passage.

Social entrepreneurship has become a vitally important concept in the business world. Global attitudes increasingly desire the promotion of the unselfish concern for the common good. Social entrepreneurs believe that business emphasis should be placed on the creation of social capital and not the traditional goals and objectives of industry that revolve around profit and return. Social capital is the value of social relations. It is engendered when entrepreneurs identify a pressing social problem and then use the principles of business and management to erect ventures that address these issues by way of social dialogue and collaboration. Thus, cooperation and social relationships facilitate economic results.

Select only one answer choice.

101. Based on the information given in the passage, what main difference can be inferred between social entrepreneurs and conventional entrepreneurs?

- A Social entrepreneurs build better relationships with clients than traditional entrepreneurs

- B Social entrepreneurs don't rely on the axioms of business while traditional entrepreneurs do

- C Social entrepreneurs are concerned with quality of life and traditional entrepreneurs are concerned with fiscal gain

- D Social entrepreneurs are more concerned with climate change than traditional entrepreneurs

- E Social entrepreneurs and traditional entrepreneurs are essentially the same

Select only one answer choice.

102. The author would agree with all of the following statements regarding social capital except

- A Social capital is the product of collaborative problem solving

- B Social capital is the salient feature of social entrepreneurship

- C Social capital is a tangible feature of social entrepreneurship

- D Business management principles support social capital

- E Social capital has monetary value

Select only one answer choice.

103. According to the information given in the passage, what is meant by the term social capital?

- A The author does not give enough information to define social capital.
- B Social capital means building community.
- C Social capital means building relationships.
- D Social capital is synonymous with social problems.
- E Social capital is money created by people sharing in a concerted effort towards a common goal.

Passage 50

Questions 104 and 105 are based on the following passage.

In the last twenty years trading on the stock market has gone from the stock room floors to computer screens. This has resulted in the rapid rise of high frequency trading, which researchers now believe leads to increased volatility in the stock market. High frequency trading makes it possible for large volumes of stocks to be traded in milliseconds, much faster than they can be tracked with the human eye. Multitudinous problems arise from high frequency trading, one of the most potent being the potential to disrupt the global economic balance more frequently and with little warning.

Select only one answer choice.

104. Based on the information given in the passage, how does the author intend to define high frequency trading?

- A High frequency trading is when stocks are traded continuously
- B High frequency trading is computer-generated stock trading on a grandiose scale
- C High frequency trading is computer generated stock trading
- D High frequency trading is stock trading that is done at a rapid pace
- E High frequency trading is when large volumes of stock are traded on the stock room floor

Select only one answer choice.

105. Based the information given in the passage, what can be inferred about the global economic balance?

    A   The global economic balance cannot be sustained if high frequency trading is continued

    B   High frequency trading keeps the global economic balance at a healthy equilibrium

    C   High frequency trading makes rapid and unforeseen fluctuations in the global market more possible

    D   Nothing can be inferred about the global economic market based on the information given in the passage

    E   The global economic balance was more stable before the introduction of high frequency trading

Passage 51

Question 106 is based on the following passage.

The economic crisis that broke through the global floodgates in 2008 has placed the system of capitalism under attack from its opponents. Capitalism, however, has been under scrutiny since its inception, and thus this is not a new phenomenon. However, as society has evolved so have the criticisms launched against capitalism; imperialistic oppression, market failure and the wasteful and inefficient use of resources are all common gripes that constitute the anti-capitalism jeremiad. One of the prominent denunciations vaulted against capitalism over the course of the last fifteen years is its opposition to sustainability. Critics claim that capitalism promotes a milieu of exploitation because of its unbridled focus on consumption. Consequently, capitalism is a danger to a world that is increasingly strapped for natural resources, the foundation stones of capitalist enterprise.

Select only one answer choice.

106. According to the information given in the passage, why is consumption seen as a negative attribute of capitalism?

- A. Consumption led to the financial crisis in the late 2000s

- B. Consumption results in the overuse of natural resources that are currently in high demand globally

- C. Consumption contributes to the destabilization of the market in a capitalist economic system

- D. Consumption is the way in which proponents of capitalism distract people from the system's penchant for imperialistic oppression

- E. Consumption leads to an increase in wasteful consumer choices

Passage 52

Questions 107 to 109 are based on the following passage.

Sustainability has become a paragon virtue in business endeavors, an essential ingredient for corporate success at a time when social, economic, and environmental issues permeate the heart of public discourse, particularly in Western societies. However, civic pressure for companies to mold themselves based on the capacity to endure is not the only reason that businesses have homed in on sustainability; over the course of the last twenty years, research has shown that there is a widening chasm between organizations characterized as high-sustainability and companies deemed low-sustainability relative to accounting measures and stock market success. Thus, sustainability is just as much about success as it is about showing a good entrepreneurial face to the public. According to a study conducted by Dr. Robert G. Eccles of the Harvard Business School, several major factors show that long-term corporate success is determined by iterations of a rudimentary principle in business: meeting the expectations of both shareholders and stakeholders.

One factor in the success rate of high-sustainability companies is a three-pronged approach to business that involves placing equal value on the organization's social, environmental, and financial performance. Traditionally, low-sustainability companies focus solely on profit and turn a blind eye towards the wider ramifications of their business practices on society. This leads them to a kind of tunnel vision that misjudges the expectations of stakeholders; additionally, they undervalue the importance of building good relationships with employees, customers and members of civil society, causing their venture to stagnate. Conversely, high-sustainability companies make both fiscal and socio-environmental issues the crux of their corporate goals and objectives, facilitating their capacity to build meaningful relationships with stakeholders by taking their needs and opinions into account and finding a way to amalgamate them with business decisions that are financially sound. This is done by a process of active engagement and the creation of shareholder sub-committees focused on environmental, social, and financial issues.

Another contributing factor to the recent primacy of high-sustainability organizations is their propensity to be more forward thinking than their low-sustainability counterparts. High-sustainability companies have long-term communications strategies that render them more attractive to long-term investors and diverse stakeholders, something that all ambitious businesses crave as well as need to stay in top form.

Like all facets of life, the business world is an evolving world. It depends on foresight, creativity, and the ability to identify new ways of presenting and reinforcing the fundamentals of enterprise, in this case the way in which the mutual happiness of shareholders and stakeholders is propelled by a wider scope that includes social and environmental responsibility.

Select only one answer choice.

107. Given the information in the passage, it can be inferred that sustainability is a paragon virtue in the business world because

- A Sustainability creates an atmosphere that is based on relationships and engagement between stakeholders and shareholders

- B Sustainability seeks to keep environmental concerns at the forefront of organizational practices, thus helping to mitigate the impact of climate change

- C Sustainability concerns itself with helping businesses maintain a high level of success in the face of the perpetually changing elements that constitute global society

- D Sustainability is about finding an adequate balance between social, economic, and environmental issues

- E Sustainability is in vogue in the realm of public discourse

Consider each of the three choices separately and select all that apply.

108. Corporate success can be seen as an iterative process because

- A It relies on the repetition of business principles to find the right method of meeting the expectations of shareholders and stakeholders

- B It is adaptive to social, fiscal and environmental changes

- C It is a forward thinking way of approaching business practices

109. Select the sentence that best illustrates the perils of fiscal aggrandizement within an organization.

Passage 53

Questions 110 and 111 are based on the following passage.

In recent years, American businesses have considered adoption of various business methods of Japanese companies. The most important of these methods, one that can influence the entire company is Just in Time. Just in Time (JIT), refers to the practice of having material delivered to the factory as it is needed, rather than having a quantity delivered and then stored in a warehouse. The practice greatly reduces overhead costs as there is no need for so much storage space. The practice calls for high coordination between suppliers and customers so that neither has to store material. JIT can lead to increases in quality, productivity, and adaptability to change. General Motors, for example, used JIT and was able to reduce its costs for inventory by 75%. The use of JIT creates the need for a number of other practices, among them is Strict Quality Control. Since the material arrives just as it is needed, there is no time for a complete inspection. The supplier has, therefore, to verify on its own the quality of the product sent to the customer. Supplier and customer have to work closely together. Another feature of JIT is single sourcing. Since JIT requires that buyer and customer work closely together, having many suppliers makes it difficult to work closely together with all of them. Companies using JIT, therefore, tend to have fewer suppliers than companies that do not rely on JIT. General Motors, for example, which does rely on JIT to some extent, uses 3,500 suppliers. Toyota, a company that completely relies on JIT, uses fewer than 250 suppliers.

Consider each of the three answer choices separately and select all that apply.

110. Based on the reading, advantages resulting from the use of Just in Time include

    A   Less redundancy in the supply system, since there are fewer suppliers

    B   No margin for error in the delivery of material

    C   Buyer and customer work closely together

111. Select the sentence that best describes the general benefits of Just in Time (JIT).

6

Practice Set 4 - Everyday Topics

This chapter is devoted to helping you develop your skill with Reading Comprehension questions using concrete examples. You will find passages related to *Everyday Topics* that are similar to the sorts of passages you will encounter on an actual GRE test. Each passage has a set of questions and a detailed explanation of the solution to each question. The questions and their solutions will be presented as follows:

In this chapter:

- A passage related to *Everyday Topics* similar to what you can expect on an actual GRE test

- Several questions about the passage similar to those you will encounter on an actual GRE test

In *Explanatory Answers for Practice Set 4: Everyday Topics*:

- A quick summary that paraphrases the main issues of the passage and points out important words or phrases that indicate the meaning or intent of the passage. Being able to answer a few basic questions about Reading Comprehension passages before you even see any of the questions is a key skill that will help you answer questions more quickly and more accurately. The summaries provided here will give you some sense of how to approach summarizing when looking at actual questions

- Detailed solutions that explain what the correct answer is, and what strategy of strategies you could use to determine the correct answer. Explanatory answers will usually refer back to the summary

Passage 54

Questions 112 and 113 are based on the following passage.

A fourth approach advocates using the power of the free market to improve public education. Supporters assert that public schools don't improve because they have no real competition. By giving parents vouchers that could be used for students to attend either public or private schools, parents could choose the best school for their child, and public schools would be forced to improve to compete. "School choice" programs for public schools are now officially part of the No Child Left Behind Act, which permits parents in failing schools to transfer their children to another public school. Only a few communities, like Milwaukee, Cleveland, Dayton, Fla., and Washington D.C., have attempted to include private and religious schools in their voucher plans. That raises concerns about the separation of church and state, but the U.S. Supreme Court has upheld Cleveland's plan.

Select only one answer choice.

112. Which of the following attitudes is a likely result of the lack of competition to enroll students in public schools?

- A   Optimism
- B   Pessimism
- C   Complacency
- D   Defeatism
- E   Lethargy

Select only one answer choice.

113. In addition to concerns about separation of church and state, what other weakness lies in choosing a private or religious school in an effort to improve public education?

    (A)   Students may have to purchase their own books and uniforms

    (B)   Private schools do not have to comply with the No Child Left Behind act

    (C)   Private schools may not offer extracurricular activities

    (D)   Religion classes may be part of the curriculum

    (E)   Private schools might not offer transportation to school

Passage 55

Questions 114 to 116 are based on the following passage.

It is an even thing: New York society has not taken to our literature. New York publishes it, criticises it, and circulates it, but I doubt if New York society much reads it or cares for it, and New York is therefore by no means the literary centre that Boston once was, though a large number of our literary men live in or about New York. Boston, in my time at least, had distinctly a literary atmosphere, which more or less pervaded society; but New York has distinctly nothing of the kind, in any pervasive sense. It is a vast mart, and literature is one of the things marketed here; but our good society cares no more for it than for some other products bought and sold here; it does not care nearly so much for books as for horses or for stocks, and I suppose it is not unlike the good society of any other metropolis in this. To the general, here, journalism is a far more appreciable thing than literature, and has greater recognition, for some very good reasons; but in Boston literature had vastly more honor, and even more popular recognition, than journalism.

Select only one answer choice.

114. The author uses which of the following formats to achieve his purpose in this passage?

  - (A)   Persuasive writing
  - (B)   Logical appeal
  - (C)   Narrative
  - (D)   Symbolism
  - (E)   Compare/contrast

Select only one answer choice.

115. According to this writer, in what way is New York similar to any other large city?

  - (A)   It is home to many writers
  - (B)   It treats literary work as a commodity
  - (C)   It is a center of commerce
  - (D)   It has great journalists
  - (E)   It has a stock exchange

Select only one answer choice.

116. Consider the content of this passage as you select the pair of descriptors that contrast New York City and Boston

  - (A)   Pragmatic versus aesthetic
  - (B)   Industrial versus agrarian
  - (C)   Competitive versus complacent
  - (D)   Stereotypical versus unique
  - (E)   Progressive versus stagnant

Passage 56

Questions 117 and 118 are based on the following passage.

Some of the increased diversity on campuses was the result of a 1978 U.S. Supreme Court ruling that allowed schools to consider an applicant's race as one factor in making an admissions decision. Many college officials say using affirmative action to ensure a diverse student body is part of what college is all about. Preparing students for the increasingly diverse world that awaits them. Advocates also argue that affirmative action is the best way to make sure minorities get the opportunities they were once denied. But in recent years, some white students have complained they are being denied admission in favor of minority students with poorer grades. Critics also say that using race as a factor, even with the best intentions, is wrong because it moves us further away from a society based on merit. But many are convinced that attending one of the nation's selective universities is the first step to joining the rest of society's elite institutions.

Select only one answer choice.

117.Which of the following assumptions is most reasonable based on the information in the passage?

- A   One has achieved success only after gaining acceptance in at least one of society's elite institutions

- B   One's overall character is enhanced by attending a selective college or university

- C   Attending a mediocre university leads to limited success after college

- D   Prior to the 1978 Supreme Court decision, colleges discriminated against minorities in their admissions practices

- E   Minority students perform better academically at selective universities

Select only one answer choice.

118. If affirmative action is responsible for some of the increased diversity at selective universities, which of the following might be another contributor to increased diversity at selective universities?

  (A)   Reduced tuition at selective institutions

  (B)   A greater number of minority high school graduates are applying to college

  (C)   The expanding availability of online colleges

  (D)   Restrictions on immigration

  (E)   A reduction in the number of Pell grants

Passage 57

Question 119 is based on the following passage.

The rise in popularity of Oxycontin, an addictive prescription pain reliever, illustrates the challenge facing authorities trying to prevent drug use. The drug was first released in 1995, and its use has particularly spiked in the Appalachian states, which are more isolated from traditional illegal drug routes. Oxycontin is obtained through fake prescriptions, other people's legal prescriptions, theft, diversion from pharmacies and the practice of "doctor-shopping," in which people go from one doctor to another seeking multiple prescriptions. The problem for officials is how to separate legitimate users and legitimate prescription-writing doctors from addicts and dealers.

Select only one answer choice.

119. Which of the following, if true, might weaken the position that isolation from traditional illegal drug routes is the reason for increased use of OxyContin in Appalachian states?

 A Residents of the Appalachian states, where coal mining is a common occupation, more commonly suffer from painful injuries

 B There are fewer pharmacies per capita in the Appalachian states

 C There are fewer doctors per capita in the Appalachian states

 D The population density in the Appalachian states is lower than in other areas of the country

 E OxyContin is more expensive than other prescription pain killers

Passage 58

Questions 120 and 121 are based on the following passage.

The year 1919 awarded coffee one of its brightest honors. An American general said that coffee shared with bread and bacon the distinction of being one of the three nutritive essentials that helped win the World War for the Allies. So this symbol of human brotherhood has played a not inconspicuous part in "making the world safe for democracy." The new age, ushered in by the Peace of Versailles and the Washington Conference, has for its hand-maidens temperance and self-control. It is to be a world democracy of right-living and clear thinking; and among its most precious adjuncts are coffee, tea, and cocoa - because these beverages must always be associated with rational living, with greater comfort, and with better cheer.

Select only one answer choice.

120. If this paragraph were an introduction to a longer piece of writing, which of the following topics would logically be the focus of the next paragraph?

- (A) How the properties of bacon sustained the soldiers during the war
- (B) How bread served as the most important food item for the troops during the war
- (C) How important right living and clear thinking are to democracy
- (D) How coffee, tea, and cocoa are associated with rational living, greater comfort, and better cheer
- (E) How coffee, tea, and cocoa might have deleterious effects on humans

Consider each of the three choices separately and select all that apply.

121. Which of the following is a possible topic for the longer piece of writing that contains this passage?

- A   Coffee has accumulated a number of honors throughout history
- B   Throughout history, a number of relatively commonplace commodities have helped to make the world safe for democracy
- C   Coffee, tea, and cocoa are essential to a world democracy of right living and clear thinking

Passage 59

Questions 122 and 123 are based on the following passage.

The debate surrounding the Second Amendment to the United States Constitution has the ability to bring out the pugnacious nature of American politicians and civilians alike. Gun control discussions often raise pulses, but more importantly, they underscore the myopic nature of the American civic milieu. For example, the Virginia Tech University Massacre in 2007 engendered public and political outrage and gun control issues took center stage in American public discourse. At the time, many Americans believed that gun control laws were too lax and that stricter regulations needed to be put in place to protect the public from firearms. However, in just five short years the gun control tides have turned. Americans have relaxed their oppositions to and de-centered their focus from firearms control, likely resulting in the new laws that allow the carrying of concealed weapons in states like Wisconsin and even on university campuses, such as the University of Texas.

Select only one answer choice.

122. What overall message does the author intend to convey to the reader about American society?

    A   America needs stricter gun control laws

    B   Issues related to the Second Amendment typically do not concern Americans

    C   American society is characterized by emotionally driven rhetoric

    D   American public discourse is often short-sighted relative to civic issues

    E   The Second Amendment is the cornerstone of American society

Select only one answer choice.

123. The author mentions "the pugnacious nature of American politicians and civilians alike" as

    A   A way to show how confused Americans are when it comes to the rules governing civil society

    B   A method of underscoring the belligerence of the American national character

    C   A means of capturing the reader's attention

    D   An argumentative strategy to convince the reader that Americans are aggressive by nature

    E   A narrative rhetorical strategy to convince the reader that Americans are short-sighted relative to civil issues

Passage 60

Questions 124 and 125 are based on the following passage.

The number of homeless female military veterans in the United States has intensified, with rates nearly doubling between 2006 and 2010 according to the most recent government surveys. While it is true that this increase can be attributed to an overall increase in female representation in the U.S. military, the trend is nonetheless deeply disturbing. Women are particularly vulnerable since many have or care for young children and a lack of access to veteran shelters that also provide family services only compounds the problem - more women and children have nowhere to go while many male veterans can still rely on traditional veteran shelters.

Select only one answer choice.

124. Rhetorically speaking, the author is appealing to the reader's

- A   Logos
- B   Pathos
- C   Metaphysical sensibilities
- D   Ethos
- E   Political sensibilities

Select only one answer choice.

125. The reader can most reasonably infer that

- A   The United States military does not take care of its veterans
- B   United States veterans are usually homeless
- C   Gender inequality is a problem among military veterans
- D   Women should not serve in the U.S. military
- E   Female veterans of the U.S. military have more children than male veterans

Passage 61

Question 126 is based on the following passage.

The term domestic violence generally conjures images of defenseless women being attacked by abusive and domineering men. However, statistics show that males account for 2 out of 5 cases of domestic violence; thus, men are frequently at the receiving end of abuse. Researchers also believe that these numbers could be misleading; in many Western societies, there is still a strong social stigma surrounding men being victims of abuse. Many men feel that it is socially unacceptable for them to display weakness or seek help in abusive situations. This may very well cause many cases of female on male domestic violence to go unreported.

Select only one answer choice.

126. The statistics relative to the domestic abuse of males are inaccurate because

     A   Women in Western society stigmatize abused men

     B   Researchers demonstrate a bias that supports the feminist agenda

     C   Men worry that reporting abuse will negatively impact their relationships with women

     D   Statistics in general can never be 100% accurate

     E   Men worry that reporting abuse will tarnish their image

Passage 62

Questions 127 to 129 are based on the following passage.

Debt is a hot topic and a major concern at all levels of American society and yet there is one group of Americans who are less troubled by the financial albatross that they bear than the rest: college students. Despite the high average student loan debt of $23,000 for graduating seniors, many students are not stressed about the money they owe - they in fact feel confident and empowered. Researchers attribute this response to student loan debt as atypical and evidence that college students see their education as an investment and feel that their level of debt indicates their commitment to opportunities for greater growth and later career advancement.

Select only one answer choice.

127. What can be inferred about American college students based on the information given in the passage?

   - (A) American college students have high levels of student debt
   - (B) American college students resent taking out student loans
   - (C) American college students are not as heavily affected by debt as their older adult counterparts
   - (D) American college students choose to view debt through a positive lens
   - (E) American college students feel that debt is not an important issue

Select only one answer choice.

128. College students' attitude to student loan debt is best described as

   - (A) Naïve
   - (B) Predictable
   - (C) Preternatural
   - (D) Banal
   - (E) Unexceptional

Select only one answer choice.

129. The author intends the term "albatross" in the passage to be analogous to

   - (A) The level of debt
   - (B) The burden of debt
   - (C) The stresses in American society
   - (D) A bank account
   - (E) Credit card debt

Passage 63

Questions 130 and 131 are based on the following passage.

One of the major roadblocks impeding equal opportunities for success in the United States is low literacy rates. While many people often lump low literacy and children together as one problem set, experts estimate that nearly 30 million American adults have literacy skills that are "below basic." This phenomenon is particularly harmful because low literacy among adults engenders a cycle of literacy problems; the children of adults with low literacy are more likely to struggle with school, drop out of school, and live in poverty. This is why literacy initiatives are such an important part of the fabric of American society: they help keep opportunities for success open to all individuals by fostering the development of critical language skills.

Select only one answer choice.

130. The two parts in bold-face demonstrate how the author

   A   Delineates the problems associated with low literacy

   B   Appeals to the reader's emotional sensibilities relative to low literacy

   C   Reinforces his or her beliefs as well as opposing beliefs relative to low literacy

   D   Reaches a solution to the problem posed in his or her original claim

   E   Makes use of paradox relative to low literacy

Consider each of the three choices separately and select all that apply.

131. The author would agree with which of the following statements?

   A   Low literacy is especially problematic in children

   B   Low literacy stonewalls equal opportunities

   C   Low literacy leads to higher crime rates

7

Practice Set 5 - Physical Sciences

This chapter is devoted to helping you develop your skill with Reading Comprehension questions using concrete examples. You will find passages related to *Physical Sciences* that are similar to the sorts of passages you will encounter on an actual GRE test. Each passage has a set of questions and a detailed explanation of the solution to each question. The questions and their solutions will be presented as follows:

In this chapter:

- A passage related to *Physical Sciences* similar to what you can expect on an actual GRE test

- Several questions about the passage similar to those you will encounter on an actual GRE test

In *Explanatory Answers for Practice Set 5: Physical Sciences*:

- A quick summary that paraphrases the main issues of the passage and points out important words or phrases that indicate the meaning or intent of the passage. Being able to answer a few basic questions about Reading Comprehension passages before you even see any of the questions is a key skill that will help you answer questions more quickly and more accurately. The summaries provided here will give you some sense of how to approach summarizing when looking at actual questions

- Detailed solutions that explain what the correct answer is, and what strategy of strategies you could use to determine the correct answer. Explanatory answers will usually refer back to the summary

Passage 64

Question 132 is based on the following passage.

Iron differs from the metals so far studied in that it is able to form two series of compounds in which the iron has two different valences. In the one series the iron is divalent and forms compounds which in formulas and many chemical properties are similar to the corresponding zinc compounds. It can also act as a trivalent metal, and in this condition forms salts similar to those of aluminum. Those compounds in which the iron is divalent are known as ferrous compounds, while those in which it is trivalent are known as ferric.

Consider each answer choice separately and select all that apply.

132. Use the information in the passage to decide which of the following statements is accurate.

   - A   Metals referred to as cuprous in a compound have a lower valence number as metals referred to as cupric in a compound

   - B   The suffix, - ous, means full of or possessing a certain quality, and the suffix, - ic, means having some characteristics of

   - C   Cuprous means possessing the qualities of copper and cupric means having some characteristics of copper

Passage 65

Question 133 is based on the following passage.

The reason for this peculiarity of mercury is that the pull between the particles of mercury themselves is stronger than the pull between them and your finger or handkerchief. In scientific language, the cohesion of the mercury is stronger than its adhesion to your finger or handkerchief. Although this seems unusual for a liquid, it is what we naturally expect of solid things; you would be amazed if part of the wood of your school seat stuck to you when you got up, for you expect the particles in solid things to cohere - to have cohesion - much more strongly than they adhere to something else. It is because solids have such strong cohesion that they are solids.

133. Select the sentence in the passage which reveals that the writer's audience is most likely comprised of laymen.

Passage 66

Questions 134 to 136 are based on the following passage.

The difference between the ways in which snow and rain are formed is very slight. In both cases water evaporates and its vapor mingles with the warm air. The warm air rises and expands. It cools as it expands, and when it gets cool enough the water vapor begins to condense. But if the air as it expands becomes very cold, so cold that the droplets of water freeze as they form and gather together to make delicate crystals of ice, snow is formed. The ice crystals found in snow are always six-sided or six-pointed, because, probably, the water or ice molecules pull from six directions and therefore gather each other together along the six lines of this pull. At any rate, the tiny crystals of frozen water are formed and come floating down to the ground; and we call them snowflakes. After the snow melts it goes through the same cycle as the rain, most of it finally getting back to the ocean through rivers, and there, in time, being evaporated once more.

Select only one answer choice.

134. The use of the phrase, "at any rate" reveals which of the following about the sentence preceding it?

    A   That the information in that sentence is essential to understanding the passage

    B   That the information in that sentence cannot be scientifically proven

    C   That the information in that sentence is an unnecessary digression

    D   That the process described in that sentence is not true in every case

    E   That the information in that sentence is not very interesting

Select only one answer choice.

135. Consider the context of this passage to decide which of the following most accurately identifies the type of writing exhibited.

　Ⓐ　Narrative

　Ⓑ　Expository

　Ⓒ　Editorial

　Ⓓ　Persuasive

　Ⓔ　Compare/contrast

Select only one answer choice.

136. Based on the information in this passage, decide which of the following meteorological events is a result of the same process described here.

　Ⓐ　A rainbow

　Ⓑ　Fog

　Ⓒ　Wind chill

　Ⓓ　Degree days

　Ⓔ　Thunder

Passage 67

Questions 137 to 139 are based on the following passage.

Sound is the sensation peculiar to the ear. This sensation is caused by rapidly-succeeding to-and-fro motions of the air which touches the outside surface of the drum-skin of the ear. These to-and-fro motions may be given to the air by a distant body, like a string of a violin. The string moves to and fro, that is, it vibrates. These vibrations of the string act on the bridge of the violin, which rests on the belly or sounding-board of the instrument. The surface of the sounding-board is thus set trembling, and these tremors, or vibrations, spread through the air in all directions around the instrument, somewhat in the manner that water-waves spread around the place where a stone has been dropped into a quiet pond. These tremors of the air, however, are not sound, but the cause of sound. Sound, as we have said, is a sensation; but, as the cause of this sensation is always vibration, we call those vibrations which give this sensation, sonorous vibrations.

Select only one answer choice.

137. What is the correct definition of peculiar as it is used in the first sentence of this passage?

- A   Odd
- B   Uncommon
- C   Distinctive in character or nature from others
- D   Belonging characteristically
- E   Belonging exclusively to some person, group, or thing

Select only one answer choice.

138. Consider the content of the passage and select the most likely audience for this information.

- A   Musicians
- B   Violin manufacturers
- C   Students
- D   Sonography technicians
- E   Acoustics engineers

139. Select the sentence that a seismologist might find useful to describe the effect of an earthquake.

Passage 68

Questions 140 and 141 are based on the following passage.

After the first four, no more asteroids were found until 1845, when one was discovered; then, in 1847, three more were added to the list; and after that searchers began to pick them up with such rapidity that by the close of the century hundreds were known, and it had become almost impossible to keep track of them. It was long supposed that Vesta was the largest, because it shines more brightly than any of the others; but finally, in 1895, Barnard, with the Lick telescope, definitely measured their diameters, and proved to everybody's surprise that Ceres is really the chief, and Vesta only the third in rank. They differ greatly in the reflective power of their surfaces, a fact of much significance in connection with the question of their origin. Vesta is, surface for surface, rather more than three times as brilliant as Ceres, whence the original mistake about its magnitude.

Select only one answer choice.

140. Which of the following statements is the most reasonable explanation for the increased frequency with which asteroids were discovered toward the end of the nineteenth century?

    A   A shift in the jet stream created larger areas of cloudless skies, making the asteroids more visible

    B   More colleges and universities offered courses in astronomy

    C   A period of frequent volcanic activity had finally subsided, reducing the amount of particulate matter in the atmosphere

    D   Advances in telescope technology made it possible to identify asteroids that had been previously overlooked

    E   Astronomers had a better understanding of asteroids' identifying characteristics

Select only one answer choice.

141. Which of the following predictions about the future of science is likely to be true based on your understanding of this passage?

    A   New discoveries and accuracy will occur at an increasingly rapid pace

    B   More asteroids will be discovered and correctly measured

    C   Astronomers are likely to discover an asteroid larger than Ceres

    D   Greater investment should be made in astronomical research

    E   The origins of asteroids will continue to be identified

Passage 69

Questions 142 to 144 are based on the following passage.

Lakes which fill rock-basins are such as are confined on all sides by the common rock of the country, so that in some cases a person can walk entirely around them without stepping off the solid rock; and in all cases they would be found to have a rocky rim inclosing them, were the superficial material removed. How such spoon-shaped depressions could be scooped out, was for a long time an enigma which eluded the search of the most painstaking observers.

As facts accumulated, however, it was noticed that the sides and bottoms of such lakes are smoothed, in many cases polished, and almost always covered with grooves and scratches; and also that in their vicinity beds of clay are usually found, intermixed with pebbles and large bowlders which, like the rocky basins, are also smoothed and frequently scratched. It was noticed, too, that the rock from which these bowlders and pebbles had been formed commonly differed from the rocks in place on the shores of the lakes. Thus, throughout New York and Ohio, huge bowlders are common, composed of crystalline rock found in place nowhere nearer than the Canadian Highlands, a hundred miles to the northward ; while the peculiar native copper of Northern Michigan is sometimes found mingled with the bowlders and striated stones of the drift far southward in Ohio.

The problem now was to discover what forces in Nature could polish and scratch both rock-surfaces and detached stones, and could also transport masses of rock, tons in weight, far from their native home.

It is well known that the loose stones and pebbles along the sea- shore are made very smooth and round, and often polished, by the action of the waves. It might be thought from this that the pebbles found on the shores of the lakes, and imbedded in the clays, were fashioned in the same manner. On one occasion, at the Cape of Good Hope, the writer, after wandering for a time along the sloping sandy beach of Table Bay, came suddenly to a little rocky cove exposed to the full swell of the South Atlantic. As each wave broke on the steep, rocky beach and retreated, it was followed by a sharp, rattling sound that could be distinctly heard above the roar of the waves ; we noticed, too, that the stones all along the shore were in motion, rolling down the beach, only to be caught up by the next white-capped wave that came in from the ocean, and again carried up the beach, and rolled and pounded against each other by the untiring waters, that were fast reducing them to sand and dust. On examining these water-worn stones, we found them all smoothed and rounded, and often beautifully polished; but in no case could we discover, even with a magnifying-glass, any that were scratched, or in any way marked similarly to the stones which we have so often examined in the clays and hard-pans that cover so great a portion of our Northern States. From this fact, and also from watching the action of the waves on many other coasts, we conclude that the sea tends to smooth and wear away the stones and rocks along its shores, but has no power to cover them with grooves and scratches; and that, instead of wearing the coast into pockets and basins, it tends only to grind down the islands and continents to one uniform level.

142. Select the sentence in this passage that best conveys the initial step that a researcher would take in the scientific process.

Select only one answer choice.

143. In order to satisfy the writer's hypothesis that the action of the waves creates smooth surfaces on the stones on the shoreline, what additional steps should he take?

- A   Collect and label samples from Table Bay
- B   Create an experiment that tests the hypothesis
- C   Do background research
- D   Publish a report of the results
- E   Seek others' perspectives

Consider each answer choice separately and select all that apply.

144. Which of the following are obstacles for this writer in constructing a working hypothesis?

- A   The apparent migration of rocks from one location to another
- B   Seemingly contradictory evidence
- C   Erroneous prior information

Passage 70

Question 145 is based on the following passage.

When observed with astronomical instruments, or photographed, we discover that its surface is not smooth, as might be supposed, but granulated, presenting a number of luminous points dispersed over a more somber background. These granulations are somewhat like the pores of a fruit, e.g., a fine orange, the color of which recalls the hue of the Sun when it sinks in the evening, and prepares to plunge us into darkness. At times these pores open under the influence of disturbances that arise upon the solar surface, and give birth to a Sun-Spot. For centuries scientists and lay people alike refused to admit the existence of these spots, regarding them as so many blemishes upon the King of the Heavens. Was not the Sun the emblem of inviolable purity? To find any defect in him were to do him grievous injury. Since the orb of day was incorruptible, those who threw doubt on his immaculate splendor were fools and idiots.

Consider each answer choice separately and select all that apply.

145. What purpose is served by the writer's use of euphemisms for the sun?

  A   They serve to illustrate the mythical significance attributed to the sun by humans prior to the invention of scientific instruments used to observe the sun

  B   They serve to demonstrate that early humans realized how important the sun was in providing heat and light to aid in their daily activities

  C   They serve to shed light on the disdain that common people had for anyone who challenged their beliefs

Passage 71

Question 146 is based on the following passage.

Since silver is not acted upon by water or air, and has a pleasing appearance, it is used to coat various articles made of cheaper metals. Such articles are said to be silver plated. The process by which this is done is called electroplating. It is carried on as follows: The object to be plated (such as a spoon) is attached to a wire and dipped into a solution of a silver salt. Electrical connection is made in such a way that the article to be plated serves as the cathode, while the anode is made up of one or more plates of silver. When a current is passed through the electrolyte silver dissolves from the anode plate and deposits on the cathode in the form of a closely adhering layer. By making the proper change in the electrolyte and anode plate objects may be plated with gold and other metals.

Select only one answer choice.

146. Use the information in the passage to select what appears to be the main purpose of electroplating.

- (A) To fool consumers
- (B) To significantly increase the value of base metals
- (C) To add shine to otherwise dull objects
- (D) To make anodes and cathodes useful
- (E) To add aesthetic appeal to affordable, commonplace objects

Passage 72

Questions 147 and 148 are based on the following passage.

The article claims that Mr. Gary has made a discovery of a neutral line or surface, at which the polarity of an induced magnet, while moving in the field of the inducing pole, is changed. The alleged discovery appears to be an exaggerated statement of some curious facts, which, although not new, are not commonly recognized. If a bar of iron be brought up, end on, near a magnetic pole, the bar becomes an induced magnet, but an induced magnet quite different from what our elementary treatises seem to predict. On the first scrutiny it is a magnet without a neutral point, and only one kind of magnetism - namely, that of the inducing pole. Moreover, the single pole is pretty evenly distributed over the whole surface, so that if iron filings be sprinkled on the bar they will be attracted at all points and completely cover it. Now, if while the bar is covered by filings it be moved away from the inducing pole, the filings will gradually and progressively fall, beginning at the end nearest the inducing pole and continuing to some point near the middle of the bar; the filings at the remote end will generally be held permanently. When the bar is carried beyond the field of the inducing pole it is simply a weak magnet of ordinary properties - i. e., of two poles and a neutral point between them.

Consider each answer choice separately and select all that apply.

147. Based on your understanding of the information in the passage, select which of the following statements is likely to be true about induced magnets.

    A   An induced magnet assumes the polarity possessed by the end of the existing magnet to which it is attached

    B   The end of the induced magnet that is farthest from the original magnet retains its magnetism longer than the closer end when the induced magnet is removed from the original

    C   The bar that becomes an induced magnet must be magnetized prior to placing it next to the magnet

Select only one answer choice.

148. What does the use of the words "alleged" and "exaggerated" imply about the writer's tone in this passage?

    A   He is skeptical

    B   He is reluctant

    C   He is expressing admiration

    D   He is convinced

    E   He is critical

Passage 73

Question 149 is based on the following passage.

Satellites can be placed in variations on geostationary orbits. The Japanese "Michibiki" satellite, launched in 2010, was intended to augment the American Global Positioning System (GPS) satellite navigation network. The GPS satellites provide coded timing signals that allow a receiver to determine its location on Earth, but GPS signals are not always easy to pick up in Japan's mountainous regions or skyscraper-studded cities like Tokyo. Michibiki was placed in an orbit that varied from above to below the geostationary distance, with the orbital plane at 45 degrees to the equator. Given this orbit, instead of hanging over the equator at a fixed location, it performed a daily figure-8 loop from Australia in the south to Japan in the north. The higher and smaller lobe of the figure-8 was over Japan, with the result that Michibiki remained high in the sky there for eight hours of its orbit, providing GPS augmentation signals to locations where GPS reception was otherwise spotty. Two more satellites were to be launched in the series to provide 24 hour a day coverage.

149. Select the sentence in the passage that leads the reader to conclude that an area's terrain should be used in calculating the orbits of GPS satellites.

Passage 74

Questions 150 to 152 are based on the following passage.

Our nuclear paranoia may be nowhere near as high as it was during the Cold War, but we still live in an age characterized by atomic energy. Hence the fears associated with the dangers of radiation still play a prominent role in public discourse. The recent meltdown at the Fukushima Daiichi nuclear power plant only serves to reinforce the fact that we cannot forget how high the risks really run vis-a-vis nuclear disaster.

Science, however, claims to have found a method of assuaging our fears of both atomic disaster and atomic dependence. Researchers at the United States Department of Energy's Lawrence Berkeley National Laboratory are in the process of developing a method of decontaminating human bodies that have been exposed to high levels of radiation. As many people know, radiation contamination is the one of the most dangerous aspects of a nuclear meltdown, typically resulting in a slow and often painful degeneration of health in which sickness (sometimes for generations) and death are the common end results.

The Berkeley Lab researchers claim that they can treat the ravages of radiation orally with a pill; depending on how fast the medicine is administered, one pill could remove 90% of the actinide toxins in a mere 24 hours. In 2 weeks, the body could be contaminant free.

While it is no doubt of the utmost importance to find a way to cure the effects of radiation, one must be skeptical of the treatment method proposed by the Berkeley Lab scientists because it is often times the case that things that sound too good to be true are, in fact, too good to be true. A few pills over the course of a few weeks curing radiation exposure sounds a bit suspect and makes one wonder what the side effects of such a treatment will be. Such a fast cure to such a grave problem shines a light of doubt on the efficacy and safety of these anti-radiation drugs.

If our society is characterized by paranoia, then it is certainly also characterized by a need for quick fixes to problems. Until more proof can be shown, the radiation treatment proposed by the Berkeley Lab researchers sounds too much like a miracle cure in an age where we need everything to happen as fast as, well, a nuclear meltdown. Until this new treatment has the FDA stamp of approval (and even then medications can remain suspect), the verdict will remain out as to whether or not science has found a viable cure for actinide contamination.

Select only one answer choice.

150. This passage can best be described as

  A A narrative

  B Objective prose

  C A scientific theory

  D Persuasive prose

  E Comparative prose

Consider each of the three choices separately and select all that apply.

151. The two sections highlighted in bold-face are related to each other in which of the following ways?

  A The first section is an assertion, the second sections seeks to undermine that assertion

  B The two bold-faced sections present assertions that are congruent with each other

  C The first section is the scientist's main claim, the second section is the author's main claim

152. Select the sentence that demonstrates the author's use of the concession and rebuttal rhetorical strategy.

Passage 75

Question 153 is based on the following passage.

Referring to the Higgs boson particle as the God particle is a bit of a misnomer; physicists agree that finding the Higgs boson will not prove or disprove the existence of spiritual beings. However, as gauche as it may be to say it, if physicists are able to finally locate the elusive elementary particle, then the scientific ramifications would be otherworldly indeed: the origins of particle mass in the universe would be explicated and physicists would know that their current hypotheses relative to string theory are on the right track.

Select only one answer choice.

153. The Higgs boson particle is all of the following except

- (A)   The God particle
- (B)   The origin of particle mass in the universe
- (C)   A hypothesis
- (D)   An elementary particle
- (E)   Scientific support for string theory

Passage 76

Questions 154 to 156 are based on the following passage.

Scientific progress is often measured in terms of medical progress; chemists, biologists, and even physicists work hard to find ways to keep humans healthy and whole and in doing so advance their respective scientific fields. Furthermore, many of the medical discoveries engendered by the cooperation of doctors and scientists push the boundaries of our imaginations. Recent developments within the field of chemistry have led to such a groundbreaking discovery: new "smart" material that could potentially help light be transmuted for medicinal purposes. Chemists report that their new polymer (plastic-like) material could help diagnose diseases and engineer new human tissues; whether or not these claims can be substantiated is another matter.

Select only one answer choice.

154. According to the passage, what is so avant-garde about chemists' recent discoveries relative to the new "smart" polymer?

- Ⓐ The "smart" polymer will lead to diagnosing more diseases and could even help scientists and doctors engineer new human tissues
- Ⓑ The "smart" polymer will give chemistry a competitive edge among the other sciences represented in the medical community
- Ⓒ The new polymer could help light be harnessed as a curative property
- Ⓓ The "smart" polymer is the cooperative product of chemists, physicists, and biologists
- Ⓔ There is nothing avant-garde about the new "smart" polymer

Select only one answer choice.

155. The section highlighted in bold-face is intended to underscore

- Ⓐ The fact that scientists and doctors often cooperate
- Ⓑ The fact that scientists and doctors are creative
- Ⓒ The fact that medicine evolves in unforeseen ways
- Ⓓ The fact that medical discoveries could not occur without the cooperation of doctors and scientists
- Ⓔ The fact that our imaginations are limited

156. Select the sentence that belies the author's excitement vis-a-vis the new "smart" polymer.

Passage 77

Questions 157 and 158 are based on the following passage.

Star Wars showed us planets with more than one sun and now scientists are doing the same. The Earth only orbits one sun, but astrophysicists now believe in the ubiquity of other planets in the universe that orbit two stars. These so-called circumbinary planets possess rapidly changing flows of energy and wildly varying climates due to the orbital motion around two suns. Scientists believe that since the climate and seasonal change on such planets are in constant flux, the evolution of life in a circumbinary system would be vastly different than on earth. However, scientists can only speculate as to what this difference would entail; they are still unsure of how exactly life could manifest differently on different planets and in different solar systems.

Select only one answer choice.

157. The author discusses Star Wars

- (A) In order to draw a parallel between science and science fiction
- (B) To show how science fiction films often predict scientific truths
- (C) As a stylistic device to peak the reader's interest in the text
- (D) As a narrative rhetorical strategy to peak the reader's interest in the text
- (E) In order to promote the Star Wars films

Consider each of the three choices separately and select all that apply.

158. Circumbinary planets can help us understand

- A How life materializes and evolves on other planets
- B Climate change on Earth
- C The role of the sun(s) in climate control

Passage 78

Questions 159 to 161 are based on the following passage.

Chemists are one mind-blowing step closer than ever to building artificial life forms from scratch. Whether or not this is a good idea is another matter; we are faced here with the "just because we can doesn't mean we should" dilemma. Biochemical researchers have now been able to employ a novel chemical reaction that begets self-assembling cell membranes. Cell membranes are the structural foundation stones for life on Earth and scientists hope that this research break through will allow them to better understand the very origins of life on Earth; one of the great mysteries in science is how non-living matter transmuted to living matter and scientists argue that is important to unlock the secret to the basic chemical and biological principles necessary for the original formation of life. Such research would help us answer the fundamental questions of who we are where we came from. However, some secrets are meant to stay hidden and the ability to create artificial life could open a Pandora's box with far reaching consequences from exploitation if the technology fell into the wrong hands to annihilation of natural life as we know it.

Select only one answer choice.

159. The author makes his or her point primarily by

  A   Offering an objective evaluation of the facts

  B   Dramatically appealing to the reader's fear of the unknown

  C   Providing both a view and counterview

  D   Castigating the mindset of the scientists

  E   Using a specific source of authority to back up his or her claims

Select only one answer choice.

160. The author refers to a Pandora's Box in order to

  A   Test the reader's intelligence

  B   Highlight the fact that artificial life could never be controlled

  C   Show that the creation of artificial life would be evil

  D   Reinforce his point by way of a trope

  E   Distract the reader with a red herring

Select only one answer choice.

161. In the last sentence the author apparently intends to

- (A) Explicate how non-living matter transformed into living matter
- (B) Underscore why the scientific research mentioned in the passage is important
- (C) Generalize an argument to make it more appealing to a wider audience
- (D) Give the reader more details related to the information previously discussed in the passage
- (E) Persuade the reader to believe an opinion by way of a rhetorical strategy.

Passage 79

Question 162 is based on the following passage.

Dark matter is still a mysterious phenomenon to astrophysicists. There are large portions of the universe in which mass does not emit or scatter light or any other kind of electromagnetic radiation, so scientists deem these areas to be composed of dark matter. However, there is still no concrete evidence for the existence of dark matter; scientists can only infer that it exists based on the studied gravitational effects of visible matter and the discrepancies in mass that occur in calculations relative to the mass of galaxies and clusters of galaxies. Thus, dark matter provides a good example of how little we really know about the structures that compose our universe.

162. Select the sentence that, according to the author, best describes the current state of astrophysics.

Passage 80

Question 163 is based on the following passage.

In physical geography, the earth can be divided into categories of climactic conditions, each with endemic communities of plants, animals, and soil organisms. These groups are known as biomes and it is critically important to understand and protect them because they play a vital role in sustaining the balance of life on the planet. There are four main types of biome: aquatic, forest, desert, and grassland. While each type of biome is different, all are equally important threads woven into the same tapestry: planet earth.

163. Select the sentence that uses metaphor as a rhetorical strategy.

Passage 81

Question 164 is based on the following passage.

In the wake of global climate change hysteria, everyone is looking for reasons to explain fluctuating weather patterns, from lay people to meteorologists. Extremely hot summers have everyone convinced global warming is on the rampage and extremely cold winters have everyone convinced a new ice age is coming. Scientists, however, now believe that they have found a way to explain the recent phenomenon of extreme winters: harshly hot summers. Research suggests that hot summers contribute to the melting of ice in the world's Arctic regions, which in turn causes extreme cold and heavy snowfall in the winters of temperate climates. The exact cause of the harshly hot summers is still up for debate, but one thing is certain: Just as extreme behavior begets more extreme behavior in humans, so too does extreme weather beget extreme weather.

Consider each of the three answer choices separately and select all that apply.

164. The author's attitude towards the public and scientific reaction to climate change can best be described as

  A   Petrified

  B   Incredulous

  C   Dubious

Passage 82

Question 165 is based on the following passage.

The origin of the universe is a hotly debated topic in the scientific community, but despite the fierce polemics, the Big Bang theory is still the prevailing explanation.

Proponents of the Big Bang theory insist that the universe once existed in an incredibly dense and hot state until it exploded out and expanded rapidly, causing cooling and the formation of stars, galaxies, and eventually life. Most scientists estimate this event to have occurred around 14 billion years ago.

Consider each of the three answer choices separately and select all that apply.

165. Which of the following are analogous to the term "polemic" in the passage?

     A   Contingency

     B   Brouhaha

     C   Argument

Passage 83

Questions 166 and 167 are based on the following passage.

In particle physics, antimatter is the inverse of matter; antimatter is composed of antiparticles while regular matter is comprised of particles. Antimatter was originally conceptualized in the late 1920s by physicist Paul Dirac as a means of better understanding the behavior of electrons and thus the behavior of our universe. Dirac theorized that nature's predisposition to binary pairs could help him explain the functioning of electrons. He hypothesized that electrons could only exist if there was an antielectron - the opposite of an electron with an opposite electrical charge, but proof of their existence wasn't possible until it could be tested in particle accelerators; a process that could not be undertaken until the 1960's. Today, most antimatter research is centered in Geneva, Switzerland at CERN, the European Organization for Nuclear Research.

Select only one answer choice.

166. Dirac's antimatter hypothesis relies on the assumption that

- (A) Scientific possibilities are never limited
- (B) Electrons are the key to unlocking the structure of the universe
- (C) Every extant thing has an inverse
- (D) The universe can be fully delineated and understood
- (E) Scientific ideas are sometimes ahead of their times in terms of technological capabilities

Select only one answer choice.

167. This passage can best be described as

- (A) A narrative
- (B) A testimony
- (C) A scientific theory
- (D) Persuasive prose
- (E) Comparative prose

Passage 84

Questions 168 and 169 are based on the following passage.

For expeditions in the Antarctic, wind chill, the atmosphere's cooling power, is the most difficult weather issue facing explorers. Winds blow at high speeds in the coastal areas and, especially in East Antarctica, cold air flows down from the mountains. Called katabatic winds, they blow steadily, but can become almost chaotic, and when they reach a certain level of speed can pick up loose snow, causing a phenomenon known as an Antarctic Blizzard in which human movement is difficult. In such "blizzards" no snow actually falls and the sky above the "storm" can be clear. One year, at a camp known as Mirny Station, the katabatic winds reached speeds in excess of 110 miles per hour on seven different occasions. In the years from 1911 – 1914, during the expedition to Antarctica of the Australian Douglas

Mawson, wind speed at his Adelie Coast camp averaged 40 miles per hour most of the time he was there. In 1960, winds thought to be between 140 and 155 miles an hour destroyed an airplane on the ground. Not all winds in Antarctica are so powerful. Near the South Pole, in fact, average speeds run from about nine miles an hour in the summer to about 17 miles per hour in the winter.

Consider each of the three answer choices separately and select all that apply.

168. Katabatic winds are probably caused at least in part by

- A   Atmospheric issues

- B   Terrain conditions

- C   The fact that the interior areas are cooler than the coastal areas

Select only one answer choice.

169. The sentence that best indicates the problems caused by winds in Antarctica begins

- A   For expeditions

- B   Winds blow

- C   Called katabatic

- D   In such blizzards

- E   In 1960

This page is intentionally left blank

8

Practice Set 6 - Social Sciences

This chapter is devoted to helping you develop your skill with Reading Comprehension questions using concrete examples. You will find passages related to *Social Sciences* that are similar to the sorts of passages you will encounter on an actual GRE test. Each passage has a set of questions and a detailed explanation of the solution to each question. The questions and their solutions will be presented as follows:

In this chapter:

- A passage related to *Social Sciences* similar to what you can expect on an actual GRE test

- Several questions about the passage similar to those you will encounter on an actual GRE test

In *Explanatory Answers for Practice Set 6: Social Sciences*:

- A quick summary that paraphrases the main issues of the passage and points out important words or phrases that indicate the meaning or intent of the passage. Being able to answer a few basic questions about Reading Comprehension passages before you even see any of the questions is a key skill that will help you answer questions more quickly and more accurately. The summaries provided here will give you some sense of how to approach summarizing when looking at actual questions

- Detailed solutions that explain what the correct answer is, and what strategy of strategies you could use to determine the correct answer. Explanatory answers will usually refer back to the summary

Passage 85

Questions 170 and 171 are based on the following passage.

The Japanese remained almost entirely ignorant of these preparations. Many of the Japanese military command were suffering from "senshobyo (victory disease)". They had easily won almost every battle they had fought, and they had no reason to believe they would not win just as easily in the future. The defeat at Midway had not been made public and did not disturb this belief. Few senior military officers believed there would be a serious Allied counterstroke against Japan until well into 1943.

There were those among them who were more realistic in their thinking, including Lieutenant Commander Itoo Haruki of the Naval Intelligence Center in Tokyo. In late July, his unit identified two new Allied radio callsigns, both operating on the 4.205 megahertz band and communicating with Pearl Harbor. On 1 August, Japanese radio direction finders pinpointed the location of the stations as Melbourne and Noumea. Itoo correctly guessed these were headquarters for Allied operational forces, massing for an attack on New Guinea or the Solomons. He relayed an urgent warning to Truk, the main Japanese base in the central Pacific, and Rabaul. The warning was ignored.

Select only one answer choice.

170. Based on the information in the passage, select the most likely symptom of senshobyo from the following list.

    A   Optimism

    B   Courage

    C   Overconfidence

    D   Complacency

    E   Satisfaction

Select only one answer choice.

171. What purpose is served by the writer's including the specific details of Lieutenant Commander Haruki's intelligence?

  - A   To show the level of efficiency in the Naval Intelligence Center in Tokyo

  - B   To establish a foundation for Haruki's warning

  - C   To provide information about the location of the Allies in the Pacific

  - D   To justify Haruki's rise to the level of Lieutenant Commander

  - E   To demonstrate the lack of preparedness on the part of the Japanese Navy

Passage 86

Questions 172 to 174 are based on the following passage.

This distinction must be borne in mind - that while the early chiefs were spokesmen and leaders in the simplest sense, possessing no real authority, those who headed their tribes during the transition period were more or less rulers and more or less politicians. It is a singular fact that many of the "chiefs", well known as such to the American public, were not chiefs at all according to the accepted usages of their tribesmen. Their prominence was simply the result of an abnormal situation, in which representatives of the United States Government made use of them for a definite purpose. In a few cases, where a chief met with a violent death, some ambitious man has taken advantage of the confusion to thrust himself upon the tribe and, perhaps with outside help, has succeeded in usurping the leadership.

Select only one answer choice.

172. Which of the following terms describes tribal structure prior to interference by the American government?

  - A   Matriarchal

  - B   Patriarchal

  - C   Oligarchal

  - D   Egalitarian

  - E   Tyrannical

Select only one answer choice.

173. What question might be created in the mind of the reader after reading this passage?

   A   How did tribal chiefs get their names?

   B   How many tribes were negotiating with the American government?

   C   What other misconceptions about Native Americans have been perpetuated?

   D   Why did the chiefs meet with violent deaths?

   E   Did early politicians model their behavior after that of tribal chiefs?

Select only one answer choice.

174. Which of the following is the best definition for the word "singular" in the context of this passage?

   A   Extraordinary

   B   Unusual or strange

   C   Distinctive; unique

   D   Separate; individual

   E   A form in the singular

Passage 87

Questions 175 to 178 are based on the following passage.

The Baluch character is influenced by its environment as much as by its origin, so that it is impossible to select any one section of the general community as affording a satisfactory sample of popular Baluch idiosyncrasies. They are not a homogeneous race. Peoples of Arab extraction intermixed with people of Dravidian and Persian stock are all lumped together under the name of Baluch. The Marri and Bugti tribes, who occupy the most southern buttresses of the Suliman Mountains, are Sind Baluchis, almost certainly of Arab extraction. They came to Sind either with the Arab conquerors or after them, and remained there mixed up with the original Hindu inhabitants. The Arab type of Baluch extends through the whole country at intervals, and includes all the finest and best of Baluch humanity. Taking the Sind Baluch as the type opposed to the Afridi Pathan, the Baluch is easier to deal with and to control than the Pathan, owing to his tribal organization and his freedom from bigoted fanaticism or blind allegiance to his priest. The Baluch is less turbulent, less treacherous, less bloodthirsty and less fanatical than the Pathan. His frame is shorter and more spare and wiry than that of his neighbour to the north, though generations have given to him too a bold and manly bearing. It would be difficult to match the stately dignity and imposing presence of a Baluch chief of the Marri or Bugti clans. His Semitic features are those of the Bedouin and he carries himself as straight and as loftily as any Arab gentleman. Frank and open in his manners, fairly truthful, faithful to his word, temperate and enduring, and looking upon courage as the highest virtue, the true Baluch of the Derajat is a pleasant man to have dealings with. As a revenue payer he is not so satisfactory, his want of industry and the pride which looks upon manual labour as degrading making him but a poor husbandman. He is an expert rider; horse-racing is his national amusement, and the Baluch breed of horses is celebrated throughout northern India. Like the Pathan he is a bandit by tradition and descent and makes a first-rate fighting man, but he rarely enlists in the Indian army. He is nominally a Mahommedan, but is neglectful of the practices of his religion.

175. Select the sentence in the passage that explains why the Baluchi are not likely to be farmers.

Consider each of the three answer choices separately and select all that apply.

176. Which of the following is the best explanation for the Baluch's reluctance to join the Indian army?

| A | They feel that their superior fighting skills make joining the Indian army beneath their dignity |

| B | Their allegiance to their own tribes is stronger than their allegiance to India |

| C | Their tendency to flout social expectations makes it difficult for them to develop a sense of patriotic duty |

Select only one answer choice.

177. The writer's use of the phrase, influenced by its environment as much as by its origin, in the first line of the passage and the phrase, tradition and descent, in the next-to-last sentence allow the reader to reach which of the following conclusions about the Baluch?

  - A   The Baluch scoff at the traditions of Indian culture

  - B   Heredity has determined a greater portion of the Baluch character than environment has

  - C   Environment has determined a greater portion of the Baluch character than heredity has

  - D   The Baluch's behavior and character has been formed by both nature and nurture

  - E   Their tribal organization is more tolerant of individual differences

Select only one answer choice.

178. In which of the following texts would you be likely to find this passage about the Baluch?

  - A   A gazetteer

  - B   An atlas

  - C   An almanac

  - D   A digest

  - E   An anthology

Passage 88

Question 179 is based on the following passage.

Botel Tobago is an island in the South Seas which has lately been visited by a party of United States naval officers. They were surveying a rock east of the South Cape of Formosa, and called at this island. They found a curious race of Malay stock. These aborigines did not know what money was good for. Nor had they ever used tobacco or rum. They gave the officers goats and pigs for tin pots and brass buttons, and hung around the vessel all day in their canoes waiting for a chance to dive for something which might be thrown overboard. They wore clouts only, ate taro and yams, and had axes, spears, and knives made of common iron. Their canoes were made without nails, and were ornamented with geometrical lines. They wore the beards of goats and small shells as ornaments.

Select only one answer choice.

179. Based on the information in this passage, select the list of adjectives that best describes the inhabitants of Botel Tobago.

    A   Aggressive, amenable, cunning

    B   Naive, narcissistic, opportunistic

    C   Vain, opportunistic, overt

    D   Herbivorous, humble, hardy

    E   Social, stoic, omnivorous

Passage 89

Question 180 is based on the following passage.

In this way will the whole problem of freedom be solved, that natural laws be ascertained by scientific discovery, and the knowledge of them be universally diffused among the masses. Natural laws being thus recognized by every man for himself, he cannot but obey them, for they are the laws also of his own nature; and the need for political organization, administration and legislation will at once disappear. Nor will he admit of any privileged position or class, for "it is the peculiarity of privilege and of every privileged position to kill the intellect and heart of man. The privileged man, whether he be privileged politically or economically, is a man depraved in intellect and heart." "In a word, we object to all legislation, all authority, and all influence, privileged, patented, official and legal, even when it has proceeded from universal suffrage, convinced that it must always turn to the profit of a dominating and exploiting minority, against the interests of the immense majority enslaved."

Select only one answer choice.

180. Based on your understanding of the purpose served by this passage, determine which of the following terms identifies its structure.

- Ⓐ   Manifesto
- Ⓑ   Proclamation
- Ⓒ   Edict
- Ⓓ   Fiat
- Ⓔ   Mandate

Passage 90

Question 181 is based on the following passage.

Toch estimates that 50% of home schooled children attend college, the same percentage as children educated in public schools. But are these students skilled enough to compete successfully with conventionally-schooled students in the college setting? Galloway concludes that home schoolers and traditionally educated students demonstrate similar academic preparedness for college and academic achievement. And according to Rudner , achievement test scores of home schooled students are high. The students' average scores were typically in the 70th to 80th percentile, with 25% of home schooled students enrolled one or more grades above their age-level peers in public and private schools. Christopher Klicka, Senior Counsel for the Home School Legal Defense Association, reports that home schoolers tend to score above the national average on both the SAT and ACT, the primary tests used by colleges in evaluating college applicants. A study of 2219 students who reported their home schooled status on the SAT in 1999 showed that these students scored an average of 1083--67 points above the national average of 1016; similarly, the 3616 home schooled students who took the ACT scored an average of 22.7--1.7 points above the national average of 21.

Select only one answer choice.

181. What additional information is needed to support a conclusion that home schooled students typically perform better on standardized college entrance exams than do traditionally educated students?

- A   Socioeconomic statistics of the students
- B   Student scores on other standardized tests
- C   The curriculum of both home schoolers and traditional classroom teachers
- D   At least two previous or subsequent years' SAT and ACT results
- E   The colleges to which the students were accepted

Passage 91

Questions 182 and 183 are based on the following passage.

Total fertility rate is the average number of children that would be born per woman if all women lived to the end of their childbearing years and bore children according to a given fertility rate at each age. The total fertility rate (TFR) is a more direct measure of the level of fertility than the crude birth rate, since it refers to births per woman. This indicator shows the potential for population change in the country. A rate of two children per woman is considered the replacement rate for a population, resulting in relative stability in terms of total numbers. Rates above two children indicate populations growing in size and whose median age is declining. Higher rates may also indicate difficulties for families, in some situations, to feed and educate their children and for women to enter the labor force. Rates below two children indicate populations decreasing in size and growing older. Global fertility rates are in general decline and this trend is most pronounced in industrialized countries, especially Western Europe, where populations are projected to decline dramatically over the next 50 years.

Select only one answer choice.

182. Which of the following is a probable challenge for western European countries as their fertility rates decline over the next few decades?

     A   Caring for the children who are born during this time

     B   Rising unemployment

     C   Providing for the elderly

     D   Increased poverty

     E   Reduced expenditures for education

Select only one answer choice.

183. What is a possible reason for higher fertility rates in non-industrialized countries?

     A   Lower divorce rates

     B   Fewer women in the workforce

     C   More live births

     D   Lower infant mortality

     E   Higher number of extended families

Passage 92

Question 184 is based on the following passage.

Malaysia is a destination and, to a lesser extent, a source and transit country for women and children trafficked for the purpose of commercial sexual exploitation, and men, women, and children for forced labor; Malaysia is mainly a destination country for men, women, and children who migrate willingly from South and Southeast Asia to work, some of whom are subjected to conditions of involuntary servitude by Malaysian employers in the domestic, agricultural, construction, plantation, and industrial sectors; to a lesser extent, some Malaysian women, primarily of Chinese ethnicity, are trafficked abroad for commercial sexual exploitation. Malaysia improved from Tier 3 to the Tier 2 Watch List for 2008 when it enacted comprehensive anti-trafficking legislation in July 2007; however, it did not take action against exploitative employers or labor traffickers in 2007; the government has not ratified the 2000 UN TIP Protocol (2008).

Select only one answer choice.

184. Which of the following statements most closely reflects the probable conditions that facilitate human trafficking and/or labor exploitation in Malaysia?

   A   There is a lack of employment opportunities in South and Southeast Asia

   B   Malaysia has fewer cultural taboos about sexual activity

   C   The Southeast Asian and Malaysian cultures deem it acceptable for children to work in agriculture and industry

   D   The 2000 UN TIP Protocol is too restrictive

   E   Industrialized nations outsource much of their factory production to Malaysia

Passage 93

Question 185 is based on the following passage.

These caves were inhabited by man during an immense stretch of time, and, as you dig down, you light upon one layer after another of his leavings. But note in such a case as this how easily you may be baffled by someone having upset the heap of clothes, or, in a word, by rearrangement. Thus the man whose leavings ought to form the layer half-way up may have seen fit to dig a deep hole in the cave-floor in order to bury a deceased friend, and with him, let us suppose, to bury also an assortment of articles likely to be useful in the life beyond the grave. Consequently an implement of one age will be found lying cheek by jowl with the implement of a much earlier age, or even, it may be, some feet below it.

Select only one answer choice.

185. How do archaeologists reconcile apparent contradictions in the location and age of artifacts uncovered in a dig?

    A   They examine written records of early inhabitants of the area

    B   They interview current residents of the area

    C   They create a scenario that explains the juxtaposition of artifacts from different time periods

    D   They make note of the level of preservation of the artifacts

    E   They sort the artifacts according to their function

Passage 94

Question 186 is based on the following passage.

Research into the eating habits of women shows that they are mimetic; women tend to want to mirror the way their fellow female diners enjoy their food. Psychologists theorize this has to do with the fact that women are more prone to same-gender imitation than their male counterparts - men seem to be oblivious to the behavior of other eaters in the dining group. Underpinning women's copycat eating habits is likely a stronger need to both belong to and be liked by the group, particularly the other females in the group.

Select only one answer choice.

186. All of the following can be inferred from the passage except

    A   Same-gender conformity is a more feminine trait

    B   Men are the less conventional gender

    C   Women in a dining group tend to eat the same amount of food

    D   Women value how they are perceived by others

    E   Men in a dining group eat disparate amounts of food

Passage 95

Questions 187 to 189 are based on the following passage.

Although it seems hard to imagine, humans originated in one place and then spread across the globe to create the vast network of cultures and nations that constitute our modern world. This phenomenon fascinates many, including scientists who are deeply interested in the Diaspora of modern man from the Horn of Africa to the far-reaching corners of the globe. While it is no longer disputed that modern man originated in northern Africa, many anthropologists debate the area from which human settlers organized and then colonized the rest of the world. Recent research suggests that the first humans out of Africa settled in Arabia and from there staged the global dispersal of modern man. This conclusion was drawn based on DNA comparisons between populations in Europe, North Africa, and the Near East. Scientists were able to determine that all the populations were most closely related with the Arabians samples. Thus, the Arabian settlers are the common denominator in the dispersal of modern man.

Select only one answer choice.

187. The primary purpose of this passage is to

   A   Discuss the African Diaspora of early humans

   B   Show how the interests of scientists and laymen intersect

   C   Discuss the dissemination point of modern man

   D   Show how DNA analysis can be used in anthropological research

   E   Start a debate about man's origins in Africa

Select only one answer choice.

188. The author's attitude towards DNA analysis as an anthropological research method can best be described as

  (A)   Skeptical

  (B)   Leery

  (C)   Impartial

  (D)   Favoring

  (E)   Devoted

Select only one answer choice.

189. According to the author, polemics surrounding the dispersal of early humans tend to focus on

  (A)   Whether or not early humans originated in the Horn of Africa

  (B)   Whether or not Europe or Arabia were the starting points of modern man's colonization of the globe

  (C)   The Near East's role in the dispersal of humans throughout the world

  (D)   The point of origin for organized human dispersal across the globe

  (E)   Whether or not DNA analysis is an effective way of determining the point of origin of the organized human Diaspora

Passage 96

Question 190 is based on the following passage.

According to recent psychological research published in the British Journal of Psychology, men are more likely to display altruistic behavior in the presence of attractive women. Conversely, women's behavior remains constant regardless of the attractiveness of their male company. Psychologists conclude that male behavior is determined by the need to impress prospective mates, while female behavior is based less on the need to impress and more on the need to be selective and receptive with respect to potential male partners.

Select only one answer choice.

190. The author primarily makes his or her point by

- (A)   Objectively evaluating the facts
- (B)   An emotional appeal to the reader
- (C)   Providing both a view and counterview
- (D)   Criticizing the opinions of the psychologists
- (E)   Offering a source of authority

Passage 97

Question 191 is based on the following passage.

It pays to work hard in college. Literally Researchers have concluded that slacker students in college are at the highest risk for credit card debt, unemployment, and hunkering down for a permanent stay in mom and dad's basement. Even more troubling is the fact that these students lack critical job skills - they run the highest risk of not improving their reasoning, writing, and critical thinking skills by the time they walk across the stage to accept their diploma. Many students believe college to be a time of fun and exploration, but if such experiences are not combined with hard work, future success is not a guarantee.

Select only one answer choice.

191. The author's claims about slacker students would be weakened by all of the following except

    Ⓐ   Several examples of students who were slackers yet still succeeded after college

    Ⓑ   Research that demonstrated slacker college students improving their academic skills despite low work ethics

    Ⓒ   Evidence that slacker college students obtained post-graduation jobs as easily as their hard-working counterparts

    Ⓓ   Evidence that slacker students do not struggle with financial issues any more than their hard working counterparts

    Ⓔ   Evidence that hardworking and slacker college students had similar post-graduation living conditions

Passage 98

Questions 192 and 193 are based on the following passage.

Many scholars hold Karl Marx to be one of the founding fathers of modern day social science. Karl Marx is and always has been a polemical figure, but his conceptualization of the dialectic that shapes all societal conflicts, class struggle, has fundamentally changed the way that many politicians, academics, and lay people view and analyze global power relationships. The theories of Karl Marx, known as Marxism, are most often employed as methods of critiquing not only capitalism, but also the very political systems that they engendered: socialism and communism. Thus, Marxism can be a highly useful and self-reflexive analytical tool.

Select only one answer choice.

192. According to the author, Marxism is a self-reflexive analytical tool because

   A   It accurately deconstructs power structures within capitalistic societies

   B   It can be used as a method of critically examining its own economic systems

   C   It elucidates important issues related to class conflict

   D   It helps academics set up a dialectical research framework

   E   It enables free-thinking academic exchange

Select only one answer choice.

193. The term "dialectic" in the passage is most analogous to

   A   The scientific method

   B   Reason engendered by discussion

   C   Protest

   D   Political dialogue

   E   Exploitation of workers

Passage 99

Question 194 is based on the following passage.

Art is often considered a defining characteristic of civilization, but recent anthropological finds suggest otherwise. The oldest known painting kits were recently unearthed in a South African cave, and anthropologists estimate the artifacts are over 100,000 years old. The painting kits consisted of stone and bone tools for crushing, mixing, and applying paint to cave walls, animal skins and maybe even body parts. The paint was made from red and yellow ochres and housed in sea snail shells. Thus, art predates not only modern man, but also complex human societies.

Select only one answer choice.

194. The author suggests that the painting kits found in South Africa are important because

- (A) They give us insight into the early humans
- (B) They illuminate the kinds of tools available to early humans
- (C) They give us information on the earliest forms of art as body decoration

  They show that art predates civilization
- (D) They help us trace the development of artistic methods in human
- (E) civilization

Passage 100

Question 195 is based on the following passage.

Recent studies conducted by psychologists show that combat soldier and children from abusive families have one thing unnervingly in common: changes in brain activity engendered by trauma. Children who are exposed to emotionally or verbally abusive environments experience a shift in their brain patterns associated with the amygdale and anterior insula that activates a heightened sense of awareness to danger. These changes contribute to panic attacks, anxiety, depression, and low self-esteem if left untreated by therapy and/or medication.

Select only one answer choice.

195. Based on the information given in the passage, all of the following can be inferred except

- (A) Child abuse is as emotionally damaging as active combat
- (B) Abusive and dangerous situations have the ability to change the brain at any point during a person's life
- (C) The ramifications of child abuse are treatable
- (D) Combat soldiers have a harder time recovering from traumatic experiences than children
- (E) Emotional abuse leaves a lasting physical impression on the brain

Passage 101

Questions 196 and 197 are based on the following passage.

Niccolo Machiavelli's seminal work, The Prince, is considered to be one of the first works of modern political philosophy; it is also one of the most controversial. Nonetheless, The Prince has influenced Western thought related to governance ever since its publication in 1532. Machiavelli uses his treatise to outline leadership and success relative to royal (or political) rule. In today's world it is quite controversial as The Prince negates the importance of personal virtue in leaders and lofty political idealism - realism is the goal of the treatise and the reality of the world is that successful outcomes go to the strongest in the fight for survival and the battle of the wits. Despite its controversial message, The Prince is written in eloquent, yet simple language that relays its message with surgical precision. Nearly all English speakers are well-acquainted with the polemical aphorism that lies at the thematic heart of The Prince: The end justifies the means.

Select only one answer choice.

196. The two portions in bold-face are related to each other in which of the following ways?

    A   The first bold-faced section undermines the conclusion drawn by the second bold-faced section

    B   The first bold-faced section is an extrapolation on the conclusion drawn by the second bold-faced section

    C   Both bold-faced sections challenge the author's position

    D   The first bold-faced section is a position that the author does not agree with; the second bold-faced section is a position that the author does agree with

    E   Both bold-faced sections undermine the goals and objectives of the modern day political landscape

Select only one answer choice.

197. The author most clearly makes a case for the fact that

     A   Polemical books are often among the most influential

     B   Leadership requires a combination of virtue and vice

     C   Political ideas often evolve

     D   Human nature remains the same as political systems change

     E   Political goals are best achieved by way of a Machiavellian approach

Passage 102

Questions 198 to 201 are based on the following passage.

Millions of people across the globe struggle with depression, some for only days and some for a lifetime. It is a universal mental malaise that effects people from every socio-economic background in every country. Depression is defined by psychologists as a mood disorder characterized by sadness, low activity, apathy, and hopelessness. Since depression hinders sufferers from obtaining a good quality of life, researchers make it a priority to both understand the cause of the mood disorder and discover ways to treat it.

In the 1950s psychologists and neuroscientists teamed up to proclaim that depression was the result of a chemical imbalance, more specifically low levels of serotonin, and a milieu was born that sought to frame mental health issues as curable deficiencies. Medications like Prozac, more formally known as Selective Serotonin Reuptake Inhibitors, became the main method of treatment for depression and other mood disorders.

The belief that low serotonin levels cause depression is ubiquitous, but psychologists have begun to change their tune regarding the link between so-called chemical imbalances and mental health issues. New research shows that neurotransmitters such as serotonin control moods and mental health much less than previously thought.

A study conducted in the 1990s showed that depleting the serotonin levels of people without depression did not in turn cause them to become depressed; this action in fact had little effect on their mood and behavior. This information coupled with more insight into the nuances of genetics and how they affect mood and personality has led many psychologists and medical researchers to look for new treatment methods and possibilities. Although it is still widely acknowledged that depressed people do have some type of serotonin aberration, serotonin as the primary controller of human moods is a belief that is outmoded; pills as a means of solving mood problems may hopefully become a thing of the past (bad news for pharmaceutical companies).

Whether low serotonin levels, genes, or environment are the cause of depression, one thing is clear: scientists don't really know what causes mood disorders. While this may seem like a discomforting thought for those who suffer from depression or other mental health issues, the good news is that many treatment methods such as talk therapy still have high rates of success. Life can still be lived in a world of uncertainty.

Select only one answer choice.

198. The author's attitude towards Selective Serotonin Reuptake Inhibitors (SSRIs) can best be described as

- A   Candid
- B   Positive
- C   Castigating
- D   Leery
- E   Condescending

Select only one answer choice.

199. Given the information in the passage, all of the following can be inferred except

- A   SSRIs are not a good method for treating depression
- B   Genes determine whether or not a person will become depressed
- C   Serotonin does not directly affect a person's mood
- D   Talk therapy can help heal people from depression
- E   Depression is a phenomenon common to all humans regardless of culture or ethnicity

Consider each of the three choices separately and select all that apply.

200. Depression is likely caused by

      A   Genes that contribute to a person's biological profile

      B   Environmental factors that contribute to a person's mental health profile

      C   The combination of past and present experiences, as well as biological factors

201. Select the sentence that best describes why Selective Serotonin Reuptake Inhibitors (SSRIs) have been promoted as a method of treating depression.

This page is intentionally left blank

EXPLANATORY ANSWERS

Practice Set 1 - Arts and Humanities

Passage 1 – Summary / Paraphrase

The passage is about a pre-Columbian Mexican deity, Tezcatlipoca. The main idea is that Tezcatlipoca held an especially exalted place in the pantheon of Mexican gods. The major points are (a) Tezcatlipoca was supposed to have guided his people to the valley of Mexico (b) Tezcatlipoca was credited with a tremendous range of attributes because his worshipers feared him and wished to praise him. A minor point suggests that the author believes the way that the Nahua worshipped Tezcatlipoca can be generalized to other peoples. The purpose of the passage is to explain Tezcatlipoca's position in the Mexican pantheon.

Answer to Question 1:

The correct answer is "The place he took as the head of the Nahua pantheon brought him many attributes which were quite foreign to his original character."In this case, Texcatlipoca is assumed by his followers to have attributes that are foreign to him. Because followers or believers have various needs, they will expect a variety and, perhaps, conflicting ideas do what the leader can accomplish. The leader is fated to disappoint some of his constituents, at least until he can develop the attributes that they assume he possesses.

Passage 2 – Summary / Paraphrase

The passage tells the story of Sheddad. The main idea is that although Sheddad was very powerful, he was struck down by a divine force for his impurity. The major points are (a) that Sheddad used his power to construct a lavish garden and (b) that before he had the opportunity to enjoy his garden, he was struck dead for his "impure soul". The purpose of the passage is to warn the reader that no amount of worldly power and wealth can save a bad man.

Answer to Question 2:

The correct answer is E. Shaddad has built a garden to rival the beauty of heaven and has assembled his slaves and courtiers to view it. In the construction of this garden, Shaddad has angered God, who sends the angel of death to take Shaddad's life before he can see the fruits of his labor. Shaddad's pride has caused his downfall, making E the correct answer. There is no evidence in the story to suggest that others might steal the precious metals and jewels, so A is not correct. God and the angels have no need for a beautiful garden on earth, making B an incorrect choice. Based on the words of the angel of death, one cannot presume that the garden was hidden to prevent Shaddad's heirs from claiming it, eliminating C as a correct answer. It appears that Shaddad used the resources of other countries for hundreds of years; if preventing that were the object of the lesson, it likely would have happened before the construction had been completed. D is incorrect.

Passage 3 – Summary / Paraphrase

The passage is about Social Darwinism. The main idea is that Social Darwinism was used to justify oppressive and racist views and policies. The major points are (a) that Social Darwinism is nothing more than the notion that "might makes right" dressed in a quasi-scientific guise and (b) Social Darwinism was used to justify segregation and a belief in a master race. The purpose of the passage is to explain Social Darwinism and how it was used to justify racist ideologies.

Answer to Question 3:

The correct answer is "If the struggle for survival was the way of the world, then it was only natural that human society should operate in the same way." This sentence is an example of conditional logic. Social Darwinists assumed that if this condition exists in the animal world, then it must also exist in the human world.

Answer to Question 4:

Both A and C are correct. Bullies adopt the role of predator when they select those who are weak in some way as targets of rumors or harmful insults. The Nazis used predation in the late 1930's and early 1940's to round up Jews, homosexuals, gypsies, and others that they considered inferior in an attempt to prevent sullying the Aryan race. Involuntary commitment could be the result of a court proceeding that relies on expert testimony and is not necessarily a predatory action.

Answer to Question 5:

The correct answer is C. A dovetail is a type of joint used in carpentry to make pieces of wood fit together smoothly. Social Darwinism fit well with segregationists ideas that white people were superior to black people and so had the right to repress them. Coincided implies that the two ideas occurred at the same time rather than one idea's being used to justify the other. Deviated would imply that segregationists did not agree with the idea of social Darwinism. D is a definition used in heraldry, and the definition in E suggests disagreement.

Passage 4 – Summary / Paraphrase

The passage is about supernatural powers for humans. The main idea is that, since man is created in God's image, man too must possess supernatural abilities. The major point is that the work from which the passage is excerpted hopes to demonstrate that humans possess powers "not subject to the general laws of nature"; in other words, that humans have supernatural powers. The purpose of the passage is to serve as a primer for demonstrating that humans are capable of possessing magical abilities.

Answer to Question 6:

The correct answer is B. The author states his conviction that man is undoubtedly endowed with magic powers. This belief may lead him to make the facts fit his theory, which is contrary to objective, scientific research. B is the correct answer. His belief in God should not be an impediment, as many who conduct scientific research also believe in God, making A an incorrect answer choice. The reader cannot tell from the information presented here if there is little or no research on this topic, eliminating C as the correct answer choice. The reader cannot assume that the church will not cooperate, nor that the public will scoff at his ideas, making both D and E incorrect.

Passage 5 – Summary / Paraphrase

The passage is about the author's fascination with books about WWI. The main idea is that although the author is aware that his fascination may seem horrific, he is nonetheless unable to resist it. The major point is that the author feels comfortable in the setting and characters of the war, however appalling the war itself may have been. The purpose of the passage is confessional: the author is admitting the oddities of his fascination while justifying and affirming it.

Answer to Question 7:

The correct answer is "I must confess, though, that I am a bibliophile with War books."Confession is generally a form of catharsis. One may confess to a priest or someone he/she has harmed in the past. In this case, the author thinks that others may find his love of war books strange as the author; himself was most likely a witness to the horrors about which he reads. By revealing his love of these books, he has eliminated the necessity to keep it a secret and probably feels relieved.

Passage 6 – Summary / Paraphrase

The passage is about morning as a metaphor for renewal. The main idea is that, although the author is apparently rather world weary, the beauty of the morning renews some sense of hope in the world. The major points contrast (a) the freshness and innocence of the morning to (b) the sense of the world as "trampled" and the characters as 'grey' and 'sated'. The purpose of the passage is to contrast the author's general state of mind with the symbolic purity of the morning.

Answer to Question 8:

The correct answer is B. The narrator is speaking about morning and the manner in which it is regarding this portion of the earth early in the day.

Answer to Question 9:

The correct answer is A. When the author says that this particular morning must have got lost in the year's progression, he implies that it should have occurred earlier in the year. Halcyon, when describing weather, means calm, or peaceful, or tranquil. A is the only answer that includes both of these descriptors of the day in question. There is no suggestion of a holiday celebration, making B an incorrect choice. The author mentions nothing about the emotions or attitudes of the "we" in the passage. He is describing the morning rather than people. C is not the correct choice.

Passage 7 – Summary / Paraphrase

The passage is about the author's strategy for speaking to local populations. The main idea is that the author always attempts to learn some particulars about the place where he is going to speak before overlaying the particulars with a more general theme. The major points are (a) that the author speaks to various townsfolk to find out about their town, what they are proud of, and where they see failures and (b) that the author then modifies his speech with its general themes of civic pride with certain specific features. The purpose of the passage is to reveal the author's way of addressing each town. The rhetoric suggests that the author may be somewhat cynical about his vocation.

Answer to Question 10:

The correct answer is D. The purpose of his presentation is to help the residents realize their potential for improvement. He aims to motivate them, making D the best answer. The writer gathers information in order to confirm what he believes about the inhabitants of towns everywhere. He hopes that their behavior will become new or innovative. There is nothing in this passage that he attempts to intimidate them or cause fear. He desires to use what he knows to motivate them to realize their full potential. D is the correct answer.

Answer to Question 11:

The correct answer is B. The writer's basic assumption is that, although each town has its unique characteristics, they all fail in the same way. The last two sentences provide the general idea that he uses to illuminate the specific failure of the town he is visiting. B is the correct answer. A is incorrect because he uses those visits to tailor his presentation. There is no indication that he looks down on the people in positions of power in the town, making C incorrect as well. This passage is an overview of his process and reveals nothing specific about any town, eliminating D as a possible answer. The lecture focuses on possibilities, not failures. E is incorrect.

Passage 8 – Summary / Paraphrase

The passage is about O. Henry. The main idea is that although O. Henry was a superb literary craftsman, his work is gimmicky and lacking in depth. The major points are (a) O. Henry was a unique and skillful writer (b) that his work favors sensation and surprise over genuine substance and (c) that he can be accused of lowering the overall standards of American literature. The main purpose of the passage is to severely critique O. Henry's works while giving some credit for certain topical skill.

Answer to Question 12:

The correct answer is C. The writer's use of words like caricature and cheapness describe the overall effect of O. Henry's writing, and they point to a lack of subtlety, making C the correct choice. The critic states that the reader can never be sure of himself, indicating that the stories do create tension, eliminating A as the correct answer. The writer of this passage deals with O. Henry's style extensively, so B is not the correct answer. The writer also provides information about plot elements, so it would be incorrect to assume that plot is a weakness; D is not correct. There is too little information here to select conflict resolution, answer E, as a weakness.

Answer to Question 13:

Both A and C are correct choices. The author of this passage implies that both writers entertain but fail to reach the level of important literature. Their writing lacks moral background. Answer B does not provide enough information to justify a change in the critics' opinions. One would need to know the reason for the authors' inclusion in those anthologies.

Passage 9 – Summary / Paraphrase

The passage is a critique of the human race's self-importance. The main idea is that people have always tended to view the world with an erroneous belief in their own importance and that this way of looking at things continues to influence important aspects of our beliefs. The major points are (a) people hold on to old, outmoded beliefs for fear of the unknown (b) that out of ignorance, people formed all manner of wrong beliefs about the nature of their world, tending to privilege things relatively close at hand (c) that modern science has proven the bulk of our earlier beliefs wrong and destroyed our ability to hold ourselves above the rest of creation (d) our tendency to hold onto the old is the reason for our "crude religions, our crude laws, our crude ideas, and our exalted opinion of the human race." There is a minor point that uses the story of Jacob's ladder to illustrate our way of understanding the world according to our most current knowledge. The purpose of the passage is to give the author's view of why we maintain older beliefs in the face of countervailing evidence.

Answer to Question 14:

The best choice is A. B refers to resources in their natural state, such as crude oil. C could describe a creative product like an essay or a hand-made piece of furniture. D and E describe behavior rather than beliefs and ideas.

Answer to Question 15:

The correct answer is B. The writer is contrasting what man knew in the past with what he now knows to be true. B is the correct answer. The writer is not attempting to show off his own level of education or intelligence, nor is he touting the value of telescopes, eliminating both A and E as correct choices. Answer D is what he is telling the reader but not why. The figure does nothing to enhance the words surrounding it; C is incorrect.

Answer to Question 16:

The correct answer is C. The writer has a low regard for those who refuse to revise their opinions and ideas despite the availability of new information, making C the correct choice. There is nothing in the passage that leads the reader to believe that the writer has any optimism for the human race, so A is incorrect. He does not speculate about the future of the human race, nor reveal any fears about that future, making B the wrong answer. The writer does not tout his own beliefs, so does not express superiority over others, eliminating D as the correct answer. The writer may feel that humankind is hopeless in its desire to hold on to old ideas, but it is overshadowed by his contempt for them. E is not the best answer.

Answer to Question 17:

All of the answers are acceptable choices based on the premise that the people in question were basing their statements or beliefs on what they had to go on. President Kennedy probably could not have imagined the day that scientists would say that human travel to Mars is likely. Until advances in astronomy and physics and mathematics evolved, it was reasonable to assume that everything revolved around the Earth. Columbus believed that he had found a shorter route to India and, logically, called the inhabitants of the New World Indians.

Answer to Question 18:

B is the best answer choice. The author suggests that, at each stage of history, men thought that they had discovered all of the answers only to be proven wrong by successive generations. The same is true for man today. The next best answer is just around the corner. The writer does not suggest that man has made no progress despite his fondness for old ideas. A is not a good answer choice. Although the author expresses contempt for those who cling to old ideas, he does mention the way in which new technology has created new, beneficial understanding, making C an incorrect choice.

Answer to Question 19:

The correct answer is "So to have the idea that all of this was made for man gives man a great deal of what Weber and Field used to call "Proud flesh.""Conceitedness comes from having a high opinion of oneself. The idea that the universe and everything in it was created for man's comfort and/or amusement is the height of conceitedness.

Passage 10 – Summary / Paraphrase

The passage is about the political philosophy of Thomas Hobbes. The main idea is that Hobbes developed a theory in which humans are seen as naturally inclined to do evil and require a government to reign in their naturally evil tendencies. The main points are: (a) that Hobbes believes that in a state of nature, humans are engulfed in perpetual state of conflict (b) that Hobbes believes that only in civil society governed by a social contract are humans able to escape the evils of their "natural" condition. A minor point, the mention of the age old debate between whether human nature is inherently good or bad, is used to introduce the discussion of Hobbes' ideas. The purpose of the passage is to briefly summarize Hobbes' political thought: although the passage presents a potentially controversial matter, the author avoids any indication of bias and merely presents the content.

Answer to Question 20:

"For Hobbes, society is what tames and controls the ultimately selfish and corrupt natural state of the human being."
Hobbes' view on human nature is clearly stated: it is corrupt and selfish.

Passage 11 – Summary / Paraphrase

The passage is about the relation between Pop Art and capitalism. The main idea is that while Pop Art may appear trivial on the surface, it often has deeper and more serious ramifications. The main points are: (a) that Pop Art is an artistic development of the mass production and consumerism that are the hallmarks of capitalism and (b) that Pop Artists have used the medium to both mock and critique capitalist culture, and represent and re-imagine familiar aspects of everyday life. A minor point that distinguishes British and American Pop Art develops the second major point more fully. The purpose of the passage is to inform: the author briefly summarizes several key points about the Pop Art movement. There is a slight indication that the author may be trying to convince the reader to take Pop Art seriously, as indicated by the phrase "While Pop Art seems superfluous at the surface level, it is actually produced with marked intentionality".

Answer to Question 21:

A. Wrong. The passage clearly states that there is a difference between British and

American Pop Art.

B. Correct. The passage states that British Pop artists mocked (lampooned) America's consumer culture while American Pop artists were more interested in representations of reality.

C. Wrong. Both American and British Pop Art is worthy of critique according to the passage.

D. Wrong. The passage does not discuss whether or not British or American Pop artists are more famous.

E. Wrong. The passage clearly states that British Pop Artists explored capitalism in their work since they were highly critical of American consumer culture.

Answer to Question 22:

A. Correct. The passage lists consumerism as one of Pop Art's themes relative to its exploration of capitalism.

B. Correct The passage lists mass production as one of Pop Art's themes relative to its exploration of capitalism.

C. Wrong. The passage does not indicate that Pop Artists used free markets as a part of their artistic expression relative to capitalism.

Passage 12 – Summary / Paraphrase

The passage is about the Art Nouveau movement. The main idea is that Art Nouveau developed art in directions that had never before been seen. There is a major point that Art Nouveau represents a conscious break from Neoclassicist attempts to mimic Greco-Roman aesthetics. A minor point develops the ways in which Art Nouveau differs from art based in classical aesthetics by discussing the use of asymmetry and unusual patterns. The purpose of the passage is to inform, which is reflected in the descriptive tone.

Answer to Question 23:

"Art Nouveau arose at the turn of the 20th century as a reaction against the Neoclassicist movement's propensity to simply mimic the style of the Greeks and Romans."

Art Nouveau artists wanted to find new ways of creating art because they were tired of forms that were constantly mimicking the past.

Passage 13 – Summary / Paraphrase

The passage is about Jacques Derrida's critical theory. The main idea is that Derrida believed that the critical analysis of a literary work could only be done by thoroughly investigating its context. The major points are that (a) Derrida believed that there was no objective starting point to begin the analysis of a work and (b) analysis of narrative could only begin by deconstructing the assumptions underlying the interpretive process. The main purpose of the passage is to introduce the reader to Derrida's idea about critical theory.

Answer to Question 24:

A. Wrong. While this statement is true according to the passage, it does not explicate why subjectivity is needed to deconstruct complex narratives.

B. Correct. The passage shows that Derrida insisted that textual analysis was ultimately dependent on understanding and interpreting the various contexts that inform the text, an act that is an exercise in subjectivity since subjectivity is concerned with engaging a diversity of perspectives.

C. Wrong. The passage does not give enough information about how readers read in order to make a judgment as to whether or not subjectivity accounts for the interpretive process of readers.

D. Wrong. The passage does not give enough specific information about readers to make the inference that the inner experience of the reader is what characterizes deconstructionist theory.

E. Wrong. The problem word here is interesting. While it may be true that subjectivity may allows for a wider array of textual interpretations, this does not necessarily mean that they would be more interesting than objective interpretations, or at least there is not enough information given in the passage for the reader to make such an inference.

Answer to Question 25:

A. Correct. The passage states that Derrida' believed that the contexts informing a given text's content are not outside of but in relationship with the text.

B. Correct. Texts cannot be independent of contexts: they can never exist completely alone.

C. Wrong. The passage does not indicate that Derrida believed that the text was the only form of reality - reality can still exist without a text.

Passage 14 – Summary / Paraphrase

The passage is about modernist literature. The main idea is that the events of the early to mid-20th century caused modernist writers to shift their tone from a relatively optimistic to a relatively pessimistic tone. The major points are that (a) writers such as Eliot and Pound celebrated the individualism and order of the modern age and (b) that the advent of the World Wars marked a shift to a more pessimistic tone about the same subjects. The main purpose of the passage is to describe an important aspect in the development of modern literature.

Answer to Question 26:

A. Wrong. The passage states that modernist writing shifted towards a more cynical, introspective tone to reflect the realities surrounding the World Wars, thus is evolved to mirror cultural changes.

B. Wrong. The passage makes it clear that modernist writing is characterized by concise language and structure, thus the coherency of form is a highly esteemed feature of modernist writing.

C. Correct. While the passage states that modernist writing evolved to become more introspective in nature, introspection is not a hallmark feature of modernist writing - autonomy and the exactitude of form lie at the heart of modernist writing.

D. Wrong. Since precise language is a hallmark feature of modernist writing, modernist writers avoid florid or elaborate prose.

E. Wrong. Modernist writing has a very mechanistic quality since it is chiefly concerned with form, structure, and precision.

Passage 15 – Summary / Paraphrase

The passage is about Sun Tzu's The Art of War. The main idea is that The Art of War is seminal text on military strategy that is familiar to a broad swath people. The major point is that The Art of War emphasizes the ability to be flexible and alter strategies as required by circumstances. The main purpose of the passage is to inform: the tone of the passage emphasizes summary facts about the work.

Answer to Question 27:

A. Wrong. While the author clearly delineates that The Art of War is a seminal work on military strategy, the tone does not betray a sense of buoyancy or positivity and liveliness; the author is in fact quite neutral relative to Sun Tzu's work.

B. Wrong. While the author's personal opinion can be best described as dispassionate towards The Art of War, the tone is not cold. Aloof can also be a synonym for dispassionate, but in a way that is uppity or icy and thus it is not the accurate term to describe the author's personal attitude.

C. Correct. Unaligned is a synonym for dispassionate and detached, which are the characteristics of the author's personal opinion of The Art of War. Unaligned is also a synonym for dispassionate that does not come with any overly positive or negative connotations, so it is very much a good term to use to convey neutrality.

D. Wrong. The author's personal opinion of The Art of War is neutral because it is never directly expressed, but inert is too strong of a word to equate with neutrality; to be inert is to be apathetic, immobile or indolent.

E. Wrong. The author's personal opinion of The Art of War is neutral in that the author never explicitly conveys his or her opinion. Phlegmatic is a term more appropriate for describing a demeanor that is calm and collected but not necessarily neutral and thus it is not the best option for describing the author's personal opinion towards The Art of War.

Answer to Question 28:

A. Wrong. Ambitious is not a synonym for efficacious as ambitious means the determination to succeed and efficacious means the power to produce a desired effect.

B. Wrong. Useful can be a synonym for efficacious but the author is making the point that Sun Tzu's strategy is more than just useful - it leads to military success which demands a stronger adjective.

C. Correct. Efficacious means the power to produce a desired effect and thus potent can be substituted here since potent can also mean the power to produce a desired effect and the author intends to show that Sun Tzu's military strategy is powerful and effective.

D. Wrong. Adequate can also be a synonym for efficacious, but again it does not properly describe, from the author's viewpoint, the power of Sun Tzu's military strategy.

E. Wrong. Unorganized is not a synonym for efficacious as it means not organized or incoherent and efficacious means the power to produce a desired effect.

Passage 16 – Summary / Paraphrase

The passage is about the French writer Albert Camus. The main idea is that Camus was an extremely influential thinker who changed the way we think about our world. There are two major points: (a) that Camus believed that our world is absurd because it is unable to provide the meaning that many people crave and (b) that Camus thought that our attempts to grapple with the absurd through civil society are themselves rooted in the absurd. There are minor points that (a) Camus is usually associated with the existentialist movement and (b) that he explores the idea of the absurd in his works The Stranger and The Plague. The purpose of the passage is to explain and defend Camus' place as a prominent 20th century figure.

Answer to Question 29:

A. Wrong. While the passage states that existentialism is a movement in the humanities, but does not give enough information to infer that existentialism's primary concern is the humanities (even if this may be the case).

B. Wrong. The passage does not explicitly connect existentialism with the absurdity of modern life. Absurdity is a topic that Camus explores but the reader is not given enough information to infer that absurdity and existentialism are directly linked, particularly since Camus himself shunned being called an existentialist.

C. Correct. The reader can infer that existentialism is a school of philosophical thought since the passage states that existentialism is a movement in the humanities, particularly in philosophy.

D. Wrong. The passage does not give the reader enough information to infer what existentialism teaches, only enough information to infer that it is a branch of philosophy.

E. Wrong. The passage does not indicate existentialism is a method of investigating structures in civil society; the reader is only able to make the inference that existentialism is a branch of philosophy.

Answer to Question 30:

A. Correct. The passage states that the world cannot fulfill the human need for meaning - meaning does not exist.

B. Wrong. The passage does not indicate that humans could understand the world if they had the right analytical tools.

C. Wrong. Whether or not humans pay close enough attention to the structures of civil society has no bearing on whether or not the world ultimately has meaning.

Answer to Question 31:

"This ultimately leads to the erection of civil societies that, if examined more closely, are mired in and permeated by the absurd "at every street corner."."

According to the passage, Camus believed that a direct consequence of human desire for meaning and logic in the world leads to the creation of social structures that are ultimately absurd since life has no inherent meaning.

Passage 17 – Summary / Paraphrase

The passage is about a recent theoretical development in the humanities called postcolonial theory. The main idea is that later 20th century academics reacted to the dominant occicentric paradigm with a more pluralistic theory. The main points are (a) that postcolonial theory attempts to give colonized peoples more of a voice in the humanities and (b) that postcolonial theory looks at the "cultural space" as a complex interaction of European and other cultures. The main purpose of the passage is to give a brief primer on what postcolonial theory is.

Answer to Question 32:

A. Correct. The passage states that the main consequence of European Imperialism was that is shaped global society by exercising cultural dominance.

B. Wrong. It is true that diversity could not thrive under European Imperialism, but this is more of a byproduct of the fact that European cultural norms were dominant.

C. Wrong. The passage does not discuss whether or not the colonized participated in the colonial political process.

D. Wrong. The passage clearly states that global society was heavily influenced by colonialism.

E. Wrong. The passage clearly shows the culturally hegemonic nature of European Imperialism.

Passage 18 – Summary / Paraphrase

The passage is about the debate in literary criticism over authorial intent. The main idea of the passage is that while there are two main schools of thought about authorial intent, one makes more sense than the other. There are several main points: (a) some critics believe that the author's intentions and ideologies form the content of the work where others take the view that the work is independent of external factors (b) that Kafka is an author whose work is exemplary for highlighting the points of the debate (c) that most critics tend to believe that Kafka's experiences and beliefs shaped the content of his work (d) the author believes that there is significant evidence for the received critical view and (e) a reaffirmation of the view that, in general it makes sense for authors' intentions and beliefs to strongly influence the content of their works. There are several minor points that underscore key issues raised by the major points: (a) that the often bizarre nature of Kafka's works makes them especially open to the interpretations of either school of criticism (b) that Kafka's legal training coupled with his fascination with the law in his literary works support the notion that his experiences and beliefs shaped his works. The main purpose of the passage is to describe two conflicting schools of literary criticism and use an example to demonstrate why one makes more sense than the other. The author's stance is made definitively clear in the final paragraph with the phrase "it is difficult to imagine that a writer can produce a text without having some kind of interpretive goal or objective in mind." The rhetorical bow to multiplicity of interpretive possibilities does not take away from the author's clear stance on the issue.

Answer to Question 33:

A. Correct. Kafka's literature was critical of what he saw as the arbitrariness and tyranny of the legal system and thus it can be inferred that Kafka himself was anti-authoritarian.

B. Wrong. The passage does not provide any indication that Marxist literary criticism is the most efficient way of extracting meaning from a text or knowing with certainty the intent of the author of a fictional work.

C. Wrong. The passage does not indicate that Kafka's fictional representations of the law had any bearing on actual, real-world legal practices and policies.

D. Wrong. The passage in no way indicates that the intent of the author can ever be determined with certainty.

E. Wrong. The passage makes it clear that finding absolute truth in literature is neither the goal of literary criticism nor within the realm of possibility.

Answer to Question 34:

A. Correct. According to the information given in the first paragraph, authorial intent can be defined as the intentions and ideological leanings of an author that have the potential to shape the meaning of his or her text.

B. Wrong. The passage does not indicate that authorial intent is the term for the catalyst behind an author's decision to write, rather that it is the conglomeration of an author's subjective thoughts and experiences that could influence the text.

C. Wrong. While it is true that authorial intent is the sum of an author's thoughts and experiences, the passage makes it clear that the literary community does not agree that they always shape the meaning of a text - they only have the potential to do so.
D. Wrong. Authorial intent is not shown to be a type of writing style and furthermore the New Critics rejected the concept of authorial intent all together.
E. Wrong. The first paragraph of the passage gives enough information for the reader to form a solid definition of authorial intent.

Answer to Question 35:

A. Wrong. Methodological means relating to a type of discipline and hermeneutical means interpretive therefore the two terms are not analogous.
B. Wrong. Hermeneutical means interpretive and intentional is the expression of intention or purpose; therefore the two terms are not analogous.
C. Wrong. Epistemological is related to the study of the nature of knowledge while hermeneutical is related to the interpretation of knowledge and therefore the two terms are not analogous.
D. Correct. Explicative is a synonym for interpretive and thus can also be a synonym for hermeneutical, which is also analogous to interpretive.
E. Wrong. Remedial means curative and hermeneutical means interpretive and thus both terms are not analogous.

Answer to Question 36:

A. Correct. The passage indicates that, according to Kafka, both laymen and lawmen did not understand the law or legal process.
B. Correct. The passage indicates that Kafka's imagery representations of law and legality convey his opinion that the legal system was arbitrary and oppressive.
C. Wrong. The passage in no way indicates how Kafka felt about being a trained lawyer.

Answer to Question 37:

A. Correct. The passage states that Kafka believed the legal system to be rigid and intransigent is a synonym for rigid, both meaning uncompromising.
B. Correct. The passage states that Kafka believed the legal system to be absurd and incongruous can be a synonym for absurd, both meaning senseless.
C. Correct. The passage states that Kafka believed the legal system to be absurd and inane can be a synonym for rigid, both meaning senseless.

Answer to Question 38:

"The images and metaphors that Kafka infuses his prose with regarding the law and the legal process are what constitute not only the meaning of his fiction but also his personal view on the law."

Tropes are rhetorical strategies that include metaphors and images and thus the sentence above both identifies and describes the tropes used by Kafka in his prose.

Practice Set 2 - Biological Sciences

Passage 19 – Summary / Paraphrase

The passage is about basic locational terminology in anatomy. The main idea is that students of anatomy need to master a specialized lexicon of locational terms. The major point is the discussion of key locational terms used in anatomy. The major point is supported by (a) several examples of how to use the terms when discussing the anatomy of a rabbit and (b) a brief justification for why anatomists prefer a specialized locational terminology to more general terms. The purpose of the passage is to introduce the reader to anatomical terminology.

Answer to Question 39:

All three are correct choices. The passage emphasizes the importance of using correct and uniform terminology depending on the task or occupation. When sailing, for example, it is crucial to know the parts of a ship in relation to the bow. If one were to us the word left instead of port, the listener might think that the speaker is referring to his own left rather than the left side of the boat. When performing brain surgery, the terms front, back, top, or bottom can change depending on the patient's position. Medical terminology for the parts of the brain and their relative position in the cranium remain constant enabling everyone involved in the procedure to understand what is happening. In the same way, a mechanic must know and use the correct names for parts of an engine, especially if he is working with another mechanic or ordering parts.

Passage 20 – Summary / Paraphrase

The passage is about the natural conditions in the Indian jungle. The main idea is that both predators and prey are adapted to their conditions. The major points are that (a) tigers have developed successful traits and behaviors to help them efficiently hunt prey such as deer and (b) deer have developed traits and behaviors that allow them to elude predators such as tigers. The passage mainly serves as rumination on life in a natural context. While the content is mainly factual, the rhetoric, such as the use of pronouns like "his" and "him" in discussing the animals in question suggests a tone more meditative than matter of fact.

Answer to Question 40:

Both A and B are suitable choices. If a commercial use for the reeds makes it profitable to harvest them, the tiger will be affected by the inability to camouflage himself. If he cannot make himself less visible to the deer, they will have more success evading the tigers. The tigers' inability to hunt successfully will result in starvation for some of them. Similarly, if the deer do not have an adequate food supply, they will die; there will be fewer of them to reproduce, causing a decline in successive generations. A smaller deer population means a reduction in the food supply for the tigers, and they will not survive in traditional numbers. On the other hand, if the deer's ability to detect the tiger is reduced, the tigers will more easily capture them, creating a sufficient food source and ensuring their survival.

Passage 21 – Summary / Paraphrase

The passage is about strategies for dealing with insect pests. The main idea is that while an insect may do the most harm during one point in its lifecycle, it may be easier to destroy at another point in its cycle. The major point is that it may be easier to destroy a mature insect than its larvae even though the larvae may be more harmful. There is a minor point that underscores the potential harmfulness of larvae by explaining that larvae require a large food supply to furnish their tremendous growth rate. The purpose of the passage is to provide information on pest control. Although the passage features normative language such as "it is better to", it is mainly factual; the reader is not being told that they ought to kill pests, merely the most strategic approach to dealing with them should they desire pest control.

Answer to Question 41:

The best answer is E. The first words of this passage, "from this", indicates that an explanation or example has been given in the earlier portion of the text. The content of the text here presented reinforces it. There is too little information to assume that this is a conclusion. The writer may very well continue with the topic. Answer choice A is incorrect. The writer is really restating what he has said or shown in the previous text, rather than providing an example, so B is also incorrect. The writer presents the reader with alternatives rather than issuing a warning, making C incorrect as well. There is no indication that the writer is going to further develop an idea presented in this passage, so D is the wrong answer choice.

Passage 22 – Summary / Paraphrase

The passage is about the mammalian skull. The main idea is that mammal skulls can be better understood in comparison to the skulls of lower life forms. The major point is that by comparing a mammal skull to a frog skull, one can see how they are similar, but also how the mammal skull is more developed and more complex. The purpose of the passage is to develop an illustration of the mammal skull.

Answer to Question 42:

The correct answer is E. Herpetologists study snakes and amphibians; even though the frog is an amphibian, it is not the focus of the information in this passage, so A is not the correct answer choice. Zoologists study animals. Since the apparent focus of the writer's words is the human skull, answer B is also incorrect. Endocrinologists study and treat malfunctions and disorders of the endocrine system, making C incorrect. Thoracic surgeons operate in the area of the chest, eliminating D as a correct answer choice. The correct answer is E, craniologists since they study the cranium, another word for skull.

Answer to Question 43:

The best definition is answer B. Primarily means first and does not fit in this context, so A is incorrect. In this case, answer C is also incorrect because fundamentally is not modifying the word similar in this way, nor does fundamentally mean originally similar, eliminating D as the correct choice. The structure is not indispensably similar; E is incorrect.

Answer to Question 44:

The correct answer is C. Because the author has mentioned the skull only in this passage, it would be incorrect to assume that other human anatomical structures have corresponding structures in lower life forms, making A an incorrect answer choice. The same reasoning may be applied to answer choice B. There is no indication that all of amphibian anatomy corresponds to human anatomy. Answer choice C is the best response. It may be that, because studying the frog's skull leads to a better understanding of the human skull, studying anatomical structures of other life forms leads to a better understanding of human anatomy in its various parts.

Passage 23 – Summary / Paraphrase

The passage is about strategies for cotton growing. The main idea is that through a variety of methods, farmers have succeeded in generating cotton crops with higher yields than were possible historically. The major points are: (a) that using seed selection, special cultivation, and hybridization, cotton farmers have created new varieties of cotton that produce unprecedented yields and (b) that farmers need to carefully consider numerous factors in order to optimize their results when using one of these new varieties. The purpose of the passage is to inform the reader about how cotton varietals affect yields, and advise on how to optimize them.

Answer to Question 45:

The correct answer is "Many of these attempts have succeeded, and there are now a large number of varieties which excel the older varieties in profitable yield."The writer is advising farmers to select and plant hybrid cotton. His justification for this recommendation is the success that others have had doing so. The increasing popularity of the hybrids is evidence of their effectiveness.

Answer to Question 46:

The correct answer is D. The writer reveals that hybrids are grown in ideal conditions before being made available to farmers. For farmers to produce the best crop with the highest yields, they should mimic the conditions under which the hybrid was developed. Hybridization may be a long and costly process, but this passage does not reveal any information that would make this a reasonable conclusion. A is not correct. Contrary to the conclusion expressed in answer choice B, hybrids are developed for very specific soil and climate conditions. It is likely that all plants need fertilizer to increase their yields, but it is not the only factor in a plant's success, so C cannot be correct. The price of a harvested crop depends on factors that are sometimes beyond the control of the grower. He may have planted a pricey hybrid, but there may be no demand for it at the time of harvest. E is not the best answer choice.

Answer to Question 47:

The correct answer is A. Tillage most commonly means soil that has been plowed in preparation for planting. The writer implies that each hybrid has been raised in the best tillage, meaning the best-prepared soil. A farmer can apply fertilizer, water, pesticides, and mulch and still have a crop fail because the soil was not prepared correctly. Answer A is the correct choice.

Passage 24 – Summary / Paraphrase

The passage is about effective planting. The main idea is that true grasses thrive best with the addition of another type of plant, legumes. The major points are: (a) that true grasses will exhaust the nitrogen supply in soil because they can only get nitrogen from the soil (b) that legumes such as clover are able to extract free nitrogen from the air as well as from the soil and (c) that in order to optimize planting, farmers should add legume to grass seed in order to keep the grass from exhausting all the nitrogen in the soil. The main purpose of the passage is to inform and persuade by explaining to the reader why it is optimal to add in legume.

Answer to Question 48:

The correct answer is "Hence without cost to the farmer these clovers help the soil to feed their neighbors, the true grasses." Adding fertilizer with the correct proportion of nitrogen is probably as effective as growing clover in tandem with the true grasses. The downside is the cost. Since the clover is perennial, it will grow every year without replanting, whereas chemical fertilizers must be added to the soil every year at great cost to the farmer.

Passage 25 – Summary / Paraphrase

The passage is about stocking water with fish. The main idea is that despite it seeming obvious that it is necessary to provide feed for fish that are being stocked, the issue of feeding is often forgotten. There is a major point that stocking feed after the fish have been introduced is often a failure. The main purpose of the passage is to inform. The author leaves unstated the explanation of why introducing feed after the fish does not work.

Answer to Question 49:

The correct answer is "Small attempts at stocking with creatures suitable for food, particularly after the fish have been already introduced, are not at all likely to succeed."Attempting to treat an illness is more time-consuming and expensive than taking steps to prevent the illness in the first place. One may succeed in curing the patient, but success is not guaranteed. In much the same way, stocking the body of water with food before introducing the fish is more likely to have a successful result than stocking the water with fish and, then, introducing the food. Many or all of the fish will have already died.

Answer to Question 50:

The correct answer is A. There is no evidence in the passage to suggest that the fish will migrate; a pond may not even provide an egress for that purpose. Answer choice E is not correct. Answer choice D is also incorrect based on the lack of evidence to suggest cannibalism. The writer says that an appropriate food source is necessary but does not say that fish will adapt to a new type of food, making answer choice C incorrect. Although one may stock a pond in order to catch the fish, no mention of this is made in the passage, eliminating B as the correct answer. The best answer choice is A, and failing to provide food that the fish will eat insures their death.

Answer to Question 51:

The correct answer is C. The writer's use of the word "superfluous" should lead the reader to believe that he has already discussed the creatures that are suitable as food for the fish to be stocked in the pond. The writer is now admonishing his audience that neglecting to create a food supply before putting the fish in the pond will cause the fish to die. For this reason, C is the correct answer choice.

Passage 26 – Summary / Paraphrase

The passage is about determining the age of trees. The main idea is that many methods of determining a tree's age are unreliable. The major points are that (a) scientifically rigorous measurement of growth rates has only existed since the 18th century and (b) that only the measurement of a tree's girth is reliable for telling its age. The main idea of the passage is primed by an extensive preamble that ponders questions of our knowledge of a tree's age. The purpose of the passage is to briefly discuss the longevity of trees and several methods for determining it.

Answer to Question 52:

The correct answer is "Is the period of one thousand years, the favorite figure of tradition, a common or probable period of arboreal longevity, or have our proudest forest giants attained their present size in half the time that is commonly claimed for them?"The phrase "favorite figure of tradition" suggests that scientific methods were not used to determine the ages of old trees. It may be that the only way people could judge the age of an apparently antique specimen was through a family or village oral history. As in the popular childhood game, Telephone, the initial information can undergo several transformations before reaching the final participant, so exactly when a tree was planted may be impossible to determine.

Answer to Question 53:

The correct answer is E. The writer is not talking about something that amuses; therefore, A is not the correct choice. Pleasure and amusement have similar connotations, so, for the same reasons, answer choice B is also incorrect. Answer choice C may be the easiest to eliminate, as the author is clearly not describing a performance of any kind. To entertain an idea is to consider it; one may also do this with a question, which is why E is a better answer choice than D.

Answer to Question 54:

The correct answer is A. By the end of this passage, the writer has mentioned ways in which scientists have measured the ages of trees. It is logical to assume that he will continue in this vein. He does mention, at the beginning of this passage, that it would be proper to consider where trees grow and how that affects their chances of longevity, but he does not elaborate and moves on to other topics, eliminating B as the correct answer. This same reasoning can be used to claim that answer choice C is wrong. The purpose of this passage is not to persuade, so the writer's creating an argument is not logical. Answer choice D is not correct. To this point in the passage, the writer has made no mention of specific geography, nor is it likely to be the next topic, making E incorrect.

Passage 27 – Summary / Paraphrase

The passage is about a plant known as the squirting cucumber. The main idea is that the squirting cucumber exemplifies the ingenuity of nature in providing a means for life forms to protect and propagate themselves. The major points are: (a) that the squirting cucumber exhibits unusual behavior for a plant (b) that the squirting cucumber's behavior serves to frighten away potential predators and (c) that the squirting cucumber's behavior allows the plant to spread its seeds. Several minor points provide additional information including the regions where one might find squirting cucumbers, details about the exact behavior of the plant, and the fact that the juice of the squirting cucumber has an unpleasant taste as an additional deterrent. The purpose of the passage is to inform the reader about an unusual plant and also to relate that plant to a more general point about the way that nature provides for the propagation of living things.

Answer to Question 55:

The correct answer is C. The squirting cucumber has developed a defense against animals or others who would intentionally or accidentally destroy its ability to survive. Although both the camel and the remora have adapted in order to survive, their adaptations are not defenses against their enemies. Neither A nor B are correct answers. The chameleon, on the other hand, changes its colors to make it invisible to predators. The chameleon is the only animal on the list to adapt as a means of defense, making C the only correct answer.

Answer to Question 56:

The correct answer is C. The writer's use of the words "my friend" sets a positive tone. Neither sarcastic nor antagonistic has a positive connotation; answer choices B and E cannot be correct. Satire frequently uses sarcasm to ridicule a person, institution, or idea. This is not the writer's intention here, making answer choice A incorrect. Awestruck is a bit extreme to describe the attitude of the writer toward the squirting cucumber, but it is reasonable to conclude that the writer admires the feisty little plant. C is the best answer choice.

Answer to Question 57:

The correct answer is A. The fruit expels its interior to repel predators and to reproduce itself. In its own time, the fruit eventually drops off the vine and expels its seeds; this is not done intentionally, eliminating B as a correct choice. The fruit does defend itself when disturbed, but it does not seek to be aggressive or offensive, making C an incorrect choice as well. Mutation is a form of adaptation, but there is no discussion of this likelihood in the passage; D cannot be the correct choice. Although the writer does allude to books of etiquette and another writer, he does so to make his point about the cucumber, not as a focus of the passage. E is not the correct answer.

Answer to Question 58:

The correct answer is "As long as you don't interfere with them, these hairy, green fruits do nothing out of the common in the way of personal aggressiveness." A sleeping dog will not bite or cause any other problems. In other words, leave well enough alone. Like the sleeping dog, this fruit will do nothing aggressive if you do not disturb it.

Passage 28 – Summary / Paraphrase

The passage is about the effects that hormones have on behavior. The main idea is that hormone levels have a more significant effect on mating potential than other indicators such as attractiveness. There are two major points: (a) that the behavior observed in swallows correlates to other animal species, including humans and (b) that the increased confidence and higher testosterone levels affected mating outcomes as much as the changes to the vibrancy of the birds' coloring. The purpose of the passage is to inform the reader of the important role that hormones play in animal behavior

Answer to Question 59:

A. Wrong. The passage lists confidence as one of two main factors involved in increasing male barn swallows' testosterone levels.
B. Correct. The passage claims that confidence is caused by an attractive physical appearance.
C. Wrong. The passage states beta males can turn into alpha males and thus have increased levels of testosterone, ruling out the idea that high levels of testosterone are inherent or unchangeable.
D. Wrong. The passage lists confidence as one of two main factors involved in increasing male barn swallows' testosterone levels.
E. Wrong. The passage does not attribute fluctuating levels solely to mating.

Passage 29 – Summary / Paraphrase

The passage is about primate behavior. The main idea is that sharing among primates is often not strictly altruistic. The main points of the passage are (a) that anthropologists believe that chimpanzee behavior is analogous to the behavior of early humans and (b) that chimpanzees are mainly motivated to share food and tools in exchange for sex. Major point (b) is backed up by additional facts that male chimpanzees are most likely to share food and supplies with sexually receptive females. The purpose of the passage is to inform and to draw a comparison between human behavior and that of other primates.

Answer to Question 60:

A. Correct. Since sexually receptive females in their reproductive years have a higher chance of receiving food and supplies, they have the highest chance for survival.
B. Wrong. The passage actually infers that male primates' motivation is to perpetuate the species since they are most likely to exchange food for sex with females in their reproductive years.
C. Wrong. Male primates trade food for sex as a means of survival not exploitation. Their ultimate goal is to perpetuate the species.
D. Wrong. The passage states that the food for sex process is not altruistically motivated therefore primates cannot possess a high level of magnanimity or selflessness.

E. Wrong. The passage does not infer that male primates are in any way lazy, in fact it infers the opposite: that male primates work to gather supplies to exchange.

Answer to Question 61:

A. Wrong. The passage states that primate behavior likely mirrors that of early humans, but then goes on to make it clear that sharing is the primary reason anthropologists are interested in understanding group behavior in primates.

B. Correct. The passage explores gender relationships among primates and homes in on sharing as the central reason anthropologists want to study their behavior.

C. Wrong. Since the author makes it clear that the sharing among primates is not altruistically motivated, group behavior in primates cannot teach humans about the importance of altruism.

D. Wrong. The passage indicates that group behavior in primates can only be related to humans.

E. Wrong. The sexual behavior of primates (or humans for that matter) is not the primary focus of the passage; sex is mentioned as a byproduct of the main goal of anthropological studies on group behavior in primates: sharing.

Answer to Question 62:

"According to anthropologists, observing primates in Senegal is like opening a window to the world of understanding the behavior of early humans, particularly related to sharing."

One type of trope is a metaphor employed for rhetorical purposes - to either clarify or enhance a reader or listener's understanding of something. The first sentence uses a metaphor comparing anthropological research to a window that opens to knowledge and thus makes use of the trope rhetorical device.

Passage 30 – Summary / Paraphrase

The passage is about bacterial resistance to antibiotics. The main idea is that even bacteria that are affected by antibiotics are capable of surviving an antibiotic onslaught. The main points are that (a) many antibiotic treatments work by targeting active bacteria, with the implication that they do so by cutting nutrients and (b) some bacteria are able to slow their growth rate into dormancy when there source of nutrients is threatened, thus rendering them immune to the antibiotic. The purpose of the passage is to explain how some bacteria resist antibiotics.

Answer to Question 63:

A. Correct. Starvation causes the bacteria to stop growing and lie dormant.

B. Correct. The passage states that starving bacteria are immune to medications because they are dormant; most antibiotics are only effective against active bacteria.

C. Wrong. Starvation does not change bacteria's chemical composition according to the passage.

Passage 31 – Summary / Paraphrase

The passage is about the phenomenon of ocean acidification. The main idea is that increasing acid levels in ocean waters are disrupting the growth of coral reefs that are vital to maintaining the diverse ecosystem of the ocean. There are several major points: (a) that increased levels of carbon dioxide in the atmosphere are leading to the acidification of the oceans due to the way the ocean absorbs atmospheric carbon dioxide (b) that increased acidification of ocean water prevents the proper growth of coral reefs and (c) the alteration of coral reefs could be disastrous for oceanic life, since coral reefs support a notable percentage of marine species. The main purpose of the passage is to explain and call to action; the process by which carbon dioxide affects the oceans is concisely explained, and loaded rhetoric such as the use of terms like "threat" and "terrible catastrophe" indicates that there is an implied intention we take action on atmospheric carbon dioxide levels.

Answer to Question 64:

A. Wrong. The ocean absorbs carbon from the atmosphere.

B. Wrong. While it is true that 25% of marine species depend on the coral reef ecosystem, low pH in the ocean does not mean they will all go extinct.

C. Wrong. The statement is correct except that low pH means high acidity and not low acidity and thus the answer is ultimately incorrect.

D. Wrong. While it is true that many types of coral reefs can grow in low pH environments, the passage nonetheless leads us to believe that the coral reef ecosystems are still in danger from acidification.

E. Correct. The information in the passage implies that since the base of the coral reefs cannot calcify in low pH environments the reefs as an aggregate will struggle to grow and this will harm the marine life they support.

Answer to Question 65:

A. Wrong. While it is true that the passage delineates the dangers of carbon dioxide in the world's oceans, description is not a rhetorical strategy; the goal of rhetoric is always to persuade and not describe.

B. Wrong. While the information in the passage may stimulate an emotional response in the reader, the actual rhetorical goal of the passage is to persuade the reader of the harms of ocean acidification.

C. Wrong. Persuasion is always the goal of rhetoric and this passage seeks to persuade the reader that ocean acidification is harmful, but the answer needs to be more specific - the author ultimately wants to convey the danger that coral reefs are in as a result of ocean acidification.

D. Wrong. Again, a rhetorical goal must always be persuasive and not merely descriptive; therefore, explaining the specifics of pH levels' affect on coral reefs is not a rhetorical goal.

E. Correct. The rhetorical goal of the passage is to convince the reader that ocean acidification is harmful specifically because of the damage it does to coral reefs.

Answer to Question 66:

"This is an especially vital area of exploration since coral reefs are home to 25% of all marine species."

While the passage later goes on to describe how ocean acidification damages corals reefs, the primary importance of the coral reefs, from an ecological standpoint, is that they house 25% of the world's marine species.

Passage 32 – Summary / Paraphrase

The passage is about the parasitic disease malaria. The main idea is that the pathology of malaria makes those affected by sickle-cell anemia immune. The main points are that (a) malaria requires access to the exterior of blood cells by using certain adhesive proteins and (b) that mutations to the hemoglobin of those affected by sickle cell anemia mean that they rarely, if ever, possess the adhesive proteins needed for the malaria parasite to establish itself. The purpose of the passage is to inform - the tone is mostly dry and factual.

Answer to Question 67:

A. Correct. Sickle cell anemics are protected from malaria because of a hemoglobin mutation, but this mutation does not facilitate adhesin bonding, it impedes it. The author's contention is that sickle cell anemics are protected from malaria as a result of a hemoglobin mutation that impedes adhesin bonding and thus the author's contention would be incorrect if sickle cell anemic hemoglobin mutations facilitated adhesin bonding.

B. Wrong. Adhesins can sometimes attach to the blood cells of sickle cell anemics and therefore this statement merely reinforces the author's claim that adhesin adhesions occasionally occur in sickle cell anemics, but still not frequently enough to successfully transmit the malaria virus.

C. Correct. According to the information given in the passage, the malaria parasite is not able to infect the blood of sickle cell anemics; sickle cell anemics are immune to malaria and hence this statement would weaken the author's contention if true

Passage 33 – Summary / Paraphrase

The passage is about how hormones influence primate behavior. The main idea is that exposure to oxytocin, known as the "love hormone", has been shown to increase altruistic behavior in monkeys. The main point is that since the monkeys are closely related to humans, study of the hormone's effects in the monkeys can help us better understand how it affects human behavior. There are minor points that underscore the effect of the hormone: (a) its effects on developing intimate relationships such as that between mother and child and (b) a specific instance of the prosocial behavior it helped to promote in the affected monkeys. The purpose of the passage is to explain and inform.

Answer to Question 68:

A. Wrong. Humans may be closely related to the macaque but the passage does not indicate that oxytocin will affect humans in the exact same manner as the monkeys.
B. Correct. The information in the passage implies that studying oxytocin's affects on monkeys can be used to have deeper insight into human behavior related to the hormone.
C. Wrong. While oxytocin could theoretically be used for this purpose, the passage does not indicate that the information garnered from the study on the macaques will be used to create medication to treat antisocial behavior in humans.
D. Wrong. The passage actually infers that scientists have already produced oxytocin synthetically for research purposes.
E. Wrong. The passage makes it clear that studying macaques could have long-term benefits on understanding humans relative to oxytocin.

Answer to Question 69:

A. Correct. The passage indicates that prosocial choices are about sharing, which clearly benefits the well-being of two parties, in this case the two macaques.
B. Wrong. The passage states that prosocial choices.
C. Wrong. The passage does not indicate that prosocial choices play a role in the creation of social hierarchies.
D. Wrong. According to the passage, prosocial choices are the result of changes in hormonal patterns and thus do not influence them.
E. Wrong. The passages states that prosocial choices are often made under the influence of oxytocin.

Answer to Question 70:

"Oxytocin, also known as the love hormone, bonds mothers to their children and promotes intimacy and relationships in various species including humans."
This sentence explicates why oxytocin is vital to the forging of social connections among species.

Passage 34 – Summary / Paraphrase

The passage is about the biological causes of psychiatric disorders. The main idea is that scientists hope to be able to combine their findings about the RNF123 gene with a holistic understanding of mental health. The main points are (a) that the RNF123 gene affects the hippocampus and (b) that the hippocampus is altered in people with depression and (c) that scientists are looking at this information along with the experiences of patients to form a fuller understanding of the issues affecting mental health. The purpose of the passage is to present an objective account of a current trend in the life sciences.

Answer to Question 71:

"Scientists have taken another step in the direction of better understanding the biological underpinnings of various psychiatric disorders."
While the passage ultimately indicates that scientists are interested in both genes and environment, at first their main interest is discerning the biological factors underlying mental health issues.

Passage 35 – Summary / Paraphrase
The passage is about stem cell research. The main idea is that while some scientists have promoted stem cells as having "miracle cure" potential, there is considerable trepidation about using stem cells in both the scientific community and among laymen. The main points are (a) that stem cells have been posited as a potential treatment for a wide variety of diseases and conditions (b) that there is opposition to stem cell research from those who see it as a disruption of the natural order of life and (c) there is caution from some scientists who worry that stem cell research may not be as effective as some claim. The main purpose of the passage is to briefly summarize the chief arguments for and against the use of stem cell research.

Answer to Question 72:

A. Wrong. The passage does not claim that mitosis is specifically useful because it allows scientists to use stem cells in abundance.
B. Wrong. The passage does not claim that stem cells are stronger after mitosis.
C. Correct. Diverse cells, the byproducts of mitosis, can be controlled by scientists and manipulated towards diverse medical outcomes, thus rendering mitosis a key factor in stem cell research.
D. Wrong. The passage makes it clear that mitosis is important to stem cell research because it engenders a diversity of cells.
E. Wrong. This answer is true but more information should be given to explain exactly why diversified cells are useful in stem cell research; the reason why and not just the fact that diverse cells are useful to stem cell therapy specifies the importance of mitosis.

Answer to Question 73:

A. Wrong. The author agrees that stem cell therapy is a highly sensitive issue given that he or she highlights the fact that many people believe stem cell therapy exploits human life.

B. Wrong. The author states that many medical doctors believe that stem cell therapy can have adverse effects despite the fact that it is an extremely useful treatment method. Thus, the benefits of stem cell therapy are sometimes overshadowed by its pitfalls.

C. Wrong. The author would agree that the outcomes of scientific research do not always align with social mores since stem cell therapy is a successful treatment method that also causes social controversy.

D. Correct. For the author to believe that the exploitation of natural life was the elephant in the room of the stem cell therapy debate, he or she would have to be anti-stem cell therapy; "the white elephant in the room" is a metaphor in the English language that serves as a rhetorical strategy to underline a glaring truth that is being ignored. Since the author's tone is objective regarding stem cell therapy as a whole in the passage, the author would not agree with the elephant in the room idiom for stem cell therapy, in this case because that would mean the author also believes that stem cell therapy is the exploitation of life.

E. Wrong. The entire passage is about how stem cells regenerate and can be used to treat a diverse variety of medical conditions and thus the author would agree that stem cells underscore the regenerative nature of the human body.

Answer to Question 74:

A. Correct. The passage states that some people believe that stem cell therapy exploits and interferes with natural life even though it is a very effective method of medical treatment.

B. Wrong. The passage does not explicitly state that those opposed to stem cell therapy believe it promotes a culture of death.

C. Correct. The passage states that scientists worry about the potential for stem cell therapy to worsen various medical conditions despite its ability to treat a wide array of medical issues.

Passage 36 – Summary / Paraphrase

The passage is about human genetics. The main idea is that the long-held view that our DNA was immutable has been challenged by recent evidence that suggests our genetics can in fact change in response to environmental factors. The major points are: (a) that epigenetic has discovered that a stimulus can alter a gene after conception, and that through cell division, the alterations in the gene can be passed on to further generations (b) that experimental evidence suggests that when pregnant rats are subjected to negative stimulus, it will cause behavioral problems in the baby (c) by studying and testing the genetic code of identical twins, scientists can determine the extent of genetic alteration. The purpose of the passage is to inform the reader about a cutting-edge area of genetics, and also to invite some speculation in the implications of these discoveries. The tone is largely factual, showing no obvious bias.

Answer to Question 75:

D is correct. Nascent literally means, "beginning to exist" and therefore epigenetic "being in its early stages of development" is the only correct answer. No other answer given contains a synonym for nascent.

Answer to Question 76:

A. Wrong. The passage makes it clear that the DNA methylation profiles of twins are important to epigenetic since they allow scientists to compare and understand epigenetic changes to identical DNA.

B. Correct. The main reason it is important to collect the DNA methylation profiles of identical twins is so that scientists can see the epigenetic changes that have occurred in identical DNA.

C. Wrong. While it is likely true that DNA methylation profiles gives scientists a better understanding of the process of cell division, this answer does not account for why it is specifically important for scientists to study the DNA methylation profiles of identical twins.

D. Wrong. The passage does not indicate that DNA methylation profiles help scientists understand how twins inherit their DNA; the passage places emphasis on scientists investigating what happens to the already inherited DNA in twins.

E. Wrong. This statement is correct given the information in the passage but it does not give enough information about why it is important to specifically study the DNA methylation profiles of identical twins.

Answer to Question 77:

A. Correct. The passage states that identical twins' identical DNA can help scientists identify DNA methylation patterns.

B. Correct. The passage clearly states that scientists use twins to better understand the DNA methylation process.

C. Wrong. The passage does not mention anything about twins' looks and their relationship to phenotypic expressions.

Answer to Question 78:

"It throws a wrench into Darwin's theory of evolution since it demonstrates how evolutionary changes can occur within in one generation instead of spanning thousands of years."

Darwin's theory of evolution is one of the foundation stones of modern biology and since epigenetic calls this theory into question by calming that evolutionary changes can occur within only one generation, the entire field of biology may have to reevaluate the way it conceptualizes the history of life on the planet.

Practice Set 3 - Business

Passage 37 – Summary / Paraphrase

The passage is about changing demographics in the workforce. The main idea is that people are staying more active in the workforce later into life than ever before. The major points are: (a) that adults at or near retirement age make up a significantly greater proportion of the workforce than they did a decade ago and (b) that even adults who have officially retired are more likely to remain actively engaged in paid or unpaid work than ever before. Two minor points explore the reasons behind the major points: (a) that a variety of practical concerns are keeping older workers in the workforce and (b) that shifting concepts of retirement and the desires of older adults are changing earlier notions of career. The main purpose of the passage is to inform the reader and explain some of the factors behind a demographic shift in the workforce.

Answer to Question 79:

The correct answer is D. It might be logical to conclude that older workers' remaining in the workforce for more years means that there are fewer job opportunities for younger workers or those trying to enter the workforce for the first time. If, however, the percentage of the total population represented by workers aged 55-64 is small, it should have little detrimental effect on younger workers' ability to obtain employment. The correct answer is D.

Passage 38 – Summary / Paraphrase

The passage is about the way that countries are responding to the threat of global warming. The main idea is that the response has been mixed. The major points are: (a) the United States, historically the largest producer of greenhouse gases, has not acted aggressively on climate change because of fear of the economic consequences (b) other developed nations have been more successful in curbing emissions through the use of nuclear power and cleaner natural gas (c) developing economies such as China and India are poised to become major producers of greenhouse gases and also have the possibility of developing the infrastructure for cleaner energy. The main purpose of the passage is to give an overview of how different countries are responding to global warming.

Answer to Question 80:

The correct answer is A. A fiat is an order or a decree. A is the correct answer. Because the government has decreed it, the use of paper money is acceptable, or sanctioned. Most countries have their own national currency. These characteristics of currency result from the government's decree. Solvent refers to having enough money to satisfy one's creditors.

Answer to Question 81:

The correct answer is B. The writer says that gold has no innate quality that makes it more suitable than anything else as a foundation for a monetary system. It could just as easily be tin or copper or coal. The choice is arbitrary, answer B. This arbitrary choice makes both A and D incorrect answers. Answer choice A contradicts the writer's statement that a money system based on precious metals is not necessarily more stable than one based on paper. In the same vein, gold is no more or less unreliable than any other foundation of a monetary system, making answer choice D incorrect. There is nothing in the paragraph to suggest that Latin America has greater resources for gold than other areas in the world, making C incorrect. The paragraph implies that gold was highly valued in Europe before the Spaniards and Portuguese visited Latin America, so E is not correct.

Answer to Question 82:

The correct answer is B. The value of existing Van Gogh paintings is unlikely to fall or rise. Examples in the passage show how the value of precious metals can be manipulated by controlling the supply, but, because Van Gogh is dead and cannot create new paintings, all existing paintings and any newly discovered works would remain rare and very valuable. The paintings would be carefully examined to determine their authenticity; they would not necessarily be declared counterfeit. Donating the paintings would have tax advantages only after ownership is determined. The value of the paintings would be determined only after thorough examination, making B the correct answer.

Answer to Question 83:

Both B and C are acceptable choices because they cause inflation. Advanced Placement classes are generally worth more points toward a GPA than are regular classes. As a result, they devalue the high grades that students earn in regular classes. Colleges that award supplementary points to SAT scores earned by students from culturally deprived areas devalue the true scores of other students. Answer choice A is not correct; when items are put on sale, the value of a dollar actually increases. End-of-season sales are temporary, and their intention is to get rid of old merchandise to make room for new items.

Answer to Question 84:

The correct answer is C. A medium of exchange allows individuals, groups, businesses, etc., to engage in transactions. The most common transaction involves exchanging money for goods or services. In the example in answer C, the transaction involves an exchange of services making it the only correct answer. The coupon in answer A is a gift; nothing is expected in return. Answer B only benefits the student. There is no exchange, eliminating it as the correct answer.

Answer to Question 85:

The correct answer is "Even without such a monstrous kick in the teeth, the price of gold tends to fluctuate drastically, dropping or rising relative to relatively stable fiat currencies."Because the price of gold fluctuates on a daily basis, currency values based on the gold standard would, in theory, also change daily. Businesses would be challenged to purchase inventory if they sold their goods at today's value and had to replace the goods after the price of gold had risen. Consumers would face uncertainty in their buying power from day to day.

Passage 39 – Summary / Paraphrase

The passage is about changes to patent law. The main idea is that while the privatization of research was designed to promote innovation, it has had some adverse effects as well. The major points are: (a) the government allowed commercial interests and public institutions to collaborate and share revenues in order to foster innovation (b) firms now have the right to deny foreign competitors the right to produce generic versions of products for which they hold the patent (c) the exclusivity of the licensing process makes it difficult for poorer countries to produce generic drugs to combat diseases such as AIDS. The purpose of the passage is to raise awareness of a flaw in the way the patent process works.

Answer to Question 86:

The correct answer is D. To equivocate is to use ambiguous or unclear language. The context of the passage suggests that America has difficulty deciding between economic or humanitarian concerns. The best word to express that behavior is vacillate, answer D. Hesitate would be correct if they eventually made a decision. To prevaricate is to lie. Pontification is similar to preaching, and to abrogate is to abolish. None of these other words are suitable choices in this context, eliminating answer choices A, B, C, and E.

Passage 40 – Summary / Paraphrase

The passage is about the way that countries are responding to the threat of global warming. The main idea is that the response has been mixed. The major points are: (a) the United States, historically the largest producer of greenhouse gases, has not acted aggressively on climate change because of fear of the economic consequences (b) other developed nations have been more successful in curbing emissions through the use of nuclear power and cleaner natural gas (c) developing economies such as China and India are poised to become major producers of greenhouse gases and also have the possibility of developing the infrastructure for cleaner energy. The main purpose of the passage is to give an overview of how different countries are responding to global warming.

Answer to Question 87:

The correct answer is D. Rapid growth is a challenge. It is easier to use the technologies that already exist to meet the demands of a growing economy. Stopping to install cleaner and more efficient means of production would slow the economy. The information in this passage makes no mention of the work force, so A is not the correct answer choice. There is no evidence that they are reluctant to use examples set by other countries or that they are unaware of more efficient technologies, eliminating B and C as correct answers. The passage does not reveal any ignorance about global warming on the parts of the emerging economies, eliminating E as a correct answer.

Passage 41 – Summary / Paraphrase

The passage is about the federal budget. The main idea is that spending on entitlement programs is rapidly growing in proportion to other spending. The major points are (a) some portions of the budget, such as Social Security are guaranteed funding by law, while others, however important, are funded at the discretion of congress and (b) that while discretionary programs constituted two thirds of the budget only 50 years ago, they now account for only one third of the budget while entitlements account for two thirds of spending. The purpose of the passage is to draw attention to a significant shift in the way government spending is allocated. While the issue of the budget is charged, the passage treats it matter of fatly and the rhetoric shows no bias.

Answer to Question 88:

The correct answer is D. The writer is claiming that the effect of the growth of entitlements is a reduction in discretionary spending, or that a reduction in discretionary spending is caused by an increase in entitlements. It is an example of cause-and-effect, answer D. Point-counterpoint involves two sides of an argument. In circular logic, the writer says the same thing in more than one way. Answer B is the easiest to eliminate as there is no identifiable question or answer in the statement. Loaded language relies on words that appeal to the reader's emotions, and, since the sentence in the passage is stating a fact, no emotional appeal is apparent, making E incorrect.

Answer to Question 89:

The correct answer is B. Appearing after words in quotation marks; the parenthetical phrases serve to explain those words, making answer B the correct choice. The parentheses do not affect the tone of the piece, as tone refers to the attitude of the writer towards the topic, so answer choices A and E are not correct as they both refer to the writer's tone. Sophistication describes a writer's style, and there is too little content here to identify any style. C is not correct. There is also no indication that this is part of a government publication, making D incorrect as well.

Passage 42 – Summary / Paraphrase

The passage is about health care costs. The main idea is that because of the way payments are structured in the healthcare system, there are few reasons to try to control costs. The major points are: (a) because patients may never even see their bill, they have no incentive to control costs under the current system (b) that there is a proposal to make costs more transparent, and thus drive them down, by having individuals buy their own insurance rather than being covered by their employer. The purpose of the passage is to explain some of the reasons for inflating healthcare costs and how one proposal suggests containing them.

Answer to Question 90:

The correct answer is A. The writer claims that one of the reasons for higher health-care costs is the consumer's ignorance of the actual cost. As long as the bill is paid with minimal contribution from the consumer, everyone is happy. The best answer is A. Answer B applies to a situation when one is expecting bad news, so no news is good news. It is as useful to save money that you already have as it is to earn more, answer C, does not apply in this case. Answer D is used to encourage someone to take a risk. Answer E cautions one to fix a problem while it is still minor; left alone or ignored, it could become worse.

Answer to Question 91:

The correct answer is D. If insurance companies pay at different levels for different providers, it logically follows that doctors might accept only insurance plans that offer higher reimbursement for office visits and procedures. This practice will contribute to higher health-care costs. While there is likely a shortage of medical providers in some areas of the country, it may not have an effect on the cost of health care. Doctors may set their fee structure to cover their operating expenses, but that does not affect the level at which insurance companies reimburse them. Whether doctors work in private practice or for medical centers has no effect on the level at which insurance companies reimburse practitioners for their services. There is nothing in the passage to suggest that doctors order unnecessary tests. Answers A, B, C, and E are not suitable choices.

Answer to Question 92:

The correct answer is B. There is no information in the passage to suggest that competition would lead to a reduction in the number of group plans, making A an incorrect choice. The government's offering tax credits to buy insurance would not necessarily lead to an increase in the number of regulations places on insurers, so C cannot be a correct answer. According to the passage, the public is currently ignorant of the true cost of health care, and, even if that condition persists, it should have no bearing on the effect of competition between insurers, so D is also incorrect. Insurance companies' offering competitive rates for coverage should have no bearing on what any hospital charges for services, eliminating E as a correct answer. Companies that have a healthy financial reserve will be able to lower their premiums to attract more consumers, forcing less stable companies to lower their rates in order to compete. In this scenario, many smaller companies will fail or stop offering health insurance, leaving a few large companies to dominate the market. When competition is reduced, these companies will be able to raise their rates. B is the best answer choice.

Passage 43 – Summary / Paraphrase

The passage is about measuring GDP. The main idea is that although economists prefer to calculate GDP using purchasing power parity (PPP), doing so is difficult. The major points are (a) that computing a PPP exchange rate is difficult, since it is not always possible to find equivalent sets of goods and services to base the calculation off and (b) some countries do not provide data on PPP, making GDP calculations imprecise. The purpose of the passage is to explain the challenges economists face when calculating GDP.

Answer to Question 93:

The correct answer is E. Another way of stating the information in the last sentence of the passage is to say that the OER measure is a fraction of the PPP measure, which would make the difference between the OER- and PPP-denominated GDP values for developing countries generally much greater. This eliminates answer choice A as the correct one. The reader would expect different results for industrialized countries, so answer choice B cannot be correct. This difference cannot be calculated for countries who do not participate in the World Bank's PPP project, so both C and D can be eliminated as correct answer choices. Because wealthy industrialized nations have products similar to those in the United States, it is easier for economists to assign US-dollar values to their goods and services. As a result, the difference between OER- and PPP- denominated values is likely to be smaller. E is the correct answer choice.

Passage 44 – Summary / Paraphrase

The passage is about the aim of business. The main idea is that while a net profit can only come about after the original capital outlay is recovered, net profit can actually be viewed as the creation of new capital. The major points are: (a) that net profit is the share of revenue left over after expenses are covered (b) that even with the payment of dividends; net profit is often reinvested in the business as capital. The purpose of the passage is to demonstrate that the true aim of business is the creation of capital.

Answer to Question 94:

The correct answer is B. Answer choice A is incorrect. Gross profits lead to greater net profits only if money remains after all expenses are met. That same reasoning makes answer choice B correct. If a business has money left over after subtracting initial capital from gross profits, they have made a net profit. Investors may benefit from spending their dividends, but they may also benefit from reinvesting or saving their dividends. The word "most" makes answer choice C incorrect.

Answer to Question 95:

The correct answer is D. The only way to increase net profits is to reduce expenses. Freezing wages means that they stay the same, so this action cannot lead to greater net profit, making A an incorrect choice. Concealing losses is not effective, because the losses will show up in the inventory, so B is not correct. Purchasing less inventory simply means that a business will have less inventory at the end of the period but has no effect on net profit. Answer C is not correct. Staying open more hours may generate more sales, but it also generates more expenses in wages and utilities like heat and electricity, so E is the wrong answer. The best answer is D. Spending less on electricity affects the bottom line and increases the net profitability of a business.

Passage 45 – Summary / Paraphrase

The passage is about the importance of time management in business. The main idea is that inefficient time management among higher management may lead a business to stagnate. The major point is that in spite of many platitudes about the importance of effective time management, many business leaders actually use their time poorly. A minor point reinforces this notion by explaining how poor time management affects a business. The purpose of the passage is to raise awareness of the harmful effects of poor time management.

Answer to Question 96:

A. Wrong. The passage pinpoints upper management as an area of a business where time is most often poorly managed, so the reader can infer that upper management in is in general disorganized because the ability to distribute time correctly is a feature of the ability to organize.

B. Wrong. The passage indicates that time management is a principle of business and thus it can be inferred that businesses struggle to implement their theoretical maxims in actuality.

C. Correct. While the author does draw attention to the fact that sayings like "time is money" highlight a link between time management and money, there is not enough information given to draw the conclusion that time management skills are analogous to money management skills.

D. Wrong. The passage claims that businesses lacking in time management skills also lack the ability to be self-evaluative which often leads to poor leadership, thus poor leadership is a major indicator that an organization is also time management deficient.

E. Wrong. The passage points out the fact that businesses stagnate when they lack organizational self-reflexivity and thus the reader can infer that businesses to better when they are able to critically evaluate their own methods and practices.

Answer to Question 97:

A. Correct. People in upper management should be the most responsible and time conscious given their position of power, but according to the passage they are the party that lacks critical time management skills and hence the understanding of the principles of business management - a clear incongruence.

B. Correct. Despite the fact that people know how valuable time is, as evidenced by the aphorisms" time is money" and "time is of the essence", businesses still commit the crime of wasting time.

C. Wrong. While wasting time may indeed lead to making poor business decisions, this is not a paradox; poor time management would logically lead to poor decision making. A paradox would require that the result was in logical conflict with the original statement.

Passage 46 – Summary / Paraphrase

The passage is about employers' concern with their employees' emotional attitudes. The main idea is that certain leadership behaviors can contribute to making employees more efficient. The major points are that (a) research indicates that employees tend to be more productive and creative when their work experience is positive and (b) that leadership that develops the meaning of work tasks and invites active engagement with projects fosters a positive work environment. The purpose of the passage is to persuade the reader to adopt the leadership practices described by explaining the positive effects of those practices.

Answer to Question 98:

A. Correct. The author uses deductive reasoning to underscore why improving the inner work lives of employees improves their performance in the work place.

B. Wrong. Pathos rhetoric is a persuasive strategy based on ethics and the character or reliability of the author. Since the reader has no information about the author to go on, and the author does not specifically make claims about improving the inner work life of the employee from a distinctly ethical dimension, the passage does not make use of pathos as a rhetorical strategy.

C. Wrong. The author uses both deductive reasoning and a dispassionate tone to appeal to the importance of improving inner work the work place environment.

Since ethos is a rhetorical appeal to the emotions, it cannot be applied as the rhetorical strategy of the passage in question.

D. Wrong. The author does not make comparisons to illuminate the importance of improving workplace conditions for employees; the author only deductively deduces why it is important to improve the inner work life of the employee.

E. Wrong. The author does not use narrative, or a recounting, to shed light on why improving workplace conditions benefits the inner work life of the employee and thus does not make use of narrative rhetoric.

Passage 47 – Summary / Paraphrase

The passage is about the spending habits of men. The main idea is that men tend to spend more liberally if they live in a region with a disproportionately high male population than if they live in a region with relative gender equilibrium. The main idea is supported by the mention of a relevant study. The purpose of the passage is to inform, as indicated by the dispassionate rhetoric and clear summary of research findings.

Answer to Question 99:

A. Wrong. The word dearth is not synonymous with abundance under any circumstances, regardless of the author's intent.

B. Wrong. While rarity can be a synonym for dearth, in this context dearth is more indicative of a higher rate of men than women and not the fact that women are rare.

C. Correct. The author uses this passage to discuss the implications of higher ratios of men than women on debt, and thus a dearth of women can be a synonym for a surplus of men.

D. Wrong. A total lack of women would mean that there were no women at all and the author clearly states that there are women, just less women than men.

E. Wrong. Paucity is synonymous with scarcity and thus not an adequate synonym in terms of the author's intention for dearth of women to indicate a surplus of men.

Passage 48 – Summary / Paraphrase

The passage is about gender disparity in upper management. The main idea is that while women play an increasing role in the corporate world, they are far less likely to be represented in higher management. There are two major points: (a) that the gender disparity is not the result of explicit discrimination and (b) that the relative lack of women in high management positions can be attributed to a "covert bias" that can discourage women from advancing. There is a minor point that specifies an example of "covert bias": corporate policies on maternity leave that force women to choose between their career and having a family. The purpose of the passage is to explain - the passage tackles a known phenomenon and offers an explanation of why it is the case.

Answer to Question 100:

A. Wrong. The passage does not discuss professional development and in fact infers that women have adequate professional development based on their ability to rise to the management level.

B. Wrong. The passage states that the attrition of female employees occurs after they have reached the management level, and thus women have the ability to reach the management level but are typically unable to rise beyond it.

C. Wrong. The passage does not state that U.S. businesses do not provide maternity leave, just that the maternity leave options do not allow women to easily reintegrate into the company.

D. Wrong. The passage does not mention anything about women's issues.

E. Correct. The passage states that U.S. businesses do not provide adequate maternity leave that allows for the successful re-entry of women into the company after their time off. Thus, it is difficult for women with children to balance family with work obligations and this impedes their ability to rise to the upper echelons of business organizations.

Passage 49 – Summary / Paraphrase

The passage is about social entrepreneurship. The main idea is that social entrepreneurship is a form of doing business that places a higher value on serving the common good than traditional business practices. The main points are that (a) attitudes have shifted so that people now demand businesses to conduct themselves in a more socially conscious fashion and (b) social entrepreneurship is a corollary of these shifts. There is a minor point that socially responsible business can have positive economic outcomes, although it is not developed. The purpose of the passage is to inform.

Answer to Question 101:

A. Wrong. The passage does not suggest that social entrepreneurs build better client relationships than traditional entrepreneurs. While it is true that social entrepreneurs must be adept at building relationships as means of promoting social capital, traditional entrepreneurs can be just as adept at creating client relationships as a means to the end of profit

B. Wrong. The passage clearly states that social entrepreneurs rely on the traditional principles of business and in the case of the passage above, axiom is analogous to principle.

C. Correct. It can be inferred from the passage that social entrepreneurs are more concerned with quality of life than their traditional entrepreneur counterparts because their main objective is to use business as a method of addressing social problems.

D. Wrong. The passage does not suggest that social entrepreneurs are more

concerned with climate change.
E. Wrong. The passage delineates clear differences between the two categories, particularly in their conceptions of capital.

Answer to Question 102:

A. Wrong. The author states that social capital is engendered by social dialogue and collaboration and thus the author would agree that it is a product of collaborative problem solving.
B. Wrong. The author states that social capital is the prominent feature that distinguishes social entrepreneurship from other business ventures and entrepreneurs and would thus agree that social capital is the salient feature of social entrepreneurship.
C. Correct. While it is true that social capital is a feature of entrepreneurship, the author would not agree that social capital is concrete or tangible; he or she describes it as the value of social relations which in and of itself cannot be materially embodied.
D. Wrong. The passage states that the principles of business management are used to create social relations and social capital.
E. Wrong. Since the passages states that social capital facilitates economic results, the author would clearly agree that it has monetary value.

Answer to Question 103:

A. Wrong. The author clearly gives enough information to define social capital in stating that cooperation and social relationships facilitate economic growth.
B. Wrong. The author intends social capital as capital in the traditional sense that it refers to financial assets and thus it does not mean community building.
C. Wrong. The author intends social capital as capital in the traditional sense that refers to financial assets and thus it does not mean relationship building.
D. Wrong. The author intends social capital as capital in the traditional sense that refers to financial assets and thus it does not mean social problems.
E. Correct. The passage indicates that social capital is the monetary result of people cooperating and building relationships in order to reach a goal.

Passage 50 – Summary / Paraphrase
The passage is about changes in the way stock market trading is conducted. The main idea is that increased computerization in stock market trading has led to greater volatility in the global economy. The main points are (a) computerization has facilitated high frequency trades and (b) high frequency trading can disrupt global economic equilibrium without warning. The purpose of the passage is to inform and explain; the passage summarily informs the reader about the volatility caused by high frequency trading while explaining

why this is the case.

Answer to Question 104:

A. Wrong. Stocks being traded continuously does not account for the fact that a high volume of stocks are being traded digitally as is the case with high frequency trading per the information relayed by the author in the passage.
B. Correct. High frequency trading occurs rapidly and on a massive scale with the assistance of a computer program.
C. Wrong. While high frequency trading is computer generated, this answer does not account for the fact that the author makes it explicitly clear that high frequency trading entails the rapid transference of huge quantities of stocks.
D. Wrong. It is true that high frequency trading means that stocks are being traded rapidly but this does not account for the fact that stocks are also being traded digitally as is the case per the information relayed by the author in the passage.
E. Wrong. The passage makes it clear that high frequency trading is done by computers and not on the stock room floor.

Answer to Question 105:

A. Wrong. The author does not indicate that the global market cannot be sustained if high frequency trading continues, just that high frequency trading is potentially dangerous to the global economic balance.
B. Wrong. The author makes it explicitly clear that high frequency trading has a negative impact on the global economic balance and thus it does not facilitate equilibrium, so this inference is not accurate.
C. Correct. The information in the passage indicates that the global economic balance can be affected quickly and in an unforeseen manner by high frequency trading, thus it can be inferred this will lead to trends of irregularity.
D. Wrong. The author gives plenty of information for the reader to make inferences regarding the global economic balance.
E. Wrong. The passage does not give indications regarding the state of the global economic balance before high frequency trading was introduced as a method on the stock market.

Passage 51 – Summary / Paraphrase
The passage is about the evolution of criticisms leveled against capitalism. The main idea is that critiques of capitalism tend to evolve to match the concerns of the day. The major points are (a) that critics of capitalism carry over many older complaints and (b) in light of current concerns about the environment and resource depletion, current critiques of capitalism claim that it is a danger to the world itself as well as its social structures. The main purpose of the passage is to inform the reader about the history of the ways in which capitalism has been attacked. The tone of the passage suggests that the author may be

trying to undermine current critiques of capitalism by lumping them with earlier critiques - the phrase "this is not a new phenomenon" seems dismissive in the context.

Answer to Question 106:

A. Wrong. The passage does not in any way discuss consumption leading to the financial crisis of the late 2000s.
B. Correct. The passage states that consumption leads to the exploitation of natural resources that are in high demand and since the passage states that consumption is a main focus of capitalism it is thus also a negative attribute of capitalism.
C. Wrong. While the passage does mention that market failure (a result of destabilized markets) is often seen as a negative attribute of capitalism, it does not directly link consumption with this specific issue.
D. Wrong. The passage makes no claims directly linking imperialistic oppression and consumption within the paradigm of capitalism.
E. Wrong. While it is true that consumption leads to the overuse (and waste) of natural resources, the passage does not explicitly state that consumption leads directly to wasteful consumer choices, even if the reader can make this inference based on the information given in the text.

Passage 52 – Summary / Paraphrase

The passage is about sustainability in business practice. The main idea is that businesses that show a robust concern for sustainability tend to outperform those that do not along a variety of metrics. The major points are: (a) sustainable business practice has become important for the public image of many firms, especially those in the West (b) that there is strong evidence to suggest that high-sustainability businesses tend to outperform low-sustainability businesses along traditional measures of profitability. Several minor points support the major points: (a) a Harvard study indicates that business success is determined by repeatedly meeting the expectations of both shareholders and stakeholders (b) that high-sustainability businesses are better at consistently meeting shareholder and stakeholder expectations over the long-run by being able to assimilate those needs into fiscally sound practices and (c) that due to their already-progressive practices, high-sustainability businesses are often more forward-thinking, and thus better able to attract long-term investment. The main purpose of the passage is to persuade the reader that sustainable business practices are better than non-sustainable practices by explaining why high-sustainability businesses tend to do better than low-sustainability businesses. While the rhetoric of the passage does not show overt bias, the fact that such strong emphasis is placed on the benefits of sustainability gives away the intent.

Answer to Question 107:

A. Wrong. While this statement is true, it does not account for what the passage suggests: That sustainability is such a vital factor in business because it facilitates both relationships and success by executing a forward-thinking, integrative approach to enterprise.

B. Wrong. The passage claims that environmental issues are a component of business sustainability, but it does not suggest that sustainability relative to corporations will assuage the problems associated with climate change.

C. Correct. The passage suggests that sustainability is of paramount importance in business because it will keep businesses enduring and successful despite the fact that the environmental, economic, and social milieu is in a constant state of flux.

D. Wrong. While it is true that sustainability is primarily concerned with helping businesses balance social, economic, and environmental factors related to organizational success, this answer does not specifically account for why the passage suggests that sustainability itself is vitally important: its ability to keep a company healthy and at the cutting edge despite the fact that global social, economic and environmental issues are in a constant state of flux. Sustainability is fosters adaptability, which keeps companies successful.

E. Wrong. The passage claims that sustainability is a popular topic in public discourse but again this does not account for why sustainability is crucial to the success of business endeavors.

Answer to Question 108:

A. Correct. The first paragraph in the passage states that long-term business success is determined by iterations or repetitions on business principles to meet the needs to both shareholders and stakeholders; thus an iterative process is also a repetitive process.

B. Wrong. While it is true that sustainable businesses are adaptable to social, fiscal and environmental changes, this answer does not relate to the iterative process since it does not mention iteration or repetition.

C. Wrong. The passage does not give any indication that an iterative process is a forward thinking process; an iterative process is defined by the repetition of business principles to meet shareholder and stakeholder demands.

Answer to Question 109:

"This leads them to a kind of tunnel vision that misjudges the expectations of stakeholders; additionally, they undervalue the importance of building good relationships with employees, customers and members of civil society, causing their venture to stagnate."

This sentence explicates how low-sustainability organizations' over-focus on the financial aspects of enterprise contributes to their inability to perform as successfully as high-sustainability companies; their overemphasis on the fiscal side of enterprise causes their ventures to stagnate.

Passage 53 – Summary / Paraphrase

The passage is about Just In Time (JIT) method. The main idea is that JIT method is adopted by many American businesses due to its various benefits. The purpose of the passage is to elaborate on the advantages of using JIT method.

Answer to Question 110:

The correct answer is A. B is not an advantage and C having buyer and customer work together is not necessarily an advantage.

Answer to Question 111:

The correct answer is "JIT can lead to increases in quality, productivity, and adaptability to change." It lists general advantages of Just in Time. The other options present specific advantages which may not necessarily be applicable to other manufacturers.

Practice Set 4 - Everyday Topics

Passage 54 – Summary / Paraphrase

The passage is about methods for improving outcomes in primary education. The main idea is that introducing a market system to primary education might be one way to improve outcomes. The main points: (a) that a voucher system will make primary education a free market and (b) that market forces will pressure underperforming public schools to improve their performance vis a vis their better-performing peers in order to compete. There is a minor point that some districts have tried to include private and even parochial schools, in their voucher program, raising a potential constitutional issue regarding separation of church and state. The main purpose of the passage is to inform the reader about an approach to improving outcomes in primary education: while the issue is often a charged one, the passage presents relevant information without clearly espousing a position.

Answer to Question 112:

The correct answer is C. When there is no sense of urgency to improve the way a business or school, etc. does business, that institution may suffer from complacency. When schools have a captive student body that has nowhere else to go, there is the temptation to think, "We're doing all right." It is easy to become complacent, or satisfied with the status quo. C is the best answer. Only when a school is striving to improve and is seeing some progress is there a reason to feel optimistic. Conversely, a school that is trying to improve and failing has reason to feel pessimistic or defeated. Lack of competition does not lead to A, B, or D. Lethargy implies a lack of energy, which can result from complacency. E is not the best choice.

Answer to Question 113:

The correct answer is B. If the purpose of the voucher system is to ensure that students get the best educational opportunities, then private schools who attract students under this system should have to conform to the guidelines set by the No Child Left Behind act. There is no oversight to insure that private schools offer a curriculum that is any better than that of a public school. The best answer is B. Answer A is not correct; parents do not have to select a private school and may choose not to do so because of the added expense of books and uniforms. Extracurricular activities are not a measure of excellence of education offered by a school, so C is not correct. Again, parents would be aware of religion courses offered at religious schools, and can choose to send their children elsewhere. The same reasoning applies to answer E.

Passage 55 – Summary / Paraphrase

The passage is about differences in attitudes toward literature in New York and Boston. The main idea is that although New York is a literary center, Boston society appreciates literature more than New York society. The major points are (a) New York is a center for writers and publishing and (b) New York society values commerce more than literature, while Boston society esteems literature. The purpose of the passage is to compare the attitudes of two major eastern cities toward literature. The author makes a latent assumption that his experience accurately reflects wider attitudes.

Answer to Question 114:

The correct answer is E. The writer is comparing and contrasting the attitudes of New York City's and Boston's regard for literary endeavors. The repetitive use of the word but is a standard tool for this purpose. The writer may be making a case for his point of view, but he is not asking the reader to take some action, which is the point of persuasive writing; A is not the correct answer choice. A logical appeal is a technique used in persuasive writing and not a format in itself, making B incorrect a well. A narrative is simply a story and does not describe the author's purpose here. C is incorrect. He writer has not employed symbolism to achieve his purpose here, eliminating D as a correct answer.

Answer to Question 115:

The correct answer is B. The writer claims that New York cares more for horse and stocks than it does for books and supposes that this attitude exists in other large cities. The writer tells the reader that New York is the home of many writers but does not say this about other cities, making A the wrong choice. It would be correct to say that New York City is a center of commerce and that it has great journalists, but that does not fulfill the purpose of comparison to other cities, eliminating both C and D as correct answers.

Answer to Question 116:

The correct answer is A. New York City has a more pragmatic or practical attitude toward the literary world; it cares more for the factual reporting of journalism than it does for the aesthetics of great literature. Boston, on the other hand is more enamored of literature than journalism, preferring its aesthetic sensibilities. The reader may conclude that New York is industrial in focus, but there is no evidence that Boston is an agrarian, or agricultural, city, so B cannot be correct. There is also no evidence that New York is more competitive than Boston in any sense, so answer choice C cannot be correct. Although the author reveals contrasts between the two cities, he makes no mention of New York's being a stereotypical American city or that Boston is one of a kind. D is the wrong answer. Boston is not described as being less progressive than New York, simply different from New York, maki ng answer choice E also incorrect.

Passage 56 – Summary / Paraphrase

The passage is about affirmative action. The main idea is that while affirmative action has helped to make college student bodies more diverse, it has been criticized for undermining meritocracy by advancing less deserving students on the basis of race. The major points are (a) that affirmative action guarantees greater minority representation in universities and (b) that affirmative action may sometimes disqualify students with better grades in favor of a minority candidate. The purpose of the passage is to briefly present both sides of the debate over affirmative action.

Answer to Question 117:

The best answer is C. The final sentence of the passage implies that attending a selective university paves the way for success in society. If true, then the converse would also be true, that a mediocre education leads to mediocrity in society. Answer A is incorrect; one doesn't succeed simply because he/she has gained acceptance to an elite institution, he or she must also graduate. The passage makes no mention of character, so B is also incorrect. There is nothing in the passage to indicate that colleges were discriminating against minorities based on race prior to the 1978 ruling. Using merit as a determining factor for acceptance may have inadvertently biased colleges against minority students because they received inferior high school educations. D is not the answer. There is no information in the paragraph about the academic performance of minority students at these universities, eliminating E as the best answer.

Answer to Question 118:

The correct answer is B. The most logical reason for more diversity on college campuses is the greater number of minorities applying to college, answer B. The cost of higher education at all types of colleges and universities continues to rise, so A is incorrect. The expanding availability of online colleges and course offerings makes it possible for people to obtain their education from home and, generally, at a great financial savings. Since these students do not physically attend college, they do not contribute to campus demographics. C is not the correct choice. A restriction on immigration might have the opposite effect on increased diversity on college campuses, eliminating D as an answer, and fewer Pell grants might make it more difficult for students to attend any college, so E is incorrect.

Passage 57 – Summary / Paraphrase

The passage is about prescription drug abuse. The main idea is that the difficulty of determining legitimate drug use from abuse makes the prevention of prescription drug abuse difficult. The major point is that prescription drug abusers can obtain the drug in a variety of ways, many of them difficult to distinguish from proper use. The purpose of the passage is to illustrate the difficulties authorities face in preventing prescription drug abuse.

Answer to Question 119:

The correct answer is A. Fewer pharmacies and doctors might result in a lower use of all prescription drugs, including OxyContin, so neither B nor C is correct. Population density has nothing to do with the rate of drug use; that rate would be determined per capita, regardless of how those individuals are scattered in a geographic area; D is incorrect. Because OxyContin is expensive does not make it unlikely to be abused. The cost of a particular drug has little to do with its being abused by the public, so E is also incorrect. A spike in the use of OxyContin in Appalachian states may not indicate abuse of the painkiller. Its arrival on the scene may simply mean that residents of this area finally have a more effective drug for injuries or conditions that are painful.

Passage 58 – Summary / Paraphrase

The passage is about public perceptions of coffee. The main idea is that coffee is a symbol of American values. The major points are (a) that an American general remarked that coffee helped the allies win WWI and (b) that coffee is associated with temperance and rationality, qualities needed for the functioning of democracy. The purpose of the passage is to celebrate coffee, and to associate coffee with what the author thinks are essential values of democracy.

Answer to Question 120:

The correct answer is D. It is typical of good writing that the last sentence of a paragraph previews the content of the subsequent paragraph. That being the case, it is correct to assume that the next paragraph will provide an explanation for or examples of the benefits of coffee, tea, and cocoa. D is the best answer choice. Answer choice A is incorrect; bacon is mentioned briefly in the second sentence of the passage, and the writer provides no reason to suspect that he will return to that subject. The same can be said for bread as a topic, eliminating B as a correct answer. It would be more correct to assume that coffee, tea, and cocoa contribute to clear thinking and right living than vice versa, so it is incorrect to assume that answer choice C is the best one. This writer extols the benefits of the three beverages rather than any harm they might cause; E is the wrong answer choice.

Answer to Question 121:

An argument can be made to support all three choices. Because the writer uses the word "one" in the first sentence, it is logical to expect a listing of the other awards that coffee has garnered. It could be that the writer wants to identify other everyday items that have had a greater impact on world democracy than their intrinsic value would lead one to believe. Finally, the writer might expand on the ideas about coffee, tea and cocoa that he has introduced in this passage.

Passage 59 – Summary / Paraphrase

The passage is focused on the gun control debate in the United States. The main idea of the passage is that the debate over gun control is a good example of the short-sighted nature of American civic discourse. The major point of the passage is that the reversal of the dominant public opinion on gun control within a 5 year span is a prime example of how short-sighted American public policy debates can be. There is a minor point that Americans are often aggressive in their views on topics such as gun control. The purpose of the passage is to illustrate a point about the nature of civic discourse in the United States. There is an underlying assumption that the legislative initiatives mentioned toward the end of the passage are an accurate reflection of current overall public opinion.

Answer to Question 122:

A. Wrong. The author does not clearly indicate his or her personal opinion on the state of gun control in American society, just that it is a hot-button issue that serves as a good example of rapidly fluctuating public opinions within the context of American public discourse.

B. Wrong. The author makes it very clear that gun control issues are an important aspect of American public discourse.

C. Wrong. While the passage states that American society can be very combative and intense in its debates, this is not the author's primary message since what the author really wants to convey is the fact that issues in American public discourse change rapidly - gun control can go from center stage to the periphery in a few short years.

D. Correct. The author states that the gun control debate demonstrates how myopic (short-sighted) American public discourse can be and then uses the remainder of the passage to provide an example that supports this claim.

E. Wrong. This answer cannot be inferred given the information provided by the author in the passage. The author claims that gun control issues play an important role in American society but not the central role.

Answer to Question 123:

A. Wrong. The passage does not indicate that Americans are confused by the rules governing civil society - on the contrary their knowledge of the Second Amendment illustrates that they at least have some understanding of the law. The author's primary goal in the passage is to draw attention to the short-sighted nature of civil society, not the confused nature of it.

B. Correct. The author wants the reader to understand the short-sighted nature of American civic debate by way of a belligerent character - that is anger and aggression are easily triggered when the issue of gun control comes up.

C. Wrong. While this phrase may very well capture the reader's attention, there is more to its significance: it serves to highlight the fact that American civic debate is not only myopic but also aggressive.

D. Wrong. An argumentative strategy requires that the author convince the audience of his claim through reasoning and since the author in the passage above only convinces the reader that American civic society is myopic by way of reason, the phrase in question cannot be an argumentative strategy to convince the reader of American aggression.

E. Wrong. It is correct that the author wants to convince the reader that American civil debate is short-sighted, but the phrase in question is not an example of a narrative rhetorical strategy. A narrative rhetorical strategy would require the recounting of an event, the telling of a story.

Passage 60 – Summary / Paraphrase

The passage is about homelessness among female veterans in the United States. The main idea is that homelessness among female veterans can be attributed to a combination of increased female participation in the military and a lack of veterans' services targeted specifically at women. The major point of the passage is the problematic increase in homelessness among female veterans. There are two minor points: (a) that the increase in homelessness is partly attributable to an increase in female enlistment and (b) that traditional veterans' shelters do not provide enough appropriate services for female veterans. The purpose of the passage is to inform the reader of a problem. The tone of the passage suggests that problem of homelessness among female veterans needs to be addressed. The passage implies that increasing veterans' services targeted specifically at females is a remedy for the problem.

Answer to Question 124:

A. Wrong. The passage does not appeal to the logos, or logical reason, to make his or her argument regarding the increase of homeless female veterans. The author appeals to the emotional sensibilities of the reader by showing that this homelessness is a problem through the example that homeless female veterans cannot care for their children - an emotional appeal.

B. Correct. The author uses the example of homeless female veterans not being able to care for their children to underscore the problem of homelessness among female veterans, which is a classic emotional (pathos) appeal that plays on the needs, values and emotional sensibilities of the reader.

C. Wrong. The passage in no way addresses metaphysical concerns (the fundamental question of being in the world according to philosophy) and thus does not appeal to the metaphysical sensibilities of the reader.

D. Wrong. Since the reader does not have any knowledge of which the author is, ethos does not apply here since ethos is an ethical appeal based on the reputation of the author.

E. Wrong. The political level is not addressed directly in this passage and thus the author is not appealing to the reader's political sensibilities.

Answer to Question 125:

A. Wrong. The passage does not suggest that the U.S military offers its veterans no services, just that these services are lacking particularly when it comes to helping female veterans and their children.

B. Wrong. The passage does not suggest that all U.S. military veterans are homeless, just that the homeless phenomenon is increasing among female veterans.

C. Correct. It can be inferred from the information given in the passage that gender inequality exists among U.S. military veterans because veteran services are not inclusive of women and their children, thus leaving them more vulnerable.

D. Wrong. The passage in no way indicates that women should not serve in the U.S. military, just the fact that female veterans need more assistance.

E. Wrong. Based on the information given in the passage it cannot be inferred that more female veterans have children than male veterans overall, but it can be inferred that more female veterans are responsible for their children than male veterans.

Passage 61 – Summary / Paraphrase

The passage is about domestic violence. The main idea is that, contrary to popular belief, men are quite often the target of domestic violence. There are two major points: (a) 40% of domestic violence victims are male and (b) due to societal attitudes toward male weakness, domestic violence incidents involving men may be underreported. The main purpose of the passage is to (a) debunk the myth that men are rarely the victims of domestic violence and (b) give one potential reason that domestic violence against men may be underreported.

Answer to Question 126:

A. Wrong. The passage does not suggest women stigmatize abused men, it suggests that Western society as a whole stigmatizes abused men.

B. Wrong. The passage does not suggest that researchers of the domestic abuse of males harbor any pro or anti female bias.

C. Wrong. The passage does not indicate that reporting domestic abuse harms the overall quality of the male victim's relationships with women.

D. Wrong. The passage does not give general drawbacks of statistical methodology as a reason for faulty statistics relative to male domestic abuse.

E. Correct. The passage states that men face social stigma if they admit to being victims of domestic abuse; society equates this with male weakness. Hence, male domestic abuse is underreported.

Passage 62 – Summary / Paraphrase

The passage is about college students' attitudes toward their student loan debt. The main idea is that college students have an unusual attitude about their debt burden. There are two major points: (a) students are optimistic about their ability to use their education to succeed, and thus inclined to take a positive view of their debt. There is also an implied point (b) that most other Americans who are in debt do not share this positive view of their debt. There is a minor point that student views on empowerment through education are a key influence on their feelings about their debt burden. The main purpose of the passage is to point out an atypical attitude within the broader context of how people respond to being in debt.

Answer to Question 127:

A. Wrong. This answer is not an inference about American college students given that it is a fact taken directly from the passage.

B. Wrong. The passage indicates that American college students feel that debt is a positive thing as it is evidence of their commitment to the future and a wider array of opportunities.

C. Wrong. The passage does not provide enough information about other adult debt levels to infer this comparison; additionally, the passage states that American college students are heavily affected by high levels of student loan debt.

D. Correct. The passage states that American college students see student loan debt as a way of advancing their careers and opportunities and thus it can be inferred that they are choosing to view debt through a positive lens.

E. Wrong. The passage states that American college students don't view student loan debt as a negative thing, which does not indicate that American college students feel that debt as an issue lacks importance - it is just not a negative issue for them.

Answer to Question 128:

A. Wrong. The passage states that researchers see students' reaction to their debt level as atypical or unusual and since naïve means child-like; naïve is not a term that accurately reflects the attitude of college students.

B. Wrong. The passage states that researchers see students' reaction to their debt level as atypical or unusual and since predictable means reliable or typical; predictable is not a term that accurately reflects the attitude of college students.

C. Correct. The passage states that researchers see students' reaction to their debt level as atypical or unusual and since preternatural means unusual and is thus a synonym for atypical; preternatural is a term that accurately reflects the attitude of college students.

D. Wrong. The passage states that researchers see students' reaction to their debt level as atypical or unusual and since banal means trite or commonplace; banal is not a term that accurately reflects the attitude of college students.

E. Wrong. The passage states that researchers see students' reaction to their debt level as atypical or unusual and since unexceptional means typical or usual; unexceptional is not a term that accurately reflects the attitude of college students.

Answer to Question 129:

A. Wrong. An albatross is a figure of speech for a burden and so it cannot be synonymous with the level of debt because that would require albatross to refer to an actual number.

B. Correct. An albatross is a figure of speech for a burden and in the passage it is used to indicate the burden of debt.

C. Wrong. An albatross is a figure of speech for a burden and thus it cannot be used as a figure of speech that represents the stresses in American society.

D. Wrong. An albatross is a figure of speech for a burden does not indicate anything about a bank account; furthermore, substituting bank account for albatross in the passage would be illogical syntactically and semantically.

E. Wrong. An albatross is a figure of speech for a burden and credit card debt is a debt and thus a burden. However, the passage does not mention credit card debt specifically and thus credit card debt cannot be substituted for albatross.

Passage 63 – Summary / Paraphrase

The passage is about the difficulty of achieving equal educational opportunities in the United States. The main idea is that while there is a tendency to focus on literacy rates and children, the problem of low literacy has broader implications. There is an explicitly stated major point that low literacy among adults engenders poor educational results in the children of the affected population. In addition, there is an implied major point that literacy is crucial to equal opportunity. The purpose of the passage is to rally support for literacy initiatives by explaining why they are important. Rhetorical cues such as the use of the word 'harmful' and the discussion of adverse outcomes indicate that the passage is a call to action.

Answer to Question 130:

A. Wrong. The author actually delineates or describes the problems associated with low literacy in the section of the passage not in bold-face; the sections in bold-face demonstrate how the author finds a solution to his or her claim.

B. Wrong. The author actually appeals to the reader's emotional sensibilities in the part of the passage that are not highlighted in bold-face by invoking the problems children face when they struggle with low literacy.

C. Wrong. The author's beliefs are congruent and the author only discusses one belief and no opposing beliefs relative to low literacy: it obstructs equal opportunities.

D. Correct. The two-bold face parts demonstrate how the author presents his or her claim that low literacy obstructs access to equal opportunities and then reaches the solution to the problem: literacy initiatives.

E. Wrong. Since the two bold-face parts are congruent and serve to illustrate the author's contention that low literacy impedes equal opportunities in society; thus, they are not paradoxical.

Answer to Question 131:

A. Wrong. The author spends the majority of the passage highlighting why low literacy is a major problem among adults, which leads to a cycle of low literacy perpetuated by the children of low literacy adults.

B. Correct. The passage discusses how low literacy rates in American adults impede equal opportunities.

C. Wrong. The passage does not indicate the effect of low literacy in American adults on crime rates.

Practice Set 5 - Physical Sciences

Passage 64 – Summary / Paraphrase

The passage is about the chemical properties of iron. The main idea is that iron can form two chemically distinct series of compounds. The major points are that: (a) iron can form a series of compounds with chemical similarities to zinc compounds and (b) that iron can also form a series of compounds that are chemically similar to aluminum compounds. The primary purpose of the passage is to inform the reader about the chemical properties of iron compounds.

Answer to Question 132:

All three statements are accurate. The prefix di- means two, and the prefix tri- means three. It logically follows that the suffix -ous is used with metals that have a lower valence number than those with the suffix -ic. Using the knowledge of common words, the reader can agree that the definitions of the two suffixes are correct. For example, beauteous means possessing beauty. If B is correct, then C must also be correct.

Passage 65 – Summary / Paraphrase

The passage is about the way that particle structure affects how matter interacts with matter. The main idea is that mercury is unusual in that it behaves like a solid even in a liquid state. The major points are: (a) that particles in solids cohere to each other more strongly than they adhere to the particles in other objects (b) that liquid mercury particles also cohere to one another more strongly than they adhere to the particles in other objects. The main purpose of the passage is to inform.

Answer to Question 133:

The correct answer is "In scientific language, the cohesion of the mercury is stronger than its adhesion to your finger or handkerchief." The writer's use of the phrase "in scientific language" implies that the text before this is not written in scientific language. The writer also follows this sentence with an example that uses a common object to illustrate the topic of the passage. This indicates that the intended audience is not other scientists.

Passage 66 – Summary / Paraphrase

The passage is about how snowflakes and raindrops form. The main idea is that snowflakes and raindrops form through a very similar process. The major points are: (a) raindrops form when water vapor reaches cooler temperatures and begins to condense to form droplets and (b) that snowflakes form in almost the exact same conditions except that it is cold enough to freeze the newly condensed water. There is a minor point that speculates on why snowflakes have the crystalline structure they have, and another that mentions that snow and rain are both part of the water cycle. The purpose of the passage is to inform.

Answer to Question 134:

Answer C is the best choice. The writer has wandered away from the topic of how rain and snow are formed in the upper atmosphere. He uses the phrase, in any case, to let the reader or audience know that he is returning to the original topic. Answer A is incorrect because the information is not essential to the main topic of the effect of cooling air on water vapor. Although the writer appears to be speculating about the manner in which snowflakes develop six points, the phrase, in any case, does not address that, making B incorrect. Answer D is incorrect for the same reason. There is no evidence that the writer does not find the information interesting, eliminating E as the correct answer.

Answer to Question 135:

The correct answer is E. The writer in this passage reveals how rain and snow are formed in the same manner although temperatures in the upper atmosphere determine whether raindrops or snowflakes are formed. His is mentioning both similarities and differences, therefore, the passage compares and contrasts, answer E. A narrative tells a story which is not the writer's goal here, making A an incorrect choice. Expository writing reveals, usually information about setting or characters. B is not the correct answer choice. Both editorials and persuasive writing present a point of view and support for that point of view, and this passage does not attempt to persuade, so neither C nor D are correct choices.

Answer to Question 136:

The correct answer is B, fog. Fog forms when cool air on the surface comes in contact with warm air vapor and small droplets of water form. A rainbow forms when light passes through water droplets in the air; A is incorrect. Wind chill is a measure of the effect of wind on the ambient air temperature, so C cannot be correct. A degree day is a measure of heating or cooling and not a weather event at all, making D incorrect. Thunder is, essentially, the sound made by lightning. Answer E is also incorrect.

Passage 67 – Summary / Paraphrase

The passage is about sound. The main idea is that sound is a sensation caused by clearly delineated physical phenomena. The major points are: (a) that sound is a sensation rather than a physical phenomenon (b) that the sensation of sound is caused by a physical phenomenon known as "sonorous vibration" and (c) the sonorous vibrations cause the sensation of sound by reaching the skin of the ear. A minor point that compares sonorous vibrations to ripples in water serves to illustrate the phenomenon. The main purpose of the passage is to clarify and explain the link between a physical phenomenon and a bodily sensation.

Answer to Question 137:

The correct answer is D. Sound is neither odd nor uncommon to the ear; it is the exact opposite. Neither A nor B is the correct answer. The definition in C means unusual; it is not the correct choice. Answer E would be correct if the author had written that the peculiar ability of the ear is to hear sound. In this case, if the reader were to replace peculiar with belonging characteristically in the sentence, the meaning would remain the same.

Answer to Question 138:

The best answer is C, students. The passage is about the sensation of sound and is not related to any particular field of interest. The writer uses the violin as an example of an object that vibrates when a bow is applied, but he is not addressing musicians specifically, making A an incorrect choice. The content is not an instruction manual for manufacturers of violins as it doesn't deal with the specific measurements or materials needed to build the instrument, eliminating B as a correct answer. Sonography technicians administer sonograms to diagnose medical issues or to provide pictures of a fetus in utero. The passage has nothing to do with this procedure, so D is incorrect. Acoustics engineers design buildings or rooms to make sound in the rooms as clear as possible. Answer choice E is also not correct. The use of the violin as an example of how vibrations affect the eardrum would be appropriate for students, making C the best answer.

Answer to Question 139:

The correct answer is "The surface of the sounding-board is thus set trembling, and these tremors, or vibrations, spread through the air in all directions around the instrument, somewhat in the manner that water-waves spread around the place where a stone has been dropped into a quiet pond."This sentence, in fact, uses some of the same language that is used to report earthquakes such as tremors and trembling. The effects of an earthquake are similar in that the movement of the earth radiates out from the epicenter.

Passage 68 – Summary / Paraphrase

The passage is about asteroids. The main idea is that astronomers originally had little knowledge of asteroids. The main idea is developed by two major points: (a) until the mid-19th century, astronomers had little accurate notion of how many asteroids there were and (b) astronomers mistakenly believed that Vesta was the largest asteroid due to its relative brightness, whereas the largest asteroid is in fact Ceres. A minor point explains that the mistake in determining the relative size of the asteroids stemmed from differences in the reflectivity of Ceres and Vesta. The purpose of the passage is to inform the reader about the history of our knowledge of asteroids.

Answer to Question 140:

Answer choice D is the most reasonable explanation. When one considers that several years passed between sightings before spotters began seeing them with increasing regularity, the logical conclusion is that, in some way, the spotters were better able to see the asteroids. The writer makes no mention of weather affecting the spotters' ability to identify more asteroids, so answer choice A is not the most reasonable. Offering more courses in astronomy does not inevitably lead to more astronomers; B is also incorrect. There is nothing in this passage to suggest that there had been a period of volcanic activity, the ash from which may have blocked the view of the sky, so C is incorrect. It is not clear in this passage that astronomers were confused about the characteristics of asteroids, eliminating E as the most reasonable explanation.

Answer to Question 141:

The best answer is choice A. After periods of relatively slow advances in the discovery and accurate measurement of asteroids, the pace of both increased rapidly. It would be fair to predict that this pace would continue or increase. An important idea in this passage is the revision of current or previous understanding about objects in the universe. Regardless of the scientific field, ideas and theories are under continuing scrutiny as the ability to examine objects becomes more advanced. After all, humans for centuries believed that the Earth was the center of the universe. Although the other 4 answer choices are likely true, their truth doesn't have an impact on the entirety of science.

Passage 69 – Summary / Paraphrase

The passage is about the geology of a certain region. The main idea is that the author is unable to find a geologic explanation for the rock-basin lakes discussed in the first paragraph. The major points are (a) that some lakes are formed in a basin scooped out of solid rock (b) that the lake bottoms are often scratched or grooved apparently by rocks or boulders that are sometimes found nearby (c) that erosion by the ocean was ruled out as a possible cause for these lakes due to dissimilarities in the geology. Two minor points serve to develop two of the major points: (a) the rock-basin lakes are described as "spoon-shaped" in order to give the reader a clearer impression of the phenomenon and (b) the effects of tidal erosion are discussed prior to being ultimately dismissed. The purpose of the passage is to discuss a geological mystery and rule out one possible solution.

Answer to Question 142:

The correct answer is "The problem now was to discover what forces in Nature could polish and scratch both rock-surfaces and detached stones, and could also transport masses of rock, tons in weight, far from their native home." In the first paragraph of the passage, the writer reveals observations that he has made. These observations lead him to state the problem, which, in turn, leads him to investigate in order to find a solution to the problem or to answer a question. Without clearly stating the problem, the writer would have no direction for his investigation, and the scientific process would not continue.

Answer to Question 143:

The correct answer is B. The writer's hypothesis appears to be based on his observations at Table Bay. At the very least, he should visit several other locations to discover if the conditions at Table Bay are typical. Ideally, the writer should conduct a series of experiments to test his hypothesis. The writer should collect and label samples from Table Bay, but that is not sufficient to prove his hypothesis. The comment, "as facts accumulate", leads the reader to believe that background research has already been done and should be done before developing a hypothesis, so C is not the correct answer choice. Scientists should never publish the results of their research before testing the hypothesis, making answer choice D incorrect as well. Seeking the perspectives of other scientists might be helpful in formulating a hypothesis, perhaps in order to create an experiment, but it is not a step that would prove the hypothesis to be correct. E is not the correct answer.

Answer to Question 144:

Both A and B are acceptable choices. How to explain the appearance of boulders in New York and Ohio that seem to have their origins in regions to the north plays a role in the writer's question about the condition of the rocks in and around lakes. The bottoms of the lakes and boulders in the vicinity have scratches in their otherwise smooth surfaces while rocks on the edges of the lakes are smooth without scratches. How can these two conditions occur in the same location? There is no evidence that the writer is testing the veracity of previous conclusions, making choice C incorrect.

Passage 70 – Summary / Paraphrase

The passage is about sun spots. The main idea is that although the surface of the sun appears to be perfectly placid, it is actually covered with potential sun spots. The major points are (a) that observing the sun with a telescope, one can see that it is covered with "pores" (b) the pores open during times of solar disturbance, giving rise to a sun spot. There is a minor point that people refused to admit the existence of sun spots for many centuries because the sun was seen as a symbol of purity. The purpose of the passage is to briefly inform the reader about sun spots, and the history of human response to them.

Answer to Question 145:

Support exists for all three statements. Humans considered the sun to be the symbol of purity, a mythological concept. The name, King of the Heavens, denotes the sun's importance in the lives of humans. Humans thought of scientists as fools and idiots because of their attempts to demystify the sun and its power.

Passage 71 – Summary / Paraphrase

The passage is about silver plating. The main idea is that silver plating is done using a process known as electroplating. The major points explain the process of electroplating: (a) the object to be plated is dipped in silver salt (b) an electrical connection is made with the object serving as the cathode and the silver solution serving as the anode (c) a current is passed through, and the silver dissolves and deposits on the cathode. There is a minor point that minor alterations to the process allow it to be applied to gold and other metals as well. The purpose of the passage is to explain the process of silver plating.

Answer to Question 146:

The correct answer is E. The writer states that silver has a pleasing appearance. A pleasing appearance would add aesthetic appeal to an object, making answer choice E the best choice. There is no mention of planting's being done to either fool consumers or to add value to an object, eliminating A and B as correct answers. The author fails to say that electroplating makes objects shiny, so C is also incorrect. Anodes and cathodes are the poles of a battery and have plenty of uses other than electroplating, making D the wrong choice. Answer E is the best choice.

Passage 72 – Summary / Paraphrase

The passage is about induced magnets. The main idea is that induced magnets have some unusual properties that are unlike other magnets. The major points are (a) that induced magnets are caused when an ordinary magnet is brought near a magnetic pole (b) that induced magnets have a single pole evenly distributed over their surface and (c) that induced magnets become weak ordinary magnets when they are moved beyond the field of the inducing pole. A minor point details the way that iron filings behave on an induced magnet. The purpose of the passage is to inform the reader about an unusual form of magnetism.

Answer to Question 147:

Both A and B are correct. The conclusion in answer B can be derived from the next-to-last sentence in the passage, "the filings at the remote end will generally be held permanently". Answer choice A is confirmed in the fifth sentence of the passage, "the single pole is pretty evenly distributed over the whole surface." The writer reveals that a bar of iron is used in the experiment, but there is nothing to indicate that it must first be magnetized, so C is not a correct choice.

Answer to Question 148:

The correct answer is A. Alleged is not proven, and exaggerated is beyond what is provable. The writer is expressing skepticism; he needs proof. A is the correct answer. He is not expressing reluctance to believe; in fact, he wants to believe the claim. There are no words that express admiration. The passage is a fairly straightforward narrative. Neither B nor C is correct. Convinced is the opposite of skeptical. If the writer were convinced, he would not use words like Alleged and exaggeration. If the writer were being critical, he would reveal weaknesses and/or mistakes. D and E are not acceptable choices

Passage 73 – Summary / Paraphrase

The passage is about GPS satellites. The main idea is that by exploiting new orbital patterns, GPS satellites can perfect their coverage. The major points are (a) that signals from GPS satellites were not always easy to pick up due to blockages from building or landforms (b) that by sending satellites into irregular orbits, the problem areas could be covered. The purpose of the passage is to briefly explain a problem with GPS coverage and how it was solved.

Answer to Question 149:

The correct answer is "The GPS satellites provide coded timing signals that allow a receiver to determine its location on Earth, but GPS signals are not always easy to pick up in Japan's mountainous regions or skyscraper-studded cities like Tokyo." One of the difficulties with traditional GPS in Japan occurred as a result its being a mountainous country. The reader can assume that the same difficulties would arise in other areas of the world where mountains are a dominant feature of the geography.

Passage 74 – Summary / Paraphrase

The passage is about a "miracle drug" that is being developed to treat radiation sickness. The main idea is that although scientists claim to have found a simple pill that can decontaminate a human body within two weeks, we should be guarded and skeptical of these claims. The major points are: (a) the most dangerous effect of a nuclear disaster is long-term radiation contamination, which leads to grave illness and death in those affected (b) that scientists working on decontaminating victims of radiation poisoning have discovered a pill that claims to quickly cure radiation sickness (c) that this "miracle cure" is almost undoubtedly too good to be true because (1) if a claim is too good to be true, it usually is (2) the pill may have untold side effects. The discussion is framed by a minor point that discusses our current and historic concern with fallout from nuclear disasters. The main purpose of the passage is to question the trustworthiness of the claim that a pill can rapidly cure radiation sickness. The tone is highly skeptical and shows a strong bias against the idea that the proposed miracle cure is really a cure. The author also assumes that past instances of things being too good to be true is evidence enough that the proposed cure is too good to be true, without citing any evidence against it.

Answer to Question 150:

A. Wrong. The author is not recounting the story of scientific research relative to radiation treatment, rather using this passage to persuade the reader that the anti-radiation treatments are likely ineffective and unhealthy.

B. Wrong. There is absolutely nothing objective or unbiased about this passage; it is driven by the author's personal opinions in an attempt to persuade the reader that anti-radiation drug treatments are likely ineffective and potentially harmful.

C. Wrong. The passage itself is not a scientific theory, it is a piece of persuasive prose that the author is using to try to convince the reader that the radiation treatment being developed at the Berkeley Lab is likely ineffective and predicated on a false promise: the quick fix.

D. Correct. The author uses this piece as a platform to persuade the reader to believe his or her opinion that the effectiveness and safety of the radiation treatment being developed at the Berkeley Lab is unproven and likely a false promise.

E. Wrong. The author does not draw any comparisons relative to the research and development of radiation treatment, rather uses this piece as a platform to persuade the reader to believe his or her personal opinion on the matter: the effectiveness of the radiation treatment is likely a false promise.

Answer to Question 151:

A. Correct. The first section is the claim of the Berkeley Lab scientists, which is that they can cure radiation exposure with a pill. The second section demonstrates that the author is trying to undermine the claim of the scientists by stating that their assertion is suspect and drawing attention to the fact that the side effects of the radiation treatment are still unknown.

B. Wrong. Only the first bold-faced section is an assertion; the second bold-faced section is the author's attempt to undermine the Berkeley's scientists claim that they can cure radiation exposure with a pill - it is a demonstration of the author's personal opinion. The second section is not in itself a claim and hence both sections cannot be congruent assertions.

C. Wrong. While the first section is correctly identified as the scientist's claim, the second section is not the author's main claim; it is the author's attitude or position towards the main claim of the scientists. The author's main claim is that the assertions of the scientists should not be believed until more proof can be given relative to the effectiveness of their radiation treatment.

Answer to Question 152:

"While it is no doubt of the utmost importance to find a way to cure the effects of radiation, one must be skeptical of the treatment method proposed by the Berkeley Lab scientists because things that sound too good to be true are good to be true." In this sentence the author acknowledges the efforts of the Berkeley Lab scientists (concession), but ultimately he or she uses the remainder of the sentence to demonstrate that their claims "sound too good to be true" (rebuttal).

Passage 75 – Summary / Paraphrase

The passage is about the hypothetical Higgs boson. The main idea is that while calling the Higgs boson "the God particle" may be misleading, actually finding the particle would unlock some of the profoundest mysteries of modern physics. There are two main points: (a) discovery of the Higgs boson would not have any bearing on the existence of spiritual beings (b) discovery of the Higgs boson would explain the origins of particle mass, and would indicate that string theory is on the right track. The main purpose of the passage is to clarify and inform. The author wants to debunk the notion of the Higgs boson having supernatural implications, while affirming its profound implications.

Answer to Question 153:

A. Wrong. The passage indicates that the God particle is another name for the Higgs boson particle.

B. Correct. The passage does not claim that the Higgs boson itself is the origin of particle mass in the universe, just that its discovery could potentially explain the origins of particle mass in the universe.

C. Wrong. Since the passage makes it clear that there is no proof of the Higgs boson then it is still just a hypothesis.

D. Wrong. The passage states that the Higgs boson is an elementary particle in physics.

E. Wrong. The passage states that finding the Higgs boson particle would reinforce the hypothesis of string theory.

Passage 76 – Summary / Paraphrase

The passage is about the impact of scientific progress on health. The main idea is that developments in all scientific fields can have an impact on medical progress. The main idea is supported by a major point: that chemist have recently discovered new materials that could potentially be used for a variety of medical diagnoses and treatments. The purpose of the passage is to inform the reader about the extent to which medical progress draws on broader scientific progress.

Answer to Question 154:

A. Wrong. The passage indicates that disease diagnostics and the engineering of new human tissues are indeed a byproduct of the new "smart" polymer, but since avant-garde is analogous to groundbreaking; the real merit in the new scientific discovery is the fact that the "smart" polymer could assist light in being used as a medicine.

B. Wrong. The passage does not discuss and does not give any information from which one could infer as to whether or not the development of the "smart" polymer will give chemists a competitive edge in the medical field.

C. Correct. The passage states that the new "smart" polymer is groundbreaking, which can be a synonym for avant-garde, and it specifically points out that this is true because the "smart" polymer would allow light to be transformed into a medicine.

D. Wrong. The passage does not indicate that the "smart" polymer was a product of scientific interdisciplinary cooperation.

E. Wrong. The passage makes it very clear that the "smart" polymer is special, specifically because it could facilitate the use of light for medicinal purposes.

Answer to Question 155:

A. Wrong. While it is true that the section in bold-face shows that scientists and doctors cooperate, it is primarily intended to draw attention to the fact that our medicine develops in ways we never think of or expect.

B. Wrong. The primary purpose of the section in bold-face is to draw attention to the fact that medical advances are often beyond the grasp of our imaginations, not to merely show us those doctors and scientists are creative.

C. Correct. The section in bold-face draws special attention to the fact that we cannot imagine the various ways in which medicine will evolve.

D. Wrong. The section in bold-face does not indicate that medical advances could not occur without the cooperation of scientists and doctors, rather draws attention to the fact that their cooperation creates medical advances that are hard to imagine.

E. While the section in bold-face draws attention to the fact that we cannot always imagine the medical developments, this does not mean that our imaginations in and of themselves are limited.

Answer to Question 156:

"Chemists report that their new polymer (plastic-like) material could help diagnose diseases and engineer new human tissues; whether or not these claims can be substantiated is another matter."

For the majority of the passage the author's tone towards the new "smart" polymer is one of excitement and intrigue. However, the last sentence demonstrates that the author is actually skeptical as to whether or not the new "smart" polymer can live up to the promises of the scientists.

Passage 77 – Summary / Paraphrase

The passage is about astrophysics. The main idea is that astrophysics now believes that it is not uncommon for planets in other solar systems to orbit more than one star, a notion that was once largely relegated to the realm of science fiction. The major points are (a) that the climate on a planet orbiting two stars would be quite unstable (b) that scientists are unsure of how or if life would come to be on such planets. The main purpose of the passage is to inform the reader about a recent development in astrophysics.

Answer to Question 157:

A. Wrong. The author does draw a comparison between circumbinary planets in both Star Wars and now in scientific reality, but this does not mean that the author is drawing a parallel between science fiction and science overall, not enough information is given by the author to support such a broad, sweeping claim.

B. Wrong. This is a far-fetched inference that the reader could draw from the author's mention of Star Wars, but it is not the intent of the author to invoke Star Wars as a commentary how science fiction precedes scientific knowledge.

C. Correct. The author's use of Star Wars is a stylistic device used to peak the readers interest in a scientific text by relating the content of the passage to a common cultural reference.

D. Wrong. While the author does invoke Star Wars to peak the reader's interest in the text, this is a stylistic strategy rather than a rhetorical strategy: the author is not using Star Wars as a means of persuading the reader to adhere to a particular viewpoint. Furthermore, the narrative rhetorical strategy requires a recounting of events which clearly does not take place with reference to Star Wars.

E. Wrong. The author is in no way advocating or advertising for Star Wars, merely introducing it as a stylistic strategy to peak the reader's interest.

Answer to Question 158:

A. Wrong. The passage indicates that scientists are unsure how life manifests and evolves on other planets, so circumbinary planets cannot help us better understand the way life materializes or evolves on other planets.

B. Wrong. The passage does not give enough information to indicate that researching circumbinary planets will help scientists understand climate change on Earth.

C. Correct. The passage only gives us enough information to let us know that circumbinary planets can help us better understand the way the sun controls planetary climates.

Passage 78 – Summary / Paraphrase

The passage is about advances in biotechnology. The main idea is that while biochemical research is coming ever closer to creating life, actually doing so could have severely adverse consequences. The major points are that (a) biochemists are using a new chemical reaction to create self-assembling cell membranes (b) scientists hope the understanding cell-membranes, which are one of the basic building blocks of life, will lead to insights into how non-living matter becomes life and (c) in the author's view, some questions are best left unanswered, especially in view of the potentially destructive potential of such breakthroughs. The main purpose of the passage is to caution against research that digs too deeply into the origins of life. Rhetorical devices such as the mention of Pandora's Box and the vague danger of total annihilation indicate that the author has a strong bias against the research under discussion.

Answer to Question 159:

A. Wrong. The author does provide the facts related to the potential creation of artificial life forms, but the entire passage is infused with the author's bias against this line of scientific inquiry; there is no purely objective evaluation of the facts.

B. Wrong. While the last line of the passage is certainly a dramatic way of driving home the author's point about the dangers of the creation of artificial life, the author primarily reinforces his or her claim by providing a counterview to the argument in delineating what scientists think about the matter.

C. Correct. The author's point that the creation of artificial life is problematic is driven home by the fact that the author also provides a counterview to his point, showing that the author is willing to both understand the other side and yet still maintain his or her own viewpoint.

D. Wrong. The author does not directly and harshly criticize the opinions of the scientists, just disputes them.

E. Wrong. The author provides no specific authority who agrees with his or her claims; the author's authority in this passage is merely his or her own opinions.

Answer to Question 160:

A. Wrong. Whether or not the reader understands the meaning of the Pandora's box metaphor, the author still clearly delineates what it means in the same sentence by saying that creating artificial life would engender a situation in which scientists could not undo the consequences. The author's strategy is double-layered and provides both the metaphor and its literal meaning simultaneously, showing that the Pandora's box trope is not used to test the reader's intelligence.

B. Wrong. Pandora's Box is a metaphor for an action with consequences that cannot be undone and its use does not necessitate that the consequences can never be controlled.

C. Wrong. Pandora's Box is a metaphor for an action whose consequences can never be undone and but this does not mean that the consequences are evil. Hence, invoking Pandora's Box does not show that the creation of artificial life is evil.

D. Correct. The author is making the point that the creation of artificial life may have far reaching consequences that can never be undone and uses the trope or metaphor of Pandora's Box as a rhetorical device to reinforce this point.

E. Wrong. Pandora's Box is not a red herring since it is a metaphor that reinforces the author's main claim and not a rhetorical device that distracts the reader from the issue at hand.

Answer to Question 161:

A. Wrong. The last sentence of the passage is meant to persuade the reader to believe in the author's opinion by way of a rhetorical appeal to the reader's emotions or sense of values (pathos).

B. Wrong. The author does not believe that the scientific research mentioned in the passage is important, rather that it is dangerous.

C. Wrong. The author does not generalize a specific argument in the last sentence of the passage, but instead uses the end of the passage to appeal to the sensibilities of the reader as a means of persuading the reader to agree with his or her viewpoint.

D. Wrong. The last sentence does not lay out more details related to self-assembling membranes; it actually seeks to convince the reader that scientific research vis-a-vis self-assembling membranes is dangerous.

E. Correct. The author uses the last sentence to appeal to the reader's sense of values or emotions (pathos).

Passage 79 – Summary / Paraphrase

The passage is about our understanding of the universe. The main idea is that physicists' lack of clear understanding of dark matter is a good example of how little we really understand the universe. The major points are (a) that scientists posit dark matter to explain sizable stretches of the universe that emit no light or electromagnetic radiation and (b) that there is no definite evidence that dark matter exists. The main purpose of the passage is to use dark matter to illustrate a point about the limits of human knowledge.

Answer to Question 162:

"Thus, dark matter provides a good example of how little we really know about the structures that compose our universe."

In the last sentence of the passage, the author makes it clear that he or she believe that astrophysics still has a long way to go in fully elucidating the structure and functioning of the universe.

Passage 80 – Summary / Paraphrase

The passage is about the way physical geography divides up the earth by climate zones. The main idea is that climactic zones, known as biomes, are crucial to understanding the balance of life on earth. The major points are (a) that biomes support a rich variety of plant and animal life and (b) the diversity of biomes is vital to sustaining the balance of life. A minor point specifies the major types of biome. The purpose of the passage is to raise awareness of biomes and their importance.

Answer to Question 163:

"There are four main types of biome: aquatic, forest, desert, and grassland and while all are different, all equally important because they are like threads in woven into the same tapestry: planet earth."

The last sentence creates a metaphor that likens the earth and its biomes to a tapestry and the author does this to underscore the fact that each part of the biome is unique but all are equally important.

Passage 81 – Summary / Paraphrase

The passage is about climate change. The main idea is that although people are prone to jump to conclusions about the climate based off transitory trends in the weather, the real picture is more complex. The major points are (a) that people tend to see extreme temperatures, depending on the nature of the extreme, as either a confirmation or a refutation of global warming and (b) research suggests that factors associated with extreme high temperatures can also be used to explain severe winters. The purpose of the passage is to caution the reader from drawing glib solutions about the phenomenon about climate change by showing at least one way in which doing so has been demonstrated to be wrong.

Answer to Question 164:

A. Wrong. The author is skeptical of public and scientific reaction to climate change but there is no indication that he or she is afraid of it.

B. Correct. Incredulous means skeptical or suspicious and since the author seems to be wary of the climate change hysteria permeating public and scientific discourse, incredulous is a good way to characterize the author's attitude.

C. Correct. Dubious means to be wary or suspicious of something and given the author's introductory sentence, it is clear that the author is skeptical of the climate change hysteria permeating public and scientific discourse.

Passage 82– Summary / Paraphrase

The passage is about the Big Bang theory. The main idea is that while the origins of the universe are still controversial, the Big Bang theory is the most widely accepted explanation. There are two major points that briefly sketch the basics of the theory: (a) that universe existed in an extremely hot and dense microcosm of itself and then exploded outward and created stars and galaxies in the process and (b) that the Big Bang is estimated to have occurred roughly 14 billion years ago. The main purpose of the passage is to give a brief, factual summary of the current position of science on the origins of the universe without commenting on whether that position is or is not correct.

Answer to Question 165:

A. Wrong. Contingency means chance or possibility and polemic means dispute so the two terms are not analogous.

B. Correct. Both brouhaha and polemic are synonyms for dispute and thus the two terms are analogous.

C. Correct. Both argument and polemic are synonyms for dispute and thus the two terms are analogous.

Passage 83 – Summary / Paraphrase

The passage is about antimatter. The main idea is that antimatter was posited as a way of understanding the behavior of electrons, but deeper understanding was not possible until the development of particle accelerators. The main points are that (a) antimatter is composed of antiparticles, just as matter is composed of particles (b) Dirac hypothesized the existence of antimatter as a way of better understanding electrons and (c) that the existence of antimatter was only proven by particle accelerators. There is a minor point that most current research on antimatter is at CERN, in Geneva. The main purpose of the passage is to familiarize the reader with some very basic points about antimatter, and give a brief, factual account of how it was initially posited.

Answer to Question 166:

A. Wrong. While this may be the case, the author does not point to this line of thinking as the impetus behind Dirac's investigations into antimatter.

B. Wrong. The author does not claim that understanding electrons is the key to unlocking the universe, nor does the author show this to be the reasoning behind Dirac's hypothesis.

C. Correct. Dirac's antimatter hypothesis is founded on the presupposition that everything has an opposite.

D. Wrong. The passage does not indicate that Dirac believed in the idea that the universe could be fully delineated nor did he use such thinking to formulate his antimatter hypothesis.

E. Wrong. The passage discusses that Dirac conceptualized antimatter in the late 1920s but that it couldn't be tested until at least the 1960s, so it can be reasonably inferred that technological capabilities and scientific ideas do not always align.

Answer to Question 167:

A. Correct. The author is recounting the conceptualization of the anti-matter hypothesis.

B. Wrong. A testimony relays a truth or conviction that something is true; this passage is merely recounting the development of the antimatter hypothesis.

C. Wrong. The passage itself is not a scientific theory, it is a recounting of the development of a scientific hypothesis.

D. Wrong. The author is not directly trying to persuade the reader to believe in the antimatter hypothesis.

E. Wrong. The author does not draw any comparisons relative to the development of the antimatter hypothesis.

Passage 84 – Summary / Paraphrase

The passage highlights the issues faced by explorers in Antarctica due to the cold winds. The author starts by explaining how the katabatic winds are formed and proceeds to warn that these winds though steady can turn wild at times. He gives two examples to support his statement. He concludes by saying that not all winds in the Antarctic are so chaotic.

Answer to Question 168:

The correct answer is B and C. The reading makes no mention of atmospheric issues such as storm fronts. It does point out that the winds come off of the cold air from the mountains, implying that the coastal areas are warmer, thus B and C are correct.

Answer to Question 169:

The correct answer is C. The correct answer has a generality that the other options lack. Further, the correct answer actually indicates problems. The other sentences either indicate no actual problems or refer to specific events, not general problems.

Practice Set 6 - Social Sciences

Passage 85 – Summary / Paraphrase

The passage is about the attitude of Japanese officers during World War II. The main idea is that Japanese officers were underprepared for an allied counterattack. There are two main ideas: (a) that many Japanese commanders were overconfident due to the ease of early victories and (b) even those who were more alert to the possibility of an allied counterstrike tended to be ignored by the prevailing opinion. Two minor points amplify and develop the major points: (a) that the Japanese defeat at Midway had gone unpublicized and (b) that Lt. Commander I too had specific intelligence that was ignored. The primary purpose of the passage is to give insight into the prevalent attitudes in the Japanese military that led to their lack of preparedness.

Answer to Question 170:

The correct answer is A. The Japanese were probably optimistic about winning the war, but optimism is not likely to be considered a symptom of disease. Based on previous battle victories, they would feel optimistic when going into battle. Answer A is correct. Courage is a positive emotion and, like optimism, not symptomatic of disease, so B is not correct. Complacency and satisfaction are similar in meaning; it is doubtful that the Japanese would be satisfied until the war ended with their ultimate victory. D and E are incorrect choices. In this context, overconfidence is the best choice. Their overconfidence made them overlook warnings that could have changed the outcome of the war.

Answer to Question 171:

The correct answer is B. The writer includes these details to let the reader know that Haruki had not made a rush to judgment in warning the Japanese command, answer B. One example of work by the Naval Intelligence Center is insufficient to determine its level of efficiency of that group; A is not the correct answer. The passage is not about the location of the Allies in the Pacific; the fact that the positions were discovered is the salient information here, making C an incorrect answer. One might use this investigation by Haruki in conjunction with other actions he has taken to justify his position in the Japanese military, but one action in not enough for that conclusion, eliminating D as a correct answer. To this point in the war, the Japanese had won several naval battles, so their lack of preparedness is not a factor in their ignoring the warning. E is also incorrect.

Passage 86 – Summary / Paraphrase

The passage is about American Indian chiefs. The main idea is that the popular understanding of the role of a chief in tribal affairs did not always reflect the actual role of the individuals designated as chiefs. The mains ideas are: (a) while chiefs had traditionally been figureheads with little actual power, they were often political leaders during a key transitional period and (b) the political power of chiefs during this transitional period was due to either backing from the US government or power-plays by ambitious tribesmen. The primary purpose of the passage is to disabuse the reader of a widely-held but not entirely correct belief, and to more accurately inform the reader about the facts.

Answer to Question 172:

The correct answer is D. The writer of this passage is careful to downplay the role of so-called chiefs in the tribal structure prior to interference by the American government. They had no real power or authority. Based on the absence of other information, the reader can conclude that the tribal structure was egalitarian, that all members had the opportunity to express their opinions and that all were listened to. Answer D is the best choice. There is no evidence that the structure was either matriarchal - ruled by adult women- or patriarchal -ruled by adult males - so neither A nor B is correct. An oligarchy is ruled by a small select group, which does not appear to be the case here, eliminating C as a correct choice. A tyrant rules by fear, again, not the case with native tribes. E is also incorrect.

Answer to Question 173:

The correct answer is C. Any time that a popularly held belief is shown to be even partially incorrect, one should ask how he/she came to believe it in the first place. The writer of this passage states that the American public's understanding of a tribal chief's function is not correct according to the tribesmen. Now that the reader has a better understanding of the meaning of the title, chief, he or she may wonder what other commonly held ideas about the natives may also be incorrect or inaccurate. Answer C is the best choice. There is no mention in the passage of any specific chiefs, so curiosity about their names would not arise in this context, making A an incorrect answer choice. The purpose of the passage is to clarify the position of the chief in a tribe and not about the actual negotiations that took place between tribes and the American government, so it is not likely that the reader would have questions about the number of tribes involved in the negotiations, making B an incorrect answer choice. The violent deaths of chiefs is mentioned as an event that led to Americans taking advantage of the tribes, and the reason for their deaths is not important in this case. D is not the best answer choice. Although the writer mentions that chiefs served "more or less" as politicians, he does so to clarify their positions in the tribes. There is no evidence that the chiefs' behavior influenced the behavior of the Americans, eliminating E as a correct answer.

Answer to Question 174:

The correct answer is C. Extraordinary would be used in the sense of an achievement or accomplishment and does not apply in this context, so A is not the correct choice. Answer E refers to the use of the word in grammar, so it is not the correct choice. It is not a separate or individual idea, either, eliminating D as the correct answer. Distinctive or unique means that it stands alone as an example; there is no other like it. Answer C is to the best choice. Answer B is not the best choice in this case because this "singular" fact is neither unusual nor strange.

Passage 87 – Summary / Paraphrase

The passage is about the Baluch tribes. The main idea is to explain that the Baluch are not a single homogeneous population. The major points (a) characterize Baluch tribesmen along ethnic lines explaining that the Balcuh draw from Arab, Persian and Dravidian stock and (b) characterize the Baluch in terms of stereotypical character and bearing. There is an extensive discussion of stereotypical attributes of a variety of different Baluch tribesmen. The main purpose of the passage is to characterize the Baluch people. The rhetoric of the passage is fairly chatty and anecdotal, suggesting that it is likely an ethnographic piece from an earlier time when stereotypical observations were favored over scientific rigor.

Answer to Question 175:

The correct answer is "As a revenue payer he is not so satisfactory, his want of industry and the pride which looks upon manual labour as degrading making him but a poor husbandman." A Husbandman is a farmer; the Baluch's disdain for manual labor, a requirement for farming, makes it unlikely that they would be farmers.

Answer to Question 176:

Both B and C are reasonable choices. Because they are tribal by nature, the Baluchi are most likely to feel little connection to the interests of India. They have little in common with the native people of India. Their predilection to banditry along with their reluctance to contribute financially to society makes them unlikely to observe the strict standards required by military service. There is nothing in the passage to suggest that they feel superior to soldiers in the Indian army, eliminating A as a correct answer choice.

Answer to Question 177:

The best answer choice is D. Environment and tradition would nurture the character of the Baluch, while origin and descent would determine the nature of the Baluch. The author's use of these terms suggests that both nature and nurture have had equal influences on the resulting character of the Baluch. Answer choices B and C claim that either nature or nurture has had a greater effect on their resulting character, eliminating them as reasonable answer choices. There is nothing in the passage to suggest that the Baluch scoff at the traditions of Indian culture, making A incorrect. Answer choice E may be a correct inference on the part of the reader, it does not respond to the phrases used in the question, making it incorrect also.

Answer to Question 178:

The correct answer is D, digest. A gazetteer includes only geographical information, so A is incorrect. An atlas also deals with geography, making answer B incorrect. An almanac, published annually, includes a calendar, information about weather, when to plant a garden, etc. It is not the most likely place to find the passage above; C is incorrect. An anthology is a collection of writings by the same author or writings by different authors in the same genre, such as a poetry anthology. E is not the correct choice.

Passage 88 – Summary / Paraphrase

The passage is about a previously unknown tribe of indigenous islanders. The main idea of the passage is to summarily characterize the islanders. There are no major points, merely a list of information of the islanders that indicates that they had little exposure to modern life. The purpose of the passage is to describe a previously unknown tribe.

Answer to Question 179:

The correct answer is C. The writer explicitly reveals that the natives eat taro and yams, both vegetables. Because the natives have spears and knives and trade goats and pigs, the reader may conclude that they also kill and eat meat. It would be difficult, with the limited information in this passage, to believe that their diet is either restrictive or inclusive, so answer choices D and E must be eliminated. There is nothing in the passage to suggest that the natives are aggressive, so A is also incorrect. Narcissism is also not evident here, making answer choice B incorrect. Opportunistic describes people who recognize and take advantage of an opportunity, much as these natives do when they paddle around the ship waiting to dive for objects that are thrown overboard. Overt means open or obvious. It was obvious to those on the ship that the natives waited openly for items to be thrown overboard. That the natives exhibit some vanity is revealed by the writer's description of the designs on their canoes and the body ornamentation in the form of goats' beards and shells worn by the natives. Answer C is the best choice.

Passage 89 – Summary / Paraphrase

The passage is about political philosophy. The main idea is that any form of government that privileges one person over another is patently corrupt and oppressive. The major points are: (a) that once people recognize the natural laws that govern them, they will necessarily obey them, obviating the need for government and (b) that any form of government is oppressive because it will always privilege a governing minority at the expense the majority. The main purpose of the passage is to provide a rationale for anarchy.

Answer to Question 180:

The correct answer is A, manifesto. A manifesto is a declaration of intentions, opinions, or objectives; this passage is clearly a declaration of an opinion. A proclamation, edict, fiat, or mandate is an official declaration or instruction and is backed up by some form of authority. This fact of authority eliminates all of the other answer choices.

Passage 90 – Summary / Paraphrase

The passage is about the performance of homeschooled students. The main idea is that despite concerns about their ability to compete with those educated in public schools, they actually perform slightly better than their peers according to some measures. The major point is that homeschooled students tend to perform noticeably better on achievement tests and college entrance exams than their peers. The purpose of the passage is to debunk the common perception that homeschooled students are under-prepared for college. The rhetorical question "But are these students skilled enough to compete successfully with conventionally-schooled students in the college setting?" frames the debate

Answer to Question 181:

The correct answer is D. Typical performance cannot be determined from one set of score. Each year's testing cohort can vary considerably. Without at least three years of results, one cannot determine a trend. Home schooled students would have to perform better over time to establish a pattern of higher achievement. Socioeconomic status and curriculum can affect scores on standardized tests, but those variables can vary for each cohort as well, which further supports including several years' test results in determining a trend. Other standardized tests may measure abilities very different from those measured by the SAT or ACT, so the score have no correlation, eliminating B as the correct answer. The colleges to which the students were accepted do not determine SAT or ACT scores, so E is also incorrect.

Passage 91 – Summary / Paraphrase

The passage is about fertility rates. The main idea is that the total fertility rate is a more direct measure than the birth rate for determining a nation's potential for population change. The major points are (a) the total fertility rate measures the average number of children per woman (b) the total fertility rate tells demographers whether population is growing, declining, or holding steady (c) fertility rates are generally declining, especially in industrialized nations. The purpose of the passage is to explain a method for demographers to determine rates of population growth.

Answer to Question 182:

The best answer choice is C. As population growth declines, the median age of the population rises, eventually leading to a disproportionately large number of older people who will require more health care and/or long-term care. A is not the correct choice because fewer children will be born, decreasing the demand for child care. With fewer people competing for available jobs, it is more likely that unemployment will decline, making B incorrect. A reduction in population means that fewer people share in the wealth of the country, causing a decline in poverty. D is not the best answer. Having to spend less on education frees up budget dollars for other societal needs. E is not the correct response.

Answer to Question 183:

The correct answer is B. Non-industrialized countries likely have fewer career opportunities for women, so they are less likely to postpone having children. There is not enough information in this passage to infer that divorce rates have any effect on fertility rates, so A cannot be the correct answer. Neither the number of live births nor infant mortality has an impact on fertility rates, eliminating both C and D as correct answers. The presence of an extended family may contribute to child care, but may not have an effect on fertility rates, so E is incorrect. The correct answer is B.

Passage 92 – Summary / Paraphrase

The passage is about human rights in Malaysia. The main idea is that Malaysia is a notorious hub of human trafficking. The major points are that (a) Malaysia is a destination for people trafficked for both sexual exploitation and for forced labor and (b) that while Malaysia took action to improve its anti-trafficking laws, it has yet to tackle exploitative labor practices. The purpose of the passage is to inform the reader about the status of human trafficking in Malaysia.

Answer to Question 184:

The correct answer is A. The passage reveals that men, women and children from South and Southeast Asia willingly migrate to Malaysia to work. One can infer that jobs are in short supply in the countries that they have left. Answer A is the correct answer. There is no information in the passage about the cultural beliefs in Malaysia, so answer B cannot be correct. We also cannot infer that the Malaysian culture is more accepting of child labor, eliminating C as the correct answer. There are no details about the 2000 UN TIP Protocol and its restrictions, so D must be eliminated as an answer. Finally, the passage does not reveal that industrialized nations outsource their labor to Malaysia; E is not correct.

Passage 93 – Summary / Paraphrase

The passage is about the archaeology of cave dwellings. The main idea is that the distribution of finds is often counterintuitive. The major points are (a) over centuries of occupation, cave dwellers left behind many layers of leavings (b) the leavings are sometimes found in unexpected layers (c) the occupants of the caves may themselves dug into the layers and buried bodies and implements in a way that disturbed the layering process. The purpose of the passage is to explain how objects from a much older age can often be found alongside much newer objects in archaeological sites.

Answer to Question 185:

The correct answer is C. Depending on the age of the artifacts, there may be no written records or residents left in the area who can, through memory or oral tradition, identify the function or relative age of the artifacts, making A and B incorrect choices. The level or degree of preservation can depend on a variety of factors, including weather over time or the type of soil in which they were found, so it is not a reliable means of dating artifacts. D is not the correct answer choice. Sorting the artifacts according to their function will only make collections of artifacts that serve a similar function. Using earlier discoveries or prior knowledge about human artifacts is the most logical place to begin dating what has been found.

Passage 94 – Summary / Paraphrase

The passage is about gender differences in imitation of behaviors. The main idea is that women tend to imitate the way other women behave more than men tend to imitate the way other men behave. The main point is that studies show that women tend to imitate other women in their eating habits, where men do not exhibit a similar pattern, lending credence to an existing hypothesis that women exhibit more same-sex imitation than men. There is a minor point that speculates that the reason for this phenomenon is that women have a greater need to fit in to and be liked by groups. The purpose of the passage is to inform and explain, which is indicated by the straightforward and factual language.

Answer to Question 186:

A. Wrong. It can be inferred from the information given in the passage that women have a greater tendency to conform to their same-gender counterparts because they have a stronger need to be liked by other females.
B. Correct. Just because men are not as keen as females are to follow group behavior at the dining table does not mean that men are the less conventional gender as a whole; the passage does not allude to the fact that men are never conventional, just vis-a-vis the eating habits of their same-gender counterparts.
C. Wrong. Since the passage states that women copy each other's eating habits in a group, it can be inferred that women would then eat generally the same amount of food during a meal together.

D. Wrong. The passage states that women find it important to be liked and accepted by a group and thus the inference can be made that they value how other perceive or see and understand them.

E. Wrong. Since men who dine together do not pay attention to the eating habits of the men around them, it can be inferred that the amount of food consumed by each male in a given dining group will be different.

Passage 95 – Summary / Paraphrase

The passage is about the spread of human-kind. The main idea is that while there is a consensus among specialists that humans originated in Africa before spreading outward, there is still debate as to exactly where early humans settled first as they dispersed from northern Africa. The main point is that recent evidence suggests that the initial point of colonization was the Arabian Peninsula. There is a minor point about DNA evidence suggesting genetic similarities between relevant populations that support the major point. The purpose of the passage is to inform and persuade: much of the tone is factual, but the final sentence suggests that the author is trying to get the reader to accept the conclusion that Arabia was the first area of human colonization. The author seems to assume that the evidence cited is conclusive.

Answer to Question 187:

A. Wrong. While the African Diaspora is an important aspect of the passage, the primary purpose of the passage is to show that scientists have determined the location of modern man's dissemination (Arabia)

B. Wrong. The author mentions that many are fascinated by the spread of human culture across the globe, and this "many" includes scientists and the inference can be made that this "many" also includes laymen. However, this statement is never developed and the author never directly references laymen and thus the primary purpose of the passage could not be to discuss the ways in which the interests of scientists and laymen intersect.

C. Correct. The primary purpose of the passage is to discuss the point of origin from which modern man disseminated across the globe; this point was determined to be Arabia by way of DNA analysis.

D. Wrong. The primary goal of the passage is to discuss the point of origin for the dispersal of modern man. DNA analysis helps scientists to determine this point, Arabia, but discussing the use of DNA analysis in anthropological research is not the main purpose of the passage.

E. Wrong. There is nothing polemical about the passage; the author does not use the information relayed in the passage relative to the dispersal of modern man across the globe to instigate a debate.

Answer to Question 188:

A. Wrong. The author's tone and style do not indicate that he or she doubts the validity of DNA as an anthropological research method. The author in fact seems to be neutral towards this practice and thus is not skeptical.

B. Wrong. The author's tone and style do not indicate disbelief relative to anthropological DNA analysis; the author demonstrates candid detachment from the topic and thus is not leery.

C. Correct. The author makes use of a tone and style that do not betray any judgments towards the validity of DNA analysis as an anthropological research method; the author's attitude appears cool and detached thus impartial.

D. Wrong. The author's tone does not suggest that he or she finds DNA analysis a good or favorable anthropological research method, the author's attitude is much more detached and candid.

E. Wrong. The author in no ways exhibits an attitude of devotion or dedication to anthropological DNA analysis; the author is much more detached and observational.

Answer to Question 189:

A. Wrong. The author states that anthropologists are no longer debating whether or not early humans originated in the Horn of Africa, thus the scientific polemics do not focus on this issue.

B. Wrong. The author discusses how DNA samples of Europeans and Arabians were compared to determine the origin of the organized human Diaspora, but the author does not give information to suggest that these two specific places are the focus of scientific debate.

C. Wrong. The author names the Near East as a region subjected to DNA testing but does not give any information about the Near East's specific role in the human Diaspora and definitely does not suggest that the Near East lies at the nexus of scientific debate relative to the dispersal of modern man.

D. Correct. The author indicates that the focus point of scientific debate is the point of origin of modern man's organized dispersal across the globe.

E. Wrong. The author does not say that scientists debate the use of DNA analysis in the study of the dispersal of modern man.

Passage 96 – Summary / Paraphrase

The passage is about gender differences in altruistic behaviors. The main idea is that men are more likely than women to change their behavior based on the presence of attractive members of the opposite sex. The two main points are (a) that men are more likely to perform altruistic acts in the presence of attractive women and (b) that this behavior is caused by a need to impress potential mates. The purpose of the passage is to explain gender differences in a particular type of behavior.

Answer to Question 190:

A. Wrong. While the author does objectively evaluate the facts vis-a-vis altruistic behavior in males and females, his or her point is made most compelling by the use of a source of authority, the British Journal of Psychology.

B. Wrong. The author's approach to making his or her claim is deductive and objective and thus not rhetoric aimed at invoking an emotional response.

C. Wrong. The author does not provide a counterview to his or her claim.

D. Wrong. The author does not criticize the opinions of other psychologists.

E. Correct. The author offers a source of authority to back-up his or her claims, the best method of making a claim convincing and believable.

Passage 97 – Summary / Paraphrase

The passage is about the longer-term benefits of working hard in college. The main idea is that lazier college students tend to fare significantly worse along several measures than their more industrious peers. There are two main points: (a) that slacker students are at a higher risk of poor economic outcomes and (b) that slacker students often do not improve vital skills such as critical reasoning. The purpose of the passage is to caution students to take college seriously - rhetorical flourishes such as "even more troubling" indicate that the author has a clear bias toward what outcomes are better.

Answer to Question 191:

A. Correct. This option would not weaken the author's claims because several slacker college students who are still able to achieve success are within the margin of error; there are always a few exceptions to every rule.

B. Wrong. The authors maintains that slacker college students suffer from low academic skills like critical reasoning and this hinders their ability to succeed in the future; evidence to the contrary, such as academic skills improvement despite a low work ethic, would definitely undermine the author's claims.

C. Wrong. The author claims that one of the main problems with slacking in college is that it makes it more difficult for students with low work ethics to obtain jobs after graduation; research pointing to a different conclusion, such as there being no marked difference between low and high work ethic students obtaining jobs, would undermine the author's claims.

D. Wrong. If the financial situation of both the hardworking and slacker college students was the same, then the author's claim that it pays to work hard in college would be undermined.

E. Wrong. If the living situation of both the hardworking and slacker college students was the same, then the author's claim that slacker students suffer the consequences of living with their parents post-graduation due to their lack of academic effort would be undermined.

Passage 98 – Summary / Paraphrase

The passage is about the political philosophy of Karl Marx. The main idea is that Marxist analysis is a highly useful tool in analyzing a variety of social and political systems. There are two major points: (a) that Marxist analysis has changed the way people think about socio-political systems and (b) that while Marxist theories are often used to critique capitalism, they can also be used to critique socialism and communism, systems that are themselves based in Marxism. The purpose of the passage is to inform the reader of an under-publicized aspect of Marxism, namely its usefulness in critiquing its own systems.

Answer to Question 192:

A. Wrong. Self-reflexivity means the ability of a person (or in this case a theory) to accurately see and assess its own artificialities and contradictions and thus merely saying that Marxism deconstructs capitalistic power structures does not account for self-reflexivity at all.

B. Correct. Since self-reflexivity means the ability to self critique and find contradictions and artificialities, it is true that, according to the passage, Marxism is self-reflexive because it critically analyzes its own theories.

C. Wrong. Self-reflexivity is the ability to self-critique or analyze and thus it is not a way of delineating the specifics of class conflict in general.

D. Wrong. While it may be true that self-reflexivity, the ability to self analyze and critique, helps academics set up research frameworks, the passages states that self-reflexivity in Marxism is a particularly valuable feature because it allows for Marxism to critique its own economic theories.

E. Wrong. The passage does not indicate that self-reflexivity or engaging in self critique creates an environment of free thinking academic exchange.

Answer to Question 193:

A. Wrong. Dialectic means the method of inquiry that uses discussion as a means of eliciting reason and intellectual discovery and it stands in opposition to the scientific method which gathers information using empirical methods.

B. Correct. Dialectic means to gather intellectual information or reason by way of discussion and debate.

C. Wrong. Dialectic is a method of academic inquiry powered by discussion and protest means to express and objection to words, thoughts, or policies and thus the two terms are not analogous.

D. Wrong. Dialectic is certainly dialogue but it is not limited to the political arena.

E. Wrong. Dialectic is a method of eliciting reason via discussion not the process of worker exploitation.

Passage 99 – Summary / Paraphrase

The passage is about how art relates to civilization. The main idea is that, contrary to popular belief, art predates complex human civilizations. There are two main points: (a) that art is often considered constitutive of civilization and (b) recent archaeological finds suggest that art significantly predates civilization. The purpose of the passage is to debunk a commonly held view that the author views as false. The author of the passage makes an implicit assumption that art is well-defined, and that primitive painting is in fact art.

Answer to Question 194:

A. Wrong. The author suggests that the painting kits are an important find because they shows that art was practice among the earliest human ancestors, not just one of the characteristics of human civilization.
B. Wrong. The author does discuss the specific tools that were used by the early humans, but the main importance of the tools is that they predate human civilization.
C. Wrong. The author suggests that art was used for body decoration among the early humans, but again the main importance of the findings was the fact that they are evidence that artistic practices predate civilization.
D. Correct. According to the author, the importance of the anthropological discovery of early human painting kits is that they are a sign that artistic practices predate human civilization even though art is typically seen as a marker of human civilization.
E. Wrong. While this statement may be true, the author is more intent on getting the message across that the painting kits are an important find because they show that art predates human civilization.

Passage 100 – Summary / Paraphrase

The passage is about psychological trauma. The main idea is that apparently very different circumstances can lead to strikingly similar changes in brain activity. The main point is that soldiers exposed to combat and children exposed to abusive situations both experience a similar shift in brain patterns that is associated with a sense of danger. There is a minor point that such abnormal brain activity can lead to specific disorders if left untreated. The main purpose of the passage is to raise awareness of the potentially severe consequences of abuse: the rhetorical device of comparing childhood abuse to combat raises the stakes of the discussion and highlights severity.

Answer to Question 195:

A. Wrong. The first sentence of the passage draws a parallel between victims of child abuse and soldiers who have experience active duty, saying that both experience the same brain changes as a result of trauma.
B. Wrong. Since both children and adult soldiers can experience the same changes in the brain as a result from trauma, it is safe for the reader to infer that changes in the

brain can occur at any point in a person's life.

C. Wrong. The passage says that children from abusive environments can be treated by way of therapy and/or medication.

D. Correct. The passage does not give enough information about the treatment of soldiers who have been subjected to traumatic experiences to allow the reader to make inferences as to whether or not soldiers have a more difficult time recovering than children.

E. Wrong. The passage discusses how emotional abuse/child abuse changes the victim's brain patters which is in fact a physical change to the brain that the passage claims can only be treated by therapy or medication; thus, the changes are lasting and physical.

Passage 101 – Summary / Paraphrase

The passage is about Machiavelli's The Prince and its influence. The main idea is that The Prince has been both highly controversial and very influential on political thought. There are two main points: (a) that The Prince has been controversial for its cynical view of political life and (b) that its message of "the end justifies the means" has made a lasting impression on many readers. There is minor point that specifies some of the ways in which The Prince runs contrary to many cherished political ideals contrasting the work's brazen realism with belief in political ideals. The main purpose of the passage is to inform and briefly familiarize the reader with the work and surrounding controversy. The tone is largely factual, and while the author mentions the controversial nature of the work, they do not express an opinion on the controversy.

Answer to Question 196:

A. Wrong. Both bold-faced sections highlight how The Prince promotes political theories that are controversial in the modern political landscape and thus the first section cannot undermine the second.

B. Correct. The second bold-faced section concludes that the statement "the end justifies the means" at the heart of The Prince is well-known and controversial; the first bold-faced section outlines in more detail why The Prince is controversial.

C. Wrong. The author's position is that the Prince is a poignant yet controversial book and both of these bold-faced sections in fact support this claim.

D. Wrong. Both bold-faced sections reinforce the author's position that The Prince is a controversial yet poignant book.

E. Wrong. Both bold-face sections discuss how The Prince undermines many of the ideas relative to modern political practices, but the bold-faced sections do not undermine modern political practices themselves.

Answer to Question 197:

A. Correct. The author spends the duration of the passage discussing how The Prince was and has remained a book that is highly influential despite the fact that it is equally controversial; thus, a clear case is made for the fact that polemical books are the most influential.

B. Wrong. The author never discusses leadership in terms of combining virtue and vice, just the fact that The Prince negates the importance of personal vice in leaders. Thus, a case is not made for the concept that leadership requires a combination of virtue and vice.

C. Wrong. It can be inferred that political ideas evolve since the author points out the fact that modern political ideas clash with Machiavellian political ideas, but this is still an inference and not a clear case or argument for a specific fact.

D. Wrong. The author does not directly discuss human nature even though it does show how political systems change and evolve.

E. Wrong. The author does not make a case for how the Machiavellian approach works when it moves from the realm of theory to the practical world of practice and thus this does not make a case for the Machiavellian approach as the best political method.

Passage 102 – Summary / Paraphrase

The passage is about the causes of depression. The main idea is that after years of scientific consensus that depression is caused by low serotonin levels, there has been recent support for the idea that depression may not correlate as clearly with chemical imbalance as was previously thought. The main points are: (a) starting in the 1950s, scientists studying behavior and the brain agreed that depression was caused by serotonin deficiency (b) the notion that chemical imbalance caused depression let mental health professionals treat depression using pharmaceuticals (c) recent research has suggested that depleted levels of serotonin are not the sole factor in depression, opening the door to different treatment possibilities. A minor point that genetics, and more subtle views about mood and personality, develops the main points. The purpose of the passage is polemical: the author has a clear bias against the notion that mental disorders can be treated pharmaceutically as evidenced by the phrase "pills as a means of solving mood problems may hopefully become a thing of the past" and by the tone of the final paragraph.

Answer to Question 198:

A. Wrong. Candid means impartial and since the author believes that serotonin as a cause of depression is outmoded, he or she is at least slightly skeptical of SSRI's as a treatment method for depression and thus is not rendered impartial or unprejudiced.

B. Wrong. The author is critical of SSRIs believes them to be outmoded and thus does not have a positive or affirmative attitude towards them.

C. Wrong. While the author is critical of SSRIs (calling them outmoded), castigating is too harsh of a term to describe the author's attitude as castigating means to chastise or criticize severely.

D. Correct. Leery is a synonym for skeptical and the author is clearly skeptical of SSRIs since he or she believes it is outmoded to regard serotonin as the main cause of depression.

E. Wrong. The author's tone and word choice relative to SSRIs do not indicate snobbery (condescension) but rather skeptical disbelief.

Answer to Question 199:

A. Wrong. Since the passage states that SSRIs are an outmoded, the reader can infer that they are not a good way of treating mood disorders.

B. Correct. The passage states that scientists see genes as a potential cause of depression and thus inferring that they are the definite cause of depression is incorrect.

C. Wrong. The passage discusses a study that concluded that decreased serotonin levels in healthy people did not affect their mood so the reader can infer that serotonin does not play a direct role in affecting a person's mood in general.

D. Wrong. The passage lists talk therapy as one of the successful methods of treating depression

E. Wrong. The beginning of the passage discusses how depression is a universal, global phenomenon so the reader can infer that it affects all humans regardless of culture or ethnicity.

Answer to Question 200:

A. Correct. The author makes it clear that genes contribute to a person's biological profile and thus genes could engender depression in an individual.

B. Correct. The author also makes it clear that environmental factors can contribute to a person's mood and hence could engender depression.

C. Wrong. The author does not mention past and present experiences in conjunction with biological factors as a cause of depression.

Answer to Question 201:

"In the 1950s psychologists and neuroscientists teamed up to proclaim that depression was the result of a chemical imbalance, more specifically low levels of serotonin, and a milieu was born that sought to frame mental health issues as curable deficiencies."

This sentence underscores the fact that a treatment framework was erected around depression characterizing it as a curable deficiency. The mentality of mental health practitioners thus became SSRI based, as those were pills that could be used to treat depression.

Bibliography:

www.arthistory.net

www.wikipedia.com

Boehmer, Elleke. Colonial and Postcolonial Literature. Oxford: Oxford University Press 1995.

Wright, George. Religion, Politics and Thomas Hobbes. Dordrecht, Netherlands: Springer, 2006.

Giles, Lionel. Sun Tzu: The Art of War (electronic book from Stockholm University)

Leitch, Vincent B., Cain, William E., Finke, Laurie, Johnson, Barbara, and McGowan, John. The Norton Anthology of Theory and Criticism, Second Edition. New York: W.W. Norton & Compan y, Inc. 2010.

http://www.biologynews.net/archives/2012/01/04/a_gene_for_depression_localized.html

http://www.biologynews.net/archives/2012/01/05/whiff_of_love_hormone_helps_monkeys_show_a_little_kindness.html

http://www.macroevolution.net/severe-malaria.html#.TxLdjW_bink

http://www.macroevolution.net/ocean-acidification.html#.TxLHP2_bink

http://www.macroevolution.net/bacteria.html#.TxLBcG_bink

http://www.macroevolution.net/chimpanzees-behavior.html#.TxK73W_bink

http://www.usatoday.com/tech/science/2008-06-03-1268515476_x.htm

http://www.inc.com/robert-kaplan/how-to-get-the-important-stuff-done.html

http://www.mckinseyquarterly.com/Governance/Leadership/How_leaders_kill_meaning_at_work_2910

http://mba.yale.edu/news_events/CMS/Articles/7494.shtml

http://mba.yale.edu/news_events/CMS/Articles/7446.shtml

http://mba.yale.edu/news_events/CMS/Articles/7395.shtml

http://www.time.com/time/nation/article/0,8599,1891416,00.html

http://www.guardian.co.uk/society/2010/sep/05/men-victims-domestic-violence

http://usnews.msnbc.msn.com/_news/2012/01/24/10227869-number-of-homeless-female-veterans-more-than-doubles

http://bucks.blogs.nytimes.com/2011/06/15/college-students-surprising-attitude-toward-debt/

http://www.scilearn.com/blog/low-literacy-united-states.php

http://www.physorg.com/news/2011-11-smart-material-medical-potential-tissue-penetrating.html

http://www.huffingtonpost.com/2012/01/04/higgs-boson-questions_n_1184594.html

http://www.sciencedaily.com/releases/2012/01/120111154035.htm

http://www.sciencedaily.com/releases/2012/01/120125132822.htm

http://science.nasa.gov/astrophysics/focus-areas/what-is-dark-energy/

http://www.sciencedaily.com/releases/2012/01/120112193430.htm

http://press.web.cern.ch/livefromcern/antimatter/history/AM-history02-a.html

http://todayhealth.today.msnbc.msn.com/_news/2012/02/01/10292865-bite-for-bite-women-diners-copy-each-other

http://www.sciencedaily.com/releases/2012/01/120126123705.htm

http://www.sciencedaily.com/releases/2012/02/120202093836.htm

http://www.cbsnews.com/8301-505145_162-57366295/really-bad-news-for-college-slackers/

http://en.wikipedia.org/wiki/Karl_Marx

http://www.guardian.co.uk/science/2011/oct/13/stone-age-painting-kits

References:

Rebate, Jean-Michel M.Loving Freud Madly: Surrealism between Hysterical and Paranoid Modernism. Journal of modern literature 25.3 (2002): 58-74

Miller, Peter "A thing or two about twins."National Geographic. January 2012: 38-65.
Cloud, John. "Why your DNA isn't your destiny." Time. January 6, 2010.

http://www.guardian.co.uk/sustainable-business/sustainability-key-corporate-success?newsfeed=true

http://www.sciencedaily.com/releases/2012/03/120306181212.htm

http://www.npr.org/blogs/health/2012/01/23/145525853/when-it-comes-to-depression-serotonin-isnt-the-whole-story

VERBAL INSIGHTS ON THE REVISED GRE GENERAL TEST
Price: $10.95

Verbal Insights on the revised GRE General Test provides intensive practice you need to succeed on the verbal section of the revised GRE. This book offers elaborate strategies and confidence-building exercises to boost your GRE verbal score. Towards the end, the book offers THREE full length Verbal Practice tests as per the revised GRE Guidelines along with answer key and detailed explanation.

ISBN-10: 1461152755   **ISBN-13:** 978-14-61152-75-0

ANALYTICAL WRITING INSIGHTS ON THE REVISED GRE GENERAL TEST
Price: $9.95

Analytical Writing Insights on the revised GRE General Test, as the name suggests, covers everything you need to know about the Analytical Writing section of the GRE revised General test. It features the different question types, scoring pattern, solved essays, tips, tricks and strategies separately for both the analytical writing tasks.

ISBN-10: 1463577125   **ISBN-13:** 978-14-63577-12-4

MATH INSIGHTS ON THE REVISED GRE GENERAL TEST
Price: $10.95

Math Insights on the revised GRE General Test provides intensive practice you need to succeed on the Quantitative section of the revised GRE. This book offers elaborate strategies and confidence-building exercises to boost your GRE Quantitative score. Towards the end, the book offers FOUR Math Practice tests as per the revised GRE Guidelines along with answer key and detailed explanation.

ISBN-10: 1479266698   **ISBN-13:** 978-14-79266-69-2

**GRE ANALYTICAL WRITING:
SOLUTIONS TO THE REAL
ESSAY TOPICS**
Price: $9.95

*GRE Analytical Writing: Solutions to the Real
Essay topics* includes *twenty five* sample Analyze an Issue essays
and *twenty five* sample Analyze an Argument essays along with
the rubrics, prompts and tips to use when writing your own
essays.

ISBN-10: 1466399570   **ISBN-13:** 978-14-66399-57-0

**GRE READING COMPREHENSION:
DETAILED SOLUTIONS TO
200 QUESTIONS**
Price: $12.95

*GRE Reading Comprehension: Detailed Solutions to 200
Questions* is designed to help students analyze and interpret
complex and unfamiliar passages in the minimum possible time
by employing simple, yet effective test-taking strategies. With
over 200 Reading Comprehension questions straddling all
possible topics, formats and question types, students get the
most intensive practice opportun-ities to sail through Reading
Comprehension questions on the GRE.

ISBN-10: 1479216925   **ISBN-13:** 978-14-79216-92-5

**GRE WORD LIST:
491 ESSENTIAL WORDS**
Price: $9.95

Limitless as the English lexicon is, how do you know where to
begin and how much to cover? Thankfully, with *GRE Word List:
491 Essential Words* there's now an easy answer. These 491
words have been selected by GRE experts after extensive
analysis of the new verbal section, and form the perfect
foundation for acing the exam.

ISBN-10: 1479216763   **ISBN-13:** 978-14-79216-76-5

NOTES

Printed in Great Britain
by Amazon.co.uk, Ltd.,
Marston Gate.